Horror Framing and the General Election

Lexington Studies in Political Communication

Series Editor: Robert E. Denton, Jr., Virginia Tech University

This series encourages focused work examining the role and function of communication in the realm of politics including campaigns and elections, media, and political institutions.

Recent Titles in This Series

Horror Framing and the General Election: Ghosts and Ghouls in Twenty-First-Century Presidential Campaign Advertisements, by Fielding Montgomery
Political Rhetoric, Social Media, and American Presidential Campaigns: Presidential Candidates' Use of New Media, by Janet Johnson
The Rhetoric of the American Political Party Conventions, 1948–2016, by Theodore F. Sheckels
President Trump and the News Media: Moral Foundations, Framing, and the Nature of Press Bias in America, by Jim A. Kuypers
Media Relations and the Modern First Lady: From Jacqueline Kennedy to Melania Trump, edited by Lisa M. Burns
Alternative Media Meets Mainstream Politics: Activist Nation Rising, edited by Joshua D. Atkinson and Linda Kenix
Political Humor in a Changing Media Landscape: A New Generation of Research, edited by Jody C Baumgartner and Amy Becker

Horror Framing and the General Election

Ghosts and Ghouls in Twenty-First-Century Presidential Campaign Advertisements

Fielding Montgomery

LEXINGTON BOOKS
Lanham • Boulder • New York • London

Published by Lexington Books
An imprint of The Rowman & Littlefield Publishing Group, Inc.
4501 Forbes Boulevard, Suite 200, Lanham, Maryland 20706
www.rowman.com

6 Tinworth Street, London SE11 5AL, United Kingdom

Copyright © 2021 by The Rowman & Littlefield Publishing Group, Inc.

Chapters 1 and 6. Copyright © 2019 by Michigan State University. Portions of chapters 1 and 6 originally appeared as an article in *Rhetoric & Public Affairs Vol. 22*, Iss. 2, 2019.

All rights reserved. No part of this book may be reproduced in any form or by any electronic or mechanical means, including information storage and retrieval systems, without written permission from the publisher, except by a reviewer who may quote passages in a review.

British Library Cataloguing in Publication Information Available

Library of Congress Cataloging-in-Publication Data Available

ISBN: 978-1-7936-4321-6 (cloth)
ISBN: 978-1-7936-4323-0 (pbk.)
ISBN: 978-1-7936-4322-3 (electronic)

*To my wife Annie, who made me watch horror
films until I actually enjoyed them.*

Contents

List of Figures and Tables ix

Acknowledgments xi

1 Introduction 1
2 Al Gore versus George W. Bush in the 2000 Election 25
3 John Kerry versus George W. Bush in the 2004 Election 47
4 John McCain versus Barack Obama in the 2008 Election 71
5 Mitt Romney versus Barack Obama in the 2012 Election 93
6 Hillary Clinton versus Donald Trump in the 2016 Election 115
7 Donald Trump versus Joe Biden in the 2020 Election 145
8 Conclusion 187

Bibliography 205

Index 215

About the Author 227

List of Figures and Tables

FIGURES

Figure 1.1	*Frankenstein* (1931)	5
Figure 1.2	*Midsommar* (2019)	8
Figure 2.1	*The Exorcist* (1973)	31
Figure 3.1	*The Grudge* (2004)	53
Figure 3.2	Bush, "Wacky"	62
Figure 4.1	*Night of the Living Dead* (1968)	77
Figure 6.1	Democratic National Committee, "Peace Little Girl (Daisy)"	122
Figure 6.2	*Dracula* (1931)	131
Figure 7.1	*Get Out* (2017)	174

TABLES

Table 2.1	Al Gore and George W. Bush Campaign Advertisements' Airdates	26
Table 3.1	John Kerry and George W. Bush Campaign Advertisements' Airdates	48
Table 4.1	John McCain and Barack Obama Campaign Advertisements' Airdates	72
Table 5.1	Mitt Romney and Barack Obama Campaign Advertisements' Airdates	94
Table 6.1	Hillary Clinton and Donald Trump Campaign Advertisements' Airdates	116
Table 7.1	Donald Trump and Joe Biden Campaign Advertisements' Airdates	146

Acknowledgments

This has been a project long in the making and there are countless individuals I would like to thank who have helped me at various points along my journey. First, I would like to thank Dr. Robert E. Denton, Nicolette Amstutz, Sierra Apaliski, Meaghan Menzel, Arun Rajakumar, others involved in the publication process, and the various anonymous reviewers for this piece both as an article and now as a book. Further, I would like to thank those who provided me with feedback on portions of this work for conference presentations, specifically respondents Blake Abbott and Thomas A. Salek and the anonymous conference reviewers. All of these editors, reviewers, and respondents' guidance, suggestions, and editorial assistance are truly appreciated and made this book a reality.

Next, I want to thank my master's advisor, the late Dr. Martin J. Medhurst. Dr. Medhurst was the one who pushed me to develop this project to the greatest extent possible. This work began merely as a seminar paper in his rhetorical criticism seminar at Baylor University, where through his advice, expertise, and encouragement, it became an article published in *Rhetoric & Public Affairs*, then my master's thesis, and finally this book. Dr. Medhurst was an invaluable advisor, supervisor, and mentor. This book is a testament to his belief in me and my project and his passion for developing rhetorical critics.

Further, I would like to thank my other two thesis committee members, Dr. James Kendrick and Dr. Patrick Flavin. While this project was beginning in my rhetorical criticism seminar, I was simultaneously enrolled in Dr. Kendrick's horror film class, where I learned much of the vocabulary and literature necessary to write about horror. Dr. Kendrick was another mentor who pushed me to make the most of my work. I cherish his continued mentorship and friendship. Dr. Flavin was one of my first professors to urge me to go above and beyond academically, both in terms of quality of work and in considering pursuing a graduate degree. He was my undergraduate honors thesis advisor and then my outside committee member for my master's thesis. Dr. Flavin showed me the ropes of the publication process early on through an article we coauthored in *International Political Science Review*. Much of the foundations of my still young academic career I owe to him.

Third, I absolutely want to thank my current PhD advisor at the University of Maryland, Dr. Shawn J. Parry-Giles. When I graduated from Baylor, I wasn't sure what would be my next steps for this book project. Dr. Parry-Giles immediately jumped in, providing me with consistent guidance, reassurance, and lightning-fast feedback on my drafts. I could not be happier to be her advisee.

I would also like to thank my other academic mentors who helped me at various stages through this process by offering feedback, advice, or just a general growth of knowledge and support. At Baylor, the mentorship of Dr. Leslie A. Hahner, Dr. Scott Varda, and Dr. Matt Gerber were all particularly influential in my academic journey, especially as I went to them more times than I can count for advice on picking a PhD program. At Maryland, I have been blessed by being surrounded by extremely intelligent, helpful, and accessible mentors like Dr. Carly S. Woods, Dr. Catherine Knight Steele, Dr. Trevor Parry-Giles, Dr. Damien Smith Pfister, Dr. Kristy Maddux, and Dr. Andrew Ferguson. There are, of course, countless other professors and mentors—at Baylor, Maryland, and beyond—who have guided me along the way that have my sincere gratitude.

Further, I would like to thank the multitude of brilliant graduate school peers I have had the pleasure of working with and befriending throughout my time at Baylor and Maryland. The conversations and friendships we have had and continue to foster are second to none and have encouraged me both academically and emotionally. I could not be in the position I currently am without those communities.

Finally, I owe a great deal to my family and friends who provided me with outside perspectives on portions of my work, especially when it was freshly written. I cannot thank Sandra Montgomery, Annie Montgomery, Erin C. Slattery, Samantha Olson, and Andrew Barron enough for the proofreading, edits, and other support they provided at various stages in this process. Additionally, I would like to thank all of my family and friends that provided me with the encouragement and emotional support, whether they knew it or not, to take on and complete this project.

Chapter 1

Introduction[1]

Horror and politics have been linked together for nearly as long as each has existed. Robert L. Ivie and Oscar Giner demonstrate how threat construction through fear of the "Other" has been inherent to the U.S. political system since its inception.[2] Ernest W. King and Franklin G. Mixon Jr. claim that horrors, such as the Salem witch trials, have been used by elites to create hysteria "to maintain their political-economic influence over the area."[3] Additionally, horror on the big screen has been political in nature since the introduction of the film genre.[4] Given that political ads tend to draw on the genres of film and television, understanding the generic influences of such ads provides us with a productive mode of investigating twenty-first-century presidential campaign advertisements. Such a connection between popular media genres and campaign advertisements has been made by John S. Nelson and G. R. Boynton, as well as Glenn W. Richardson Jr.[5] Horror deserves particular attention given it has been the stock-and-trade of campaign ads since at least the "Daisy" ad made it so in 1964.[6]

This project sets out to analyze the rhetorical features of horror framing present in presidential election campaign ads. I argue that the advent of televised campaign ads further fused the horror genre with U.S. presidential elections. Presidential campaigns, after all, have relied on affective fear appeals, including horror themes, across the country's history. Although horror themes were embedded in television ads of presidential campaigns from nearly their inception, they have taken on even more salience in the new millennium and the post-9/11 era. Previous studies have focused on advertisements within the context of the Cold War. But given the frightening nature of international attacks on U.S. soil, an economic collapse, a global pandemic, and other such crises that have arisen throughout the first fifth of the twenty-first century, one would expect horrific advertising to be exceptionally heightened. Thus, this

1

study sets about demonstrating the rhetorical contours of these horror ads and the role they played in the presidential candidacies of the new millennium as the United States embarked on the War on Terror, faced one of its most intense economic crises in generations, witnessed the viable candidacy of the first woman candidate, experienced the election of the first Black president, faced spikes in domestic terrorism, including violence associated with race and religion, lived through an election with allegations of Russian interference in support of a controversial candidate whose fame derived from his notorious life in business and entertainment, and witnessed a campaign in the midst of a global pandemic. More specifically, this analysis aims to paint a clearer picture of how horror frames have been used in different ways, how they differed in intensity of their usage, and how self-positive appeals to audience efficacy helped bolster these rhetorical attempts at persuasion. Further, I find that seven implications of horror framing in presidential campaign ads have been uncovered through this work: horror frames as omnipresent, normative, polarizing, demonic, invasive, insidious, and nihilistic.

In this chapter, I lay the foundation of the cinematic horror genre and past scholarship on presidential campaign ads to form the backdrop for understanding the confluence of horror themes in popular film and presidential campaign ads. In particular, the case is made that classic and conflicted horror frames dominate many presidential campaign ads in the new millennium (2000 through 2020). The intensity of these horror themes captures the increasing divisiveness of American politics as candidates come to depict their opponents at best as flawed human beings and at worst as demons and monsters. This chapter concludes by laying out the details of this study and the critical framework for understanding the ways in which presidential campaign ads portray American politics as a house of horrors.

HISTORY OF THE HORROR GENRE

Horror films have been a publicly shunned, yet central aspect of cinema since almost the birth of film as a medium itself. Kendall R. Phillips argues horror films that reach cultural significance must have resonance with the events of the day and "they must shock us."[7] Understanding how the affective appeals of shock, terror, and horror are used in campaign commercials requires, as Nelson and Boynton make clear, "comparing popular genres across media (horror in political ads versus horror in Hollywood films)."[8] Further, it is essential to understand the wide variety of forms monstrosity has assumed within the genre, since as Marina Levina and Diem-My T. Bui explain, "what is at stake in the representational analysis of monster images is the definition of humanness."[9] Thus, I engage in a review of Hollywood horror's key elements and monsters, but this could also be deemed a brief history of cultural humanness starting with the proto-horrors and classic Universal Studios horrors of the 1930s. This also helps reveal which aspects of the horror genre are deeply entrenched and which are more recently developed.[10] Both aspects are important in examining how this force of popular culture bleeds over into media outside of Hollywood film, including our political advertisements.

Many film scholars point to the Universal films of the 1930s, first with *Dracula* (1931) and followed by *Frankenstein* (1931), as the birth of a recognizable horror genre.[11] While 1931 was the year that launched horror as a definable film genre, the elements that make up this genre had been developing for years before that in the silent film era. As Harry M. Benshoff argues, some cite an earlier adaptation of Mary Shelley's book, *Frankenstein* (1910) "as the first 'horror' film."[12] While this was arguably the first horror film (existing absent a recognized genre at the time), the most consequential of the proto-horrors was almost certainly *The Cabinet of Dr. Caligari* (1920).[13] This film cemented the German Expressionist style as a mainstay of horror film, creating "an international sensation because of its unique Expressionist style."[14] Indeed, Benshoff articulates how the uniquely "distorted lines and angular shadows serve as a visual corollary for the distorted psyches of the film's villains."[15] These can very clearly be seen through *The Cabinet of Dr. Caligari*'s painted sets that have completely unrealistic buildings and windows that one could never imagine would stand on their own.[16] Thus, distorted imagery as an expression of characters' inner fears and turmoil became a primary trope of the genre before the genre was recognized as such.

However, this inner dynamic, expressed by the setting and distorted imagery, moves beyond being simply symbolic of the individual characters. Rather, it often also expresses the mindset of the creators, audience, or both. The writers of *The Cabinet of Dr. Caligari*, Hans Janowitz and Carl Mayer, had originally intended for the film to be "an outspoken revolutionary story. In it, as Janowitz indicates, he and Carl Mayer half-intentionally stigmatized the omnipotence of a state authority manifesting itself in universal conscription and declarations of war. The German war government seemed to the authors the prototype of such voracious authority."[17] While this intention had been present with the writers, the political messaging of the film was changed by director Robert Wiene when he put a framing device on the film that led to a narrative redemption of authority.[18] This framing device shows the protagonist as being locked in an insane asylum for treatment. The audience discovers Janowitz and Mayer's original story is simply the rantings of someone in need of medical assistance, which the "villain," Dr. Caligari, provides. Thus, the story is no longer about how Dr. Caligari uses his position of power to commit violent crimes, but how, even though the protagonist thinks he is evil, Dr. Caligari uses his authority to try to help the delusional protagonist.[19] Here, mental illness makes one of its earliest entries into the genre, a signifier of horror that remains to this day. Some, like Caroline Joan (Kay) S. Picart and David A. Frank, argue that the pro-authority messaging of *Caligari* represented the mood of the film's post–World War I German audience.[20] However, I disagree, since, as Siegfried Kracauer shows, the film never gained much success in Germany itself but rather gained traction in the international film audience, particularly the United States.[21] Regardless, horror films as contemporary political and social commentary became a mainstay.

Moving forward into the 1930s era of classical horror, *Dracula* "communicated the rather conservative sociopolitics of the day."[22] The political underpinnings of the movie can be seen primarily in how director Tod Browning placed all of Dracula's sexual energy in his mouth, through the act of drinking blood.[23] Thus, it is noticeable how Dracula's voyage to England is changed from its literary version where he attacks the all-male crew members to the cinematic version where the crew simply dies in a storm at sea.[24] This is because producer Carl Laemmle Jr. was uncomfortable with the idea of Dracula attacking men and thought he should only victimize women.[25] Accordingly, from its earliest days, horror films were not only explicitly political, but they even politicized what races, classes, and sexes had the "privilege" of being a victim.[26]

Both *Dracula* and *Frankenstein* also added another key element to the horror genre's setting. Both took horror and put it within decaying, gothic manors/castles, drawing from a tradition of gothic literary works such as *The Castle of Otranto*.[27] We first meet Dracula inside of such a decrepit castle in Eastern Europe.[28] Similarly, Victor Frankenstein creates his monster in a lab secluded in a decaying gothic castle up on a hill (see figure 1.1).[29] Thus, depictions of decaying settings are another critical aspect of classical horror.

Setting and victimization are not the only political elements of classical horror, as a large portion of classic horror films is also overtly xenophobic. Many of the monsters in classic horror films originate somewhere in Eastern Europe, such as in *Dracula* and *The Wolf Man* (1941).[30] In both of these films, Bela Lugosi gives life to the foreign monstrosity that infects western civilization. Thus, there are clearly dense political messages behind what is monstrous in classic horror films. With all of these overt and covert political messages inherently tied to the genre of horror, it is no wonder that politics itself would start picking up on these generic qualities of horror.

After the Universal films of the 1930s and early 1940s, horror began to noticeably decline. Mark Jancovich notes that the "1940s are rarely seen as a distinct period within the history of the English-language horror film, but merely as the decadent tail-end of the 1930s production."[31] However, there is one producer worth making note of from this period. Val Lewton, who

Figure 1.1 *Frankenstein* (1931). Screenshot captured by author.

produced films for RKO, helped relieve "a period of comparative infertility" in the horror genre, as David Punter puts it.[32] Indeed, Lewton's style has been described as "atmospheric and imaginative," preferring to merely suggest the monstrous rather than make it explicit.[33] This style can be seen at play in Val Letwon's *Cat People* (1942), which tried to capture the essence of Universal's *The Wolf Man* and merge it with a "female-centered narrative" like that in *Rebecca* (1940).[34] *Cat People* centers on a woman who morphs into a panther when jealous or aroused, clearly resembling the werewolf transformative process in *The Wolf Man*.[35] However, stylistically, these movies are completely different. In *The Wolf Man*, the transformation and the monster itself are shown explicitly using the practical effects available at the time.[36] Conversely, *Cat People* never really shows the transformation process in full or the monster itself, they are simply alluded to using shadows, camera tricks, and acting.[37] Thus, it is worth noting how embedded within the horror genre is the possibility of stylized otherization. One does not have to be shown explicitly as visually monstrous for the audience to still grasp that, through allusions and illusions, the person is in fact a monster. Such a strategy can be seen in the iconic Reagan advertisement, "Bear," which shows a bear but merely implies the Soviets as the real monstrosity.[38]

During the 1940s there was another trend arising within the horror genre, one that can likely be attributed to the rise of film noir, a genre which itself draws from German Expressionism to depict the American crime drama.[39]

As Jancovich highlights, Universal's Sherlock Holmes films, sold as a horror series, were also marketed as "whodunits" and "mysteries."[40] Thus, elements of solving a puzzle and figuring out who is to blame were injected into the horror genre. This notion of the monster not being completely obvious, once again, jived well with the subdued style of films like *Cat People*. As such, audiences are primed by the genre itself to try to figure out who represented the culpable party in horrific campaign advertisements.

Just as horror in the 1940s could largely be described as a hybrid between horror and noir, the 1950s saw the rise of the horror/science fiction hybrid.[41] These films took the political narrative lying under the surface of earlier horror films and made horror's "political/ideological agenda" far more obvious.[42] While there were many different political messages expressed by these films in this decade, some of the most notable for the purposes of this project are the invasion films. These films, such as *It Came from Outer Space* (1953), *War of the Worlds* (1953), and *The Monolith Monsters* (1957) depicted the anxiety that coincided with "a new consciousness of the relativity of spatial and temporal distance and the planet as a connected global community."[43] This new interconnectedness created two different fears: the obvious fear of external invasion (fictionally by aliens, but realistically by foreign nations), but also the fear of the "uncolonized geographic other" articulated in giant monster films such as *Them!* (1954) and *Tarantula* (1955).[44] Both invasion films and giant monster films were often set in the American Southwest because this area was geographically otherized, but still American.[45] This geographic otherization occurred for two reasons. First, the American Southwest contains large, desert landscapes that provide "[e]erie long shots of the supposedly empty landscape accompanied by voiceover musings about the limits of human knowledge."[46] The second reason this landscape became otherized was its status as "a key site of the Manhattan Project" that "remained an important testing ground for nuclear weaponry during the postwar years. Cordoned off no-go areas under the control of the US military . . . increased a sense of geographic otherness."[47]

However, the political messaging throughout these films were not all ideologically the same in that there were centrist and radical sci-fi films. Centrist sci-fi films cast extremists as the villains, while experts (e.g., scientists and government agents) and/or "average Joes and plain Janes" are cast as the heroes.[48] Radical sci-fi films, on the other hand, use covert messages to "attack the center" from either the Left or the Right.[49] Thus, the roles are often reversed, with scientists and government bureaucracy occupying the role of villain and the extremist the role of hero. This radical sci-fi lens can easily be seen in horror movies like *Invasion of the Body Snatchers* (1956), where the heroes are running from "pod people" that have taken over the center (police officers, the psychiatrist, and other officials).[50] Notably, radical ideas of what makes a hero or villain are not limited to sci-fi horrors in the 1950s. *The Cabinet of Dr. Caligari* is a great example where a radical critique of the center was changed to a centrist critique of extremism through the framing device placed on the film. Simply, 1950s sci-fi horror emphasized these differing film critiques in the context of the Cold War, with scientific advancement situated among expanding threats of both communism and McCarthyism.

The late 1950s through early 1970s were largely defined by a revival of the gothic horror of the 1930s.[51] Hammer Films led this crusade, making their own versions of Universal classics such as *The Curse of Frankenstein* (1957) and *Dracula* (1958).[52] While these films revived many of the motifs of classic, gothic horror films, some other aspects were altered. Notably, "where filmmakers at Universal had featured off-kilter sets and deep shadows inspired by German expressionism, Hammer director Terence Fisher flaunted . . . gore around securing corpses, murdering innocents, and sewing up bloody pieces of flesh and bone."[53] Thus, the more stylized horror of the 1930s was replaced in this period by graphic, in your face, horror imagery. However, this graphicness would ultimately be the demise of the gothic revival period, as "more graphic content" in films such as *Night of the Living Dead* (1968) and *The Texas Chainsaw Massacre* (1974) "made the old gothic style seem quaint."[54]

From the demise of the gothic revival, the 1980s slasher film rose. Slasher films helped better capture the rising "American youth culture,"[55] focusing largely on teenage protagonists. There are a number of elements that make up a slasher film. The most important is the "psychotic killer."[56] The killer is often the most recognizable character of these films, with villains such as Michael Myers from *Halloween* (1978), Jason Voorhees from *Friday the 13th* (1980), and Freddy Krueger from *A Nightmare on Elm Street* (1984) gaining widespread cultural recognition.[57] Often, these villains are characterized as masculine, although this gender construct has been complicated throughout.[58] Another critical aspect of the slasher film is the "Final Girl" who either "survives" or dispatches "the killer herself."[59]

However, James Kendrick notes that "there were a number of other cycles and trends" besides slashers that were present in the 1980s.[60] These include "[t]raditional horror monsters reborn via color," ghost movies, werewolf movies, zombie movies, sci-fi/horrors, and some vampire films.[61] Further, the "prevalence of genre hybrids and remakes suggested a postmodern turn in the genre."[62] This change, which often utilized campy humor, has been termed "horrality" for the films' use of "horror, textuality, morality, [and] hilarity."[63]

As slasher films began to die out in the 1990s, the horror genre entered another "slump."[64] Although critical successes such as *The Silence of the Lambs* (1991) and *Scream* (1996) came out during this time, the American horror genre was largely lost through the 1990s until the release of *The Sixth Sense* (1999) and *The Blair Witch Project* (1999).[65] However, while both of these films signaled new possibilities for the genre, neither seemed to immediately register "much of an impact on the genre as a whole."[66] Ultimately, the genre found its footing by becoming "fundamentally international" based on the success of "J-horror" films like *Ringu* (1998) and its Americanized version *The Ring* (2002).[67] The spookiness of *The Ring* was quickly supplanted by body horror films, creating a subgenre of "torture porn" films seen in *Saw* (2004) and *Hostel* (2005).[68] Bodily disfigurement is an often-used trope within horrific campaign advertisements, especially when discussing warfare or veteran sacrifices.

As the 2000s began to draw to a close, the "found footage" genre took the gimmick originated by *The Blair Witch Project* and applied it to ghost films like *Paranormal Activity* (2007) and monster films such as *[Rec]* (2007) and *Cloverfield* (2008).[69] This subgenre highlighted a growing, post-9/11 concern "with surveillance," especially in *Paranormal Activity*, which "presents near totalizing surveillance of suburban interiors."[70] Ultimately, while independent horror films have grown in the international market, the contemporary moment, at least in Hollywood, "has been largely defined by sequels and remakes."[71] Thus, it is unsurprising that presidential campaign ads have taken up a similar postmodern approach of remaking various horror styles when presenting their threat constructions. Still, there have been some noteworthy counterpoints to Hollywood's remake obsession in the 2010s. Diversity in the genre is increasing, with exemplars of feminist horror such as director Jennifer Kent's *The Babadook* (2014) and racial horror such as director Jordan Peele's *Get Out* (2017) and *Us* (2019).[72] Elevated horror is also on the rise, with indie studio A24 Films taking the lead on more artistic horrors such as *Hereditary* (2018) and *Midsommar* (2019) (see figure 1.2).[73]

Figure 1.2 *Midsommar* **(2019).** Screenshot captured by author.

PRIOR RESEARCH ON TELEVISED CAMPAIGN ADVERTISEMENTS

The advent of the television changed many facets of American life, from entertainment to how information is gathered and processed. Thus, it is no wonder that political campaigns latched onto this new medium and have, as of yet, not let go. Nevertheless, spot ads were not always how politicians utilized the medium of television. Indeed, "the half hour broadcast speech" was the norm of 1952 political campaigning.[74] However, by 1980 these half-hour speeches were "replaced by the 60-second spot."[75] Even further, 30-second spots are now common in contemporary campaign advertising.

TV spot ads have changed election campaigns in a number of ways. They have enabled "candidates to build name recognition, frame the questions they view as central to the election, and expose their temperaments, talents, and agendas for the future in a favorable light."[76] Further, "[a]ds also argue the relevance of issues to our lives," creating "a greater connection between what occurred in the political world and what occurred in their lives."[77] However, anyone who has watched a contemporary campaign ad can likely tell you that they are not all about the positives of the candidate they favor, but rather an unfavorable attack on the opposing candidate. Theodore F. Sheckels claims, "Negative television advertisements on behalf of candidates for public office are likely a permanent fixture of political campaigns, because such advertisements convey information, are memorable, and achieve their goals."[78]

Negative campaign advertising quickly picked up on horror elements, particularly the use of decaying settings and imagery as a form of visual connection between the opposing candidate and decay and decline. Kathleen Hall Jamieson shows how this functions in campaign ads, where "the favored candidate" is visually associated "with pictures of well-fed cattle, happy families, large bundles of grain, and bulging factories."[79] "The opponent, on the other hand," she argues, is "visually tied to drawings of starving cattle, poverty-ravished families, empty grain bins, and fireless factories."[80] Thus, visual representations of decay are deployed by substituting the "cause for effect" through "synecdoche,"[81] what Kenneth Burke describes as "representation."[82] In these particular political representations, the cause is the opposing candidate's character or policies and the effect is decay, decline, and destruction. This association is parallel to classic horror framing where the cause is the monster and the effect is death and decay. Attack ads, accordingly, tend to conflate the monstrous opposing candidate with the supposed horrific effects of their being elected.

Notably, these representations do not have to make sound, logical sense. Jamieson posits that this form of argument "is as powerful as it is irrational. It solicits a visceral and not an intellectual response."[83] Further,

Jamieson elaborates in her book, *Dirty Politics: Deception, Distraction, and Democracy*, that fears alter our perception of facts in negative campaign ads.[84] Additionally, she articulates the irrationality of voter response, comparing voters to pack rats because "[l]ike pack rats, voters gather bits and pieces of political information and store them in a single place.... Information obtained from news mixes with that from ads."[85] So in campaigns, voters irrationally place information together, even if some sources are clearly biased, and allow fear to guide their decision-making process.

This visceral voter response is similar, if not identical, to the somewhat irrational "fear and disgust directed at a monster" horror films are meant to impart.[86] In fact, one of the deep philosophical questions surrounding horror films is whether it is rational to fear them,[87] to which Aaron Smuts seems to lean toward "emotional reactions to fiction" as irrational.[88] Nevertheless, there is some distinction between the irrationality of horror films, which are almost always fictional, and campaign ads that, while often exaggerating and distorting facts, continue to have at least some tangential basis in reality. Still, while the grounding is potentially more real world in campaign ads than horror films, Jamieson makes clear that the audience response to campaign ads is highly irrational, much like audience response to horror.[89] Thus, the questionable rationality of audience responses to both political attack ads and horror films are likely similar because the former draws from the latter.

Yet, while the audience's response in affective form of fear may be irrational, Kim Witte has been able to predict how audiences will *act* on that fear. Witte has found that "perceived threat (beliefs about severity and susceptibility) and perceived efficacy (beliefs about response efficacy and self-efficacy)" play a crucial role in how an audience responds.[90] Thus, she concludes that high threat and high efficacy lead to "adaptive responses" whereas high threat and low efficacy creates "defensive motivation" that does not lead to productive action.[91] Indeed, P. Sol Hart and Lauren Feldman found that "positive efficacy information alone," absent "negative efficacy information," is crucial to generating audience action on a threat.[92]

Accordingly, just as classic horror films require a means to defeat the monster, and ultimately, an actual slaying of the monster, a successful political advertising strategy requires positive messages from the candidate as a viable alternative to the monstrous opposition candidate. This gives the audience a sense of efficacy in stopping the threat. According to Jamieson, a "coherent campaign" takes the acceptance speech at the candidate's party convention and "synopsizes and polishes the message."[93] Further, "The message is then systematically developed in the advertising of the general election and placed in its final form on election eve where the candidate tries on the presidency by indicating for the country his vision of the next four years under his leadership."[94] Then, if the "candidates offer consistent, coherent messages" they are often able to outlast attacks and distortions made by their opponents.[95] So, while negative campaigning is of importance in evoking the monstrous threat, it is the coherence of the entire narrative that is essential to the success of the advertising campaign.

In order to judge the coherence of a campaign strategy, Jamieson argues for the utility of "[v]iewing campaign advertising as an extended message rather than a series of discrete message units."[96] Thus, I do just that when analyzing the campaigns of 2000, 2004, 2008, 2012, 2016, and 2020 in the coming chapters. Large swaths of campaign ads are investigated, first on their own merits, before weaving them into a larger overall horror message in each chapter's conclusion. This helps to explain the utility of even purely positive advertisements in a grander narrative.

To date, the study of how the horror genre intermixes with presidential campaign ads has been woefully inadequate. Nelson and Boynton argue in their groundbreaking book, *Video Rhetorics: Televised Advertising in American Politics*, that popular genres help explain how political advertisements function as a coherent whole.[97] Further, Nelson and Boynton claim the study of genre in campaign advertising should start with *popular, cross-media genres such as horror*.[98] These popular genres require a comparison of media, such as cinematic horror and campaign advertisement horror, when possible.[99]

Glenn W. Richardson Jr. extends Nelson and Boynton's work and argues there is a gap missing in the existing research on political ads.[100] Richardson establishes how genre analysis fills this gap, positing that the "crucial connective cement that glues the components of compelling narratives together is often reinforced by generic evocations. Genres serve as emotional heuristics."[101] Richardson utilizes genres of satire, pornography, dystopia, testimonial, tabloid TV scandal, family melodrama, drugs, action-hero, and horror to capably analyze specific campaign advertisements. Specifically, Richardson applies the horror genre to the 1988 presidential election, finding that the Bush-Quayle "Revolving Door" advertisement used generic elements of horror.[102] Richardson explains some of the elements of a horror ad, "Political advertisements evoke genre through the combination of audio and visual elements (as well as text) in a way that appeals to conventional understandings of mass audiences."[103] The audio aspect of the genre usually relies heavily on soundtrack and the narrator's voice, which should be "deep and serious."[104] Visually, Richardson highlights "black-and-white film clips" and shadowy distortions, such as "rolling black clouds of smoke" as some possible visual horror cues used in campaign ads.[105] Nelson and Boynton describe other horror markers, such as a visually "pervasive gray" and an auditorily "relentless drone."[106]

While Nelson and Boynton, as well as Richardson, have opened the door for a generic study of campaign ads, both sources engage in an overview analysis of multiple genres, without doing a deep analysis on any one genre. This project extends these previous works by providing an in-depth study of one of the most readily recognizable and influential genres in terms of campaign advertisements—horror ads. Further, the choice to use horror frames in analyzing these ads is natural because many of the ads readily invite this generic reading themselves through various visual and audio cues. Even though there are a few ads in each campaign that, in and of themselves, lack horror elements, they can still perform horrific narrative functions within the larger narrative.

VISUAL RHETORIC, GENRE, AND HORROR FRAMES

This present study comes out of the traditions of presidential and visual rhetoric. I treat these campaign ads as instances of rhetorical practice targeted to voters and designed to build support for one candidacy over all others. As Mary E. Stuckey makes clear, "rhetoric" in political practice represents a "complex dance of meaning and interpretation" that imbues both political leaders and the people with "interpretative" powers that animate this "dance of democracy."[107] The aim of this project is to read these ads in their political contexts and interpret the meanings, messages, and ideologies targeted to the American people. The mission is ultimately to discern what these ads suggest about a candidate, their opponents, the voting public, the changes in campaign culture in the new millennium, and the state of American politics writ large.

A study of political ads necessarily relies heavily on visual components. According to Cara A. Finnegan, visual rhetoric is engrossed with "visual artifacts."[108] Marguerite Helmers and Charles A. Hill argue that these artifacts include "photographs and drawings, graphs and tables, and motion pictures" and the study of these mediums explores "the many ways in which visual elements are used to influence people's attitudes, opinions, and beliefs."[109] Finnegan isolates five approaches when studying visual rhetoric which include: *production, composition, reproduction, circulation*, and *reception*.[110] While each of these elements is important, this study focuses primarily on composition. As Finnegan explains, with a study focused on composition, "the critic attends to the visual features of the image itself, as well as any historical referents or commonplaces they activate."[111] These commonplaces in political ads include the words on the screen, the still and moving imagery, the colors that dominate the ads, the editing and splicing together of frames, as well as the generic features of the ads across candidacies—one of the dominant analytical tools of this study.

Karlyn Kohrs Campbell and Kathleen Hall Jamieson define "genre" in two ways. First, as a category or "classifying term" that can encompass nearly anything.[112] The second, and more useful, definition is "those similarities that make works rhetorically absorbing and consequential."[113] With this more practical parameter, Campbell and Jamieson explore "a critical use of genre" that is concerned with both "ends" and "means."[114] This critical conception captures the focus of this study that looks to the means and ends of persuasion—the rhetorical strategies reflected in the ads and the messages of horror targeted to voters.[115] More specifically, I attempt to make sense of the messages and emotional appeals broadcasted to audience members and provide potential readings of those horrific provocations.

In order to provide these readings, I rely on horror frames as outlined by Picart and Frank. In their own work, they use the classic and conflicted horror frames to analyze Holocaust films.[116] While presidential campaigns are obviously not directly comparable to the Holocaust, the idea of horror framing used by Picart and Frank is useful in analyzing the horrific elements of presidential campaign ads.

The classic horror frame is focused on depictions of monsters and monstrosities, which are often spatially and temporally bracketed.[117] While this frame frequently overlaps with the classic Hollywood horror films, it is still common in contemporary horror. As Picart and Frank argue, "The monsters in classic horror films share nothing in common with the audience; they inhabit a different space, which they leave to attack the innocent."[118] Thus, the monster's otherness spatially brackets the horrors of the film (Count Dracula and the original Wolf Man coming from Eastern Europe, or Victor Frankenstein working in isolation in a decrepit manor). Indeed, the settings and spatiality of classic horror constitute the "dark areas, of something completely other and unseen."[119] The otherization of classic horror monsters is readily apparent even beyond spatiality, as the monsters are "essentially and irreducibly other."[120] Put simply, they are meant to look monstrous and represent everything that Western notions of humans ought not to be.

Temporal bracketing is also important in the classic horror frame. As Picart and Frank make clear, "The classic horror film also breaches the ontology of normal time. The time sequence of horror is bracketed, as the transgressive monster emerges at a definitive moment and, in classic American Gothic, is eventually conquered. With the monster vanquished, normal time returns."[121] This classic horror frame "has served political purposes," as Picart and Frank argue, in that it allows people to separate themselves spatially and temporally from the monstrosities on the screen.[122]

The other frame that Picart and Frank describe is the conflicted horror frame. This frame separates itself from classic horror by weaving "evil into normality, refusing to recognize an unassailable gap between the two spheres."[123] These two spheres, as Steffen Hantke puts it, are a part of fantasy which pictures "two incompatible spheres—the predictable, mundane world of everyday life and the non-rational world of the fantastic," which "exist separately from each other."[124] As Hantke makes clear, "fantasy is generated whenever the line of separation is being crossed in one direction or the other."[125] Thus, whereas the classic frame keeps these spheres distinctly separated through otherness, spatiality, and temporality, the conflicted horror frame brings the spheres into contact with each other, making the monstrous normal, mundane, maybe even relatable in the here and now. The final form of *The Cabinet of Dr. Caligari* shows just such a framing, with the fantastical monster really just being the product of a mental patient's delusions. Typically, more contemporary horror films, like *The Silence of the Lambs*, use this conflicted frame more often, with the advent of serial killings being perpetrated not by some inhuman monster in a decrepit manor in Eastern Europe, but rather by an outwardly normal person, in the present time, in a typical urban environment. However, both frames can be found in horror films from nearly all periods, and the frames may even shift during a singular movie. One thinks of the brief moments where a sensation of sympathy is felt toward Frankenstein's monster, before its otherness takes over and it starts killing.

Certainly, themes of drama, comedy, and many other genre features are at work in these ads. In fact, comedic elements are discussed in a number of instances given their historical relation to horror. However, many of the campaign advertisements explored here openly invite a horrific reading through various audio and visual cues and other allusions to the horror genre. This makes horror framing the clear choice for a mode of analysis. Further, as Nelson and Boynton argue, "Even when popular genres are not overt and controlling in political ads, their conventions often endow the spots with meaning and coherence for viewers."[126] Thus, using the popular genre of horror as the overarching narrative measuring stick allows one to explore the predominant strategies and rhetorical coherence of an entire campaign.

THE PERILOUS PATH AHEAD

With the classic and conflicted horror frames in mind, this project performs a compositional analysis of twenty-first-century presidential campaign ads and provides insight into the continued deepening of fissures in U.S. politics and the dehumanizing images of political opponents. This work features an analysis of the 2000, 2004, 2008, 2012, 2016, and 2020 presidential elections. I focus on presidential advertising campaigns on both sides of the political spectrum as larger narratives, rather than picking single advertisements to examine. This helps to establish Jamieson's rubric of a "coherent campaign."[127]

I have chosen these elections for a couple of reasons. First, devoting this work to twenty-first-century campaigns allows one to gain insight on how these campaigns have used horror framing at the turn of the new millennium. Second, analyzing the 2000 campaigns in comparison to later campaign advertisements provides interesting comparisons in pre- and post-9/11 horror framing. While other studies have focused on Cold War–era campaign advertisements, the War on Terror and various other twenty-first-century phenomena have created an entirely new set of situational constraints for campaigns to spark fear. This study relies on ads from *The Living Room Candidate: Presidential Campaign Commercials 1952–2020*, curated by the Museum of the Moving Image. This archive is ideal for this project because it provides a wide breadth of campaign advertisements in the general election from both the Republican and Democratic nominees in a given election.[128]

Throughout this project, I seek to elaborate four main arguments. First, horror framing represents a consistently present element of televised presidential campaign rhetoric in the twenty-first century. Second, across these five elections, we see spikes in the horror framing—spikes that peak in the contentious 2016 presidential election. Third, each campaign uses horror framing in varying and unique ways. The two most prominent types are classic and conflicted horror frames, where candidates depict different types of enemies. Some treat their opponents as inhuman forces of evil, while others dismiss them as humans too deeply flawed to be president. Such narratives reflect a growing and troubling tendency to depict opposing candidates as either monsters or fools. Worth noting, some advertisements are much more apparently horrific than others. Some ads do not come across as horrific at all. However, in looking at the advertisements as a narrative whole for the given election, horrific themes become strikingly apparent. Similar to a feature-length Hollywood horror, some scenes/ads are outright terrifying, while others can be funny, upbeat, or endearing. Still, the overall narrative valence one tends to walk away with in most of the elections analyzed here is that of horror. Finally, the intensity of such horror framing and otherization, especially with the classic frame, captures the enhanced negativity of our political process. Such negativity is accompanied by dehumanizing imagery targeting political opponents and groups of people, making deliberation across differences more and more improbable. The remainder of this project winds down the haunting trail of campaign advertisements as follows.

Chapter 2 analyzes how horror framing was deployed in the televised campaign ads of two candidates in the 2000 election—Democratic Vice President Al Gore and Republican Governor George W. Bush of Texas. Both Bush and Gore used a heavy dose of positive campaign messaging, in an attempt to instill voter efficacy and set themselves apart as the "good guy" of the narrative. Both also used classic and conflicted horror frames, with Bush relying on the conflicted horror frame a little more than Gore. Whereas Bush typically attacked Gore directly by using the conflicted horror frame, Gore's attacks against Bush were done mostly through the classic frame. Further, Gore leaned heavily on deliberative, future-based policy proposals, especially those dealing with health care and the environment. Bush also provided a heavy dose of future policies related to health care and defense, while simultaneously relying on self-praise of his own economic accomplishments to set himself apart as the proven hero.

Chapter 3 explores how President Bush used horror framing in his televised reelection campaign and how Democratic candidate Senator John Kerry attempted to use these frames as a challenger in the 2004 election. In the first presidential campaign since September 11, the Bush campaign relied on horror framing early and often, using the classic frame to demonize threats to America from terrorists, enemy nations, and even technology. This framing helped to amplify the threats still facing the United States in the voters' minds. Bush then deployed the conflicted frame to attack Kerry himself, portraying him as a misguided, insidiously flawed human. Kerry's weak fortitude was juxtaposed with Bush's resilient resolve, a positive theme sprinkled throughout many of Bush's advertisements. The Kerry campaign took a different approach, attempting to avoid using horror framing for as long as possible. Kerry likely knew that his stances on defense issues would be attacked, so the campaign tried to emphasize his credentials as a veteran, while not overtly using horror to frame the threats facing America. It seems obvious in many ads that the audience can fill in the horrors facing the United States for themselves, and Kerry would not have wanted to scare people further and drive them toward Bush. However, later in the campaign there is a shift and the Kerry campaign begins using gruesome details to horrifically frame the Vietnam and Iraq wars.

Chapter 4 examines how the 2008 presidential election ads of Senator John McCain (R-AZ) and Senator Barack Obama (D-IL) used horror framing to make fear appeals to voters. Senators McCain and Obama deployed elements of the horror genre in their campaign ads, but in very different ways. McCain relied on both the classic and conflicted horror frames consistently, using the classic frame when discussing the economy and defense and the conflicted frame when attacking Obama. These conflicted attacks often relied on subtle, but deeply seated racist tropes of the horror genre. Senator Obama, on the other hand, slowly evolved his ads from a conflicted frame to a classic one, with the financial crisis of 2008 providing the impetus for a final pivot toward the classic frame. Additionally, Obama's late appeals to audience efficacy allowed these increasingly monstrous threats to have a narrative solution. McCain's calls to efficacy were too little and too contradictory to his self-proclaimed status as an experienced "maverick."

Chapter 5 explores the horror framing used in 2012 campaign advertisements by President Barack Obama and Governor Mitt Romney. The Romney campaign and the Obama campaign took nearly opposite approaches in their televised advertising. The Romney campaign relied heavily on the classic horror frame, using it to racistly demonize Obama, as well as various threats to American well-being. Positive appeals were interwoven in a few of these ads, with "The Moment" serving as the only purely positive ad analyzed here. The Obama campaign, on the other hand, used the conflicted frame early and often, with a number of positive ads spread in between.

Chapter 6 examines the 2016 campaign ads of both Hillary Clinton and Donald Trump through the method of horror framing. Clinton and Trump also deployed elements of the horror genre in their campaign ads, but again in very different ways. Clinton used both the classic and conflicted horror frames but privileged the conflicted frame over the classic when attacking Trump, while doing little in the way of attempting to promote audience efficacy through epideictic self-praise. Trump consistently evoked the classic horror frame to create distinct, otherized monsters such as immigrants, the economy, and Clinton. He also provided methods for slaying such ghouls, thus repeatedly attempting to instill audience efficacy through epideictic self-praise.

Chapter 7 provides an in-depth analysis of the 2020 campaign advertisements released by Republican President Donald Trump and the Democratic challenger, former Vice President Joe Biden. Trump once again relied on similar tactics to his 2016 campaign, using the classic horror frame to depict threats to the United States stemming from immigrants, economic decline, the Establishment, and the Radical Left. Notably, Biden was mostly framed through a conflicted lens, as the Trump campaign made him out as a puppet being strung along by the more monstrous Kamala Harris, the Establishment, and the Radical Left. Biden's campaign, on the other hand, did not deal heavily with horror framing. Instead, they relied primarily on allusions to the ongoing COVID-19 pandemic. However, Biden did lash out at Trump through classic horror framing when discussing Trump's continuation of racist policies and voter suppression.

Chapter 8 concludes this work by recounting the discoveries made in each chapter using horror framing, before providing some overarching takeaways. The conclusion explores the implications of the conflicted and classic frames, specifically how campaign horror framing is omnipresent, normative, polarizing, demonic, invasive, insidious, and nihilistic. These implications especially point to the worrisome tendencies in the nation's deliberative practices—as seen in the January 6, 2021, Capitol invasion. Through analysis of these trends, we must realize and re-envision how we talk about our country, our politics, others, and ourselves. As such, the book concludes with a potential path forward: the justified horror frame.

NOTES

1. Copyright © 2019 by Michigan State University. Portions of this chapter originally appeared as an article in *Rhetoric & Public Affairs* 22, no. 2 (2019): 281–321.

2. See Robert L. Ivie and Oscar Giner, *Hunt the Devil: A Demonology of U.S. War Culture* (Tuscaloosa: University of Alabama Press, 2015).

3. Ernest W. King and Franklin G. Mixon Jr., "Religiosity and the Political Economy of the Salem Witch Trials," *The Social Science Journal* 47, no. 3 (2010): 684.

4. John Edgar Browning, "Classical Hollywood Horror," in *A Companion to the Horror Film*, ed. Harry M. Benshoff (New York: Wiley Blackwell, 2014), 228.

5. See John S. Nelson and G. R. Boynton, *Video Rhetorics: Televised Advertising in American Politics* (Urbana: University of Illinois Press, 1997); Glenn W. Richardson Jr., "Pulp Politics: Popular Culture and Political Advertising," *Rhetoric & Public Affairs* 3, no. 4 (2000); Glenn W. Richardson Jr., *Pulp Politics: How Political Advertising Tells the Stories of American Politics* (Lanham, MD: Rowman & Littlefield, 2008).

6. Democratic National Committee, "Peace Little Girl (Daisy)," *The Living Room Candidate: Presidential Campaign Commercials 1952-2020*, September 7, 1964, http://www.livingroomcandidate.org/commercials/1964/peace-little-girl-daisy.

7. Kendall R. Phillips, *Projected Fears: Horror Films and American Culture* (Westport, CT: Praeger, 2005), 7.

8. Nelson and Boynton, *Video Rhetorics*, 60.

9. Marina Levina and Diem-My T. Bui, "Introduction: Toward a Comprehensive Monster Theory in the 21st Century," in *Monster Culture in the 21st Century: A Reader*, ed. Marina Levina and Diem-My T. Bui (New York: Bloomsbury, 2013), 5.

10. This analysis, while mentioning international horror phenomena where needed, focuses on how horror was shaped and viewed in the United States, given the focus of this work on U.S. presidential campaigns.

11. Browning, "Classical Hollywood Horror," 226; *Dracula*, directed by Tod Browning (1931; Peacock TV), Digital; *Frankenstein*, directed by James Whale (1931; Universal Pictures Home Entertainment, 2016), DVD.

12. Harry M. Benshoff, "Horror Before 'The Horror Film,'" in *A Companion to the Horror Film*, ed. Harry M. Benshoff (New York: Wiley Blackwell, 2014), 214.

13. *The Cabinet of Dr. Caligari*, directed by Robert Wiene (1920; Horrortheque, 2010), Digital.

14. Benshoff, "Horror Before 'The Horror Film,'" 216.

15. Benshoff, "Horror Before 'The Horror Film,'" 216.

16. *The Cabinet of Dr. Caligari*, Wiene.

17. Siegfried Kracauer, *From Caligari to Hitler: A Psychological History of German Film* (Princeton, NJ: Princeton University Press, 2004), 64.

18. Kracauer, *From Caligari to Hitler*, 66.

19. See *The Cabinet of Dr. Caligari*, Wiene.

20. Caroline Joan (Kay) S. Picart and David A. Frank, *Frames of Evil: The Holocaust as Horror in American Film* (Carbondale: Southern Illinois University Press, 2006).
21. Kracauer, *From Caligari to Hitler*, 77.
22. Browning, "Classical Hollywood Horror," 228.
23. Browning, "Classical Hollywood Horror," 228.
24. *Dracula*, Browning.
25. Browning, "Classical Hollywood Horror," 228.
26. Browning, "Classical Hollywood Horror," 229.
27. Horace Walpole, *The Castle of Otranto* (Edinburgh: James Ballantyne & Co., 1811).
28. *Dracula*, Browning.
29. *Frankenstein*, Whale.
30. See *Dracula*, Browning and *The Wolf Man*, directed by George Waggner (1941; Universal Pictures Home Entertainment, 2016), DVD.
31. Mark Jancovich, "Horror in the 1940s," in *A Companion to the Horror Film*, ed. Harry M. Benshoff (New York: Wiley Blackwell, 2014), 237.
32. David Punter, *The Literature of Terror: A History of Gothic Fictions from 1765 to the Present Day* (London: Longman, 1980), 247.
33. Ivan Butler, *Horror in the Cinema* (Cranbury, NJ: A. S. Barnes and Company, 1979), 51.
34. Jancovich, "Horror in the 1940s," 241; *Cat People*, directed by Jacques Tourneur (1942; Turner Home Entertainment, 2005), DVD; *The Wolf Man*, Waggner; *Rebecca*, directed by Alfred Hitchcock (1940; Criterion, 2017), DVD.
35. *The Wolf Man*, Waggner.
36. *The Wolf Man*, Waggner.
37. *Cat People*, Tourneur.
38. Reagan-Bush '84, "Bear," *The Living Room Candidate: Presidential Campaign Commercials 1952-2020*, October 2, 1984, www.livingroomcandidate.org/commercials/1984/bear.
39. Blair Davis, "Horror Meets Noir: The Evolution of Cinematic Style, 1931–1958," in *Horror Film: Creating and Marketing Fear*, ed. Steffen Hantke (Jackson: University Press of Mississippi, 2004), 193; "What is Noir?" *Film Noir Foundation*, http://www.filmnoirfoundation.org/filmnoir.html.
40. Jancovich, "Horror in the 1940s," 244. Jancovich does note that "mystery" in the 1940s did not mean the same thing it does today, being unassociated with "puzzle-solving." However, whodunit *does* suggest a puzzle solving narrative, meaning such notions were still injected into the horror genre.
41. Steffen Hantke, "Science Fiction and Horror in the 1950s," in *A Companion to the Horror Film*, ed. Harry M. Benshoff (New York: Wiley Blackwell, 2014), 255.
42. Hantke, "Science Fiction and Horror," 255.
43. Vivian Sobchack, "American Science Fiction Film: An Overview," in *A Companion to Science Fiction*, ed. David Seed (Malden, MA: Blackwell Publishing, 2005), 263. See also *It Came from Outer Space*, directed by Jack Arnold (1953; Universal Studios, 2017), Blu-ray; *War of the Worlds*, directed by Byron Haskin

(1953; Paramount Pictures, 1999), DVD; *The Monolith Monsters*, directed by John Sherwood (1957; Willette Acquisition Corp., 2015), DVD.

44. Hantke, "Science Fiction and Horror," 265; *Them!*, directed by Gordon Douglas (1954; Warner Brothers Pictures, 2020), DVD; *Tarantula*, directed by Jack Arnold (1955; Universal Studios Home Entertainment, 2013), DVD.

45. Hantke, "Science Fiction and Horror," 265.

46. Hantke, "Science Fiction and Horror," 265.

47. Hantke, "Science Fiction and Horror," 265.

48. Peter Biskind, *Seeing is Believing: How Hollywood Taught Us to Stop Worrying and Love the Fifties* (New York, Henry Holt, 1983), 129.

49. Biskind, *Seeing is Believing*, 140.

50. *Invasion of the Body Snatchers*, directed by Don Siegel (1956; Republic Pictures, 1998), DVD.

51. Rick Worland, "The Gothic Revival (1957-1974)," in *A Companion to the Horror Film*, ed. Harry M. Benshoff (New York: Wiley Blackwell, 2014), 274.

52. *The Curse of Frankenstein*, directed by Terence Fisher (1957; Horrortheque, 2010), Digital; *The Horror of Dracula*, directed by Terence Fisher (1958; Warner Bros. Digital Distribution, 2018), Blu-ray. It's worth noting that this version of the story of Dracula has a number of different titles given to it depending on the rerelease. This particular edition was dubbed *The Horror of Dracula*, but most scholars just refer to it as *Dracula* with the year of its release.

53. Worland, "The Gothic Revival," 278.

54. Worland, "The Gothic Revival," 290; *Night of the Living Dead*, directed by George A. Romero (1968; Film Detective, 2018), DVD; *The Texas Chainsaw Massacre*, directed by Tobe Hooper (1974; Dark Sky, 2014), DVD.

55. James Kendrick, "Slasher Films and Gore in the 1980s," in *A Companion to the Horror Film*, ed. Harry M. Benshoff (New York: Wiley Blackwell, 2014), 310.

56. Kendrick, "Slasher Films," 316.

57. *Halloween*, directed by John Carpenter (1978; Lionsgate Home Entertainment, 2007), DVD; *Friday the 13th*, directed by Sean S. Cunningham (1980; Paramount, 2017), Blu-ray; *A Nightmare on Elm Street*, directed by Wes Craven (1984; New Line Home Video, 2010), Blu-ray.

58. Kendrick, "Slasher Films," 318.

59. Carol J. Clover, *Men, Women, and Chain Saws: Gender in the Modern Horror Film* (Princeton, NJ: Princeton University Press, 1992), 35; Kendrick, "Slasher Films," 317.

60. Kendrick, "Slasher Films," 311.

61. Kendrick, "Slasher Films," 311–12.

62. Kendrick, "Slasher Films," 313.

63. See Philip Brophy, "Horrality: The Texture of Contemporary Horror Films," in *The Horror Reader*, ed. Ken Gelder (London: Routledge, 2000), 276–277.

64. See Steffen Hantke, "They Don't Make 'Em Like They Used To: On the Rhetoric of Crisis and the Current State of American Horror Cinema," in *American Horror Film: The Genre at the Turn of the Millennium*, ed. Steffen Hantke (Jackson: University Press of Mississippi, 2010), 7–32.

65. Adam Charles Hart, "Millennial Fears: Abject Horror in a Transnational Context," in *A Companion to the Horror Film*, ed. Harry M. Benshoff (New York: Wiley Blackwell, 2014), 329; *The Silence of the Lambs*, directed by Jonathan Demme (1991; MGM, 2009), Blu-ray; *Scream*, directed by Wes Craven (1996; Miramax, 2020), Blu-ray; *The Sixth Sense*, directed by M. Night Shyamalan (1999; Disney, 2000), DVD; *The Blair Witch Project*, directed by Daniel Myrick and Eduardo Sanchez (1999; Lionsgate, 2010), Blu-ray.

66. Hart, "Millennial Fears," 330.

67. Hart, "Millennial Fears," 330; *Ringu*, directed by Hideo Nakata (1998; Arrow Video, 2019), Blu-ray; *The Ring*, directed by Gore Verbinski (2002; Paramount Pictures, 2012), DVD.

68. Hart, "Millennial Fears," 330; *Saw*, directed by James Wan (2004; Lionsgate, 2014), DVD; *Hostel*, directed by Eli Roth (2005; Mill Creek, 2019), Blu-ray.

69. Hart, "Millennial Fears," 330; *The Blair Witch Project*, Myrick and Sanchez; *[Rec]*, directed by Jaume Balagueró (2007; Shout Factory, 2018), Blu-ray; *Cloverfield*, directed by Matt Reeves (2008; Paramount, 2017), Blu-ray.

70. Hart, "Millennial Fears," 331.

71. Hart, "Millennial Fears," 332.

72. Cheryl Eddy, "The Biggest Horror Trends of the Last Decade," *Gizmodo*, November 21, 2019, https://io9.gizmodo.com/the-5-biggest-horror-trends-of-the-last-decade-1838973130; *The Babadook*, directed by Jennifer Kent (2014; Shout Factory, 2015), DVD; *Get Out*, directed by Jordan Peele (2017; Universal Studios, 2017), Blu-ray; *Us*, directed by Jordan Peele (2019; Universal Studios, 2019), Blu-ray.

73. Eddy, "The Biggest Horror Trends"; *Hereditary*, directed by Ari Aster (2018; Lionsgate, 2018), DVD; *Midsommar*, directed by Ari Aster (2019; Lionsgate, 2019), DVD.

74. Kathleen Hall Jamieson, *Packaging the Presidency: A History and Criticism of Presidential Campaign Advertising* (New York: Oxford University Press, 1984), 446.

75. Jamieson, *Packaging the Presidency*, 446.

76. Jamieson, *Packaging the Presidency*, 446.

77. Jamieson, *Packaging the Presidency*, 446.

78. Theodore F. Sheckels, "Narrative Coherence and Antecedent Ethos in the Rhetoric of Attack Advertising: A Case Study of the Glendening vs. Sauerbrey Campaign," *Rhetoric & Public Affairs* 5, no. 3 (2002): 459.

79. Jamieson, *Packaging the Presidency*, 449.

80. Jamieson, *Packaging the Presidency*, 449.

81. Kenneth Burke, "Four Master Tropes," *The Kenyon Review* 3, no. 4 (1941): 426.

82. Kenneth Burke, "Four Master Tropes," 421.

83. Jamieson, *Packaging the Presidency*, 450.

84. Kathleen Hall Jamieson, *Dirty Politics: Deception, Distraction, and Democracy* (New York: Oxford University Press, 1992), 33.

85. Jamieson, *Dirty Politics*, 17.

86. Aaron Smuts, "Cognitive and Philosophical Approaches to Horror," in *A Companion to the Horror Film*, ed. Harry M. Benshoff (New York: Wiley Blackwell, 2014), 5.

87. Smuts, "Cognitive and Philosophical," 13.

88. Smuts, "Cognitive and Philosophical," 14.

89. Jamieson, *Dirty Politics*, 17; Smuts, "Cognitive and Philosophical," 14.

90. Kim Witte, "Putting the Fear Back into Fear Appeals: The Extended Parallel Process Model," *Communication Monographs* 59, no. 4 (1992): 345.

91. Witte, "Putting the Fear Back," 345.

92. P. Sol Hart and Lauren Feldman, "Threat Without Efficacy? Climate Change on U.S. Network News," *Science Communication* 36, no. 3 (2014): 341.

93. Jamieson, *Packaging the Presidency*, 447.

94. Jamieson, *Packaging the Presidency*, 447. Note, the use of "his" is present in the original quote and is not reflective of the 2016 election where there was obviously a woman, Hillary Clinton, filling this role.

95. Jamieson, *Packaging the Presidency*, 447.

96. Jamieson, *Packaging the Presidency*, 448.

97. Nelson and Boynton, *Video Rhetorics*, 19.

98. Nelson and Boynton, *Video Rhetorics*, 38.

99. Nelson and Boynton, *Video Rhetorics*, 60.

100. Richardson, "Pulp Politics," 609.

101. Richardson, "Pulp Politics," 611.

102. Richardson, "Pulp Politics," 617.

103. Richardson, *Pulp Politics*, 38.

104. Richardson, *Pulp Politics*, 39.

105. Richardson, *Pulp Politics*, 39.

106. Nelson and Boynton, *Video Rhetorics*, 54.

107. Mary E. Stuckey, *Political Rhetoric* (London: Routledge, 2017), xxv.

108. Cara A. Finnegan, "Studying Visual Modes of Public Address: Lewis Hine's Progressive Era Child Labor Rhetoric," in *The Handbook of Rhetoric & Public Address*, eds. Shawn J. Parry-Giles and J. Michael Hogan (West Sussex, United Kingdom: Wiley-Blackwell, 2010), 252.

109. Marguerite Helmers and Charles A. Hill, "Introduction," in *Defining Visual Rhetorics*, eds. Charles A. Hill and Marguerite Helmers (New York: Routledge, 2009), 2.

110. Finnegan, "Studying Visual Modes," 252.

111. Finnegan, "Studying Visual Modes," 252.

112. Karlyn Kohrs Campbell and Kathleen Hall Jamieson, *Presidents Creating the Presidency: Deeds Done in Words* (Chicago, IL: University of Chicago Press 2008), 14.

113. Campbell and Jamieson, *Presidents Creating the Presidency*, 15.

114. Campbell and Jamieson, *Presidents Creating the Presidency*, 15.

115. To be clear, I do not conduct any sort of quantitative study of audience response or claim that persuasion actually happened such that the election outcome was significantly influenced one way or another.

116. Picart and Frank, *Frames of Evil*, 6-8.
117. Picart and Frank, *Frames of Evil*, 6–7.
118. Picart and Frank, *Frames of Evil*, 7.
119. Rosemary Jackson, *Fantasy: The Literature of Subversion* (London: Methuen, 1981), 179.
120. Picart and Frank, *Frames of Evil*, 7.
121. Picart and Frank, *Frames of Evil*, 7.
122. Picart and Frank, *Frames of Evil*, 7.
123. Picart and Frank, *Frames of Evil*, 9.
124. Steffen Hantke, "The Kingdom of the Unimaginable: The Construction of Social Space and the Fantasy of Privacy in Serial Killers Narratives," *Literature/Film Quarterly* 26, no. 3 (1998): 181.
125. Hantke, "The Kingdom of the Unimaginable," 181.
126. Nelson and Boynton, *Video Rhetorics*, 86.
127. Jamieson, *Packaging the Presidency*, 447.
128. Additionally, *The Living Room Candidate: Presidential Campaign Commercials 1952-2020* is the most readily accessible archive for readers to quickly locate and use in conjunction with this work. The main drawback is that this archive is not a comprehensive list of every advertisement ever released by the campaigns. However, when comparing it with other potential archives, no single source seems to have a complete list. In fact, *The Living Room Candidate* has a number of advertisements that other potential archival sources are lacking. Worth further note, these campaign advertisements certainly do not constitute all that was known of the respective campaigns. Obviously, speeches, debates, newscasts, and other forms of advertising added different information and potentially amplified or competed against the ideas and horror elements present in the campaign ads. However, the breadth of these different campaign features demands this present study be limited to the televised campaign ads deployed during the general election. Additionally, I will often refer to creators and strategists of the advertisements as "candidate" or "candidate's campaign" interchangeably. Certainly, it is possible that the candidate in a given campaign had significant input on the advertising strategy. Likewise, there is a good chance some candidates put little creative effort into these ads. Thus, "candidate's campaign" is the preferable phrasing as a catch-all for both possibilities. However, that phrasing gets excessively wordy quickly. Accordingly, I use just the candidate's name as synonymous with their campaign in much of the following analysis.

Chapter 2

Al Gore versus George W. Bush in the 2000 Election

The 2000 election came at a time of relative peace and prosperity for the United States, pitting Democratic Vice President Al Gore against Republican Texas Governor George W. Bush. The terror attacks of September 11, 2001, had not yet come to pass, and the U.S. economy was "truly robust."[1] While the U.S. economy and defense were seemingly strong, the country was still reeling from the Clinton-Lewinsky scandal and President Bill Clinton's 1998 impeachment. As Clinton's vice president, Al Gore lived in the shadows of Clinton's character issue, forcing him to bolster his own presidential character. However, even though this scandal was still fresh in the public's mind, it was rarely brought up explicitly by the Bush campaign—often living in the realm of implication.

In the 2000 election, education had risen to the top of voters' concerns. In a Pew Research Center poll—which asked voters, "What one issue should candidates talk about?"—12 percent responded with education, making it the top answer.[2] The economy was close behind at 11 percent, and had risen from a mere four percent just one year before. Health care also rested at 11 percent but had dropped from 18 percent within a year. Social Security was at 10 percent but declined from 14 percent a year earlier. Taxes came in at seven percent, foreign policy at six percent, crime/drugs and gun control at five percent, and gas prices bottomed out the list at four percent.[3] Thus, education, the economy, and health care seemed poised to take the top spots in each candidate's campaigns, with other issues also deserving some attention.

With this context, this chapter looks to explore how horror framing was deployed in the televised campaign ads of both Al Gore and George W. Bush (see table 2.1). Both Bush and Gore frequently relied on mostly positive campaign messaging. These ads were used to instill voter efficacy and set themselves up as the protagonist of their respective campaign narratives.

Table 2.1 Al Gore and George W. Bush Campaign Advertisements' Airdates

Al Gore		George W. Bush	
Airdate	Title	Airdate	Title
August 22, 2000	1969	October 25, 1999	Successful Leader
August 31, 2000	Bean Counter	October 25, 1999	Hopeful
September 9, 2000	Ian	November 16, 1999	Dangerous World
September 16, 2000	Accountability	August 28, 2000	Priority MD RNC
October 7, 2000	Down	August 31, 2000	Really MD
October 10, 2000	Morph	September 25, 2000	Education Recession
October 18, 2000	Word	October 25, 2000	Priorities
2000	Matters	November 1, 2000	Muchas Gracias
2000	Question	2000	$2.2 Trillion

Both also relied on classic and conflicted horror frames in moderation, with Bush using the conflicted horror frame slightly more than Gore. While Bush tended to attack Gore directly by using the conflicted horror frame, Gore's attacks against Bush were usually accomplished with the classic frame. Further, Gore's campaign typically furnished deliberative, future-based policy proposals. Bush also administered a heavy dose of future policies, while simultaneously utilizing self-praise of his own accomplishments to distinguish himself as the proven hero.

GORE: THE PEOPLE'S DEFENDER

Gore's televised campaign relied heavily on positive, future-based policy proposals. Even in the advertisements where he used horror framing and fear appeals, he often still included his plans for defeating such threats. Gore leaned heavily on issues involving health care, the environment, and the economy.

However, according to Gerald Pomper, Gore did not fully take advantage of the economic prosperity that had preceded the election. "The economy, usually the largest influence on voters, had evidenced the longest period of prosperity in American history, over a period virtually identical with the Democratic administration."[4] This should have been a massive boost to Gore and his campaign. However, it appears that "Gore did not properly exploit the advantages offered by his administration's economic record. In his campaign appeals, Gore would briefly mention the record of prosperity but then emphasize his plans for the future."[5] Further, "Gore lost the advantages of the strong economy he inherited when, reviewing the past, he did not tie himself to this record," which meant that "the vice president turned the election away from an advantageous retrospective evaluation of the past eight years to an uncertain prospective choice based on future expectations."[6]

This strategy, which seemingly failed Gore, plays out in his campaign advertisements and his horror framing. While he tries to position himself as the protector of the American village, he does not rely on his past experience enough to separate himself from Bush, who also assesses himself as an economic defender. Typically, future policies should help solidify voters' sense of efficacy. However, Gore relied far too heavily on these future policies without providing the credentials to assure the public he could accomplish these protective tasks.

Gore the Future Hero: Positive Deliberative Ads

"Bean Counter" is one of the most simplistic advertisements deployed by Al Gore, which originally aired on August 31, 2000. The ad is focused entirely on health care and is just Gore speaking about it at a campaign rally. He claims, "If your doctor says you need a particular specialist for some treatment, if you've got an HMO or an insurance company, a lot of times there's some bean counter behind a computer terminal, who . . . will override the doctor's orders."[7] From here, he proposes that "we need a patient's bill of rights to take the medical decisions away from the HMOs and insurance companies and give them back to the doctors and the nurses."[8] During this speech, the camera almost exclusively rests on Gore, dressed in jeans and a denim shirt, talking into a microphone with lush greenery behind him. There are two quick shots of the crowd listening intently to him. While he speaks, there is gentle piano music playing.

If anything, this advertisement seems to go out of its way to make a potentially scary subject as gentle as possible. Gore speaks with candor about what needs to be done to stop insurance companies from having "the right to play God."[9] This is meant to give the viewers confidence that Gore will look out for their best interest. The vivid imagery, focused crowd, and soothing music all combine to assuage audience member doubts and fears about current medical practices. The ad assumes that health care is already something voters are fearful of and uses this starting point of fear to advocate for Gore as a chance for audience efficacy. While this fear is assumed, nothing this ad does audiovisually uses horror framing to further instill that fear. Rather, this is a self-positive ad that plays the role of giving in-depth policy discussion, setting Gore up as the savior that can defeat insurance companies. However, the ad is almost entirely focused on future policy, giving little account of past accomplishments that would make Gore able to deliver on these proposals.

"Accountability" is another positive, deliberative ad that gives specific education policy proposals. This commercial's original airdate was September 16, 2000. The ad begins with Gore speaking to an assembly, seemingly in a school gymnasium. The first line the audience hears is Gore saying, "George

Bush and I actually agree on accountability in education."[10] From here, Gore lists some of his proposals and the narrator echoes what Gore says. Some of these proposals include accountability, smaller class sizes, better training for teachers, more teachers, and making college tuition tax-deductible. Intercut with Gore speaking are images of happy students and teachers, as well as college graduates holding diplomas.[11]

This ad does everything it can to be upbeat and positive. The narrator has an optimistic tone; there is soft, inspiring trumpet music, and the imagery always shows either happy or determined individuals. It is unsurprising this ad would take on a positive tone, given how it starts with a bipartisan concession that both Gore and Bush agree on accountability in education. This ad makes no attempt to horrifically frame Bush or any of the problems facing education, but rather gives optimistic solutions to implied educational woes. However, it once again fails to give praise for past education policy by Gore, fixating exclusively on future potential policy.

"Matters" originally aired in 2000 and focuses entirely on Gore's positions on the environment. The advertisement begins with the soft sound of running water, soothing music, and the image of clear water, surrounded by trees and a blue sky. This transitions to Gore sitting in front of the camera. He is the only person to speak in the ad. He says, "In this election, the environment itself is on the ballot. And there's a big difference between us."[12] This is the only somewhat direct reference to opposing candidate Bush in the entire advertisement. Gore continues by saying, "I'll never put polluters in charge of our environmental laws," that he's worked to protect air and water, and "I believe that if we act now we can reverse the tide of global warming."[13] Gore ends by emphasizing that this election matters because "Our air and water are at stake, and I need your help to protect them."[14]

This ad, while discussing potentially frightening issues like global warming and pollution, does not use any audiovisual horror framing methods. The advertisement starts with soothing images and sounds and carries the soft music throughout as Gore talks. While Gore is speaking, there are no effects or distortions. Rather, the ad simply shows Gore speaking to the audience. Thus, "Matters" acts exclusively as a self-positive appraisal of Gore's future environmental policies. Bush isn't even mentioned by name. In a larger horror narrative, this can work to position Gore as the savior that can battle environmental threats.

Gore's Monstrosities: The Past, HMOs, and Conservative Economics

Al Gore's "1969" advertisement, which first aired on August 22, 2000, uses a heavy dose of the classic horror frame before realigning itself as a positive and motivational advertisement. The classic horror comes from the ad's opening, where a dark and serious voice says "1969. America in turmoil."[15] While the narrator speaks, shadowy images of protests and unrest are displayed as ominous music plays. In the midst of this, the narrator says, "Al Gore graduates college. His father, a US senator, opposes the Vietnam War. Al Gore has his doubts, but enlists in the army."[16] Here, images of a young Al Gore and his father play before revealing a wounded soldier. The first color image of the advertisement is then shown, depicting Al Gore in his army uniform. More images of Al Gore in the trenches and at military camps are presented.

From this point forward, the "1969" advertisement becomes noticeably more positive and upbeat. The narrator, discussing Gore, says that "the last thing he thinks he'll do is enter politics."[17] The music lightens substantially, taking on more of an inspirational tone than an ominous one. The narrator recounts Gore's personal story, with Gore starting a family and becoming a reporter before deciding "that to change what was wrong with America, he had to fight for what was right."[18] Here, the narrator starts quickly listing Gore's political achievements as colorful videos relating to each are displayed. Gore's work on the environment, welfare, social security, health care, education, and taxes are all highlighted. While images of clean water and happy people are shown, a determined Gore is repeatedly visualized, seeming to be hard at work solving these problems. The advertisement ends by showing Gore happily walking with his family as the narrator says, "Al Gore. Married 30 years. Father of four. Fighting for us."[19]

"1969" is one of only a handful of advertisements in the Gore campaign that uses classic horror framing, but that framing is quickly overtaken by epideictic self-praise. This ad is also a rarity in that it focuses heavily on Gore's past, not the future. The advertisement clearly starts in a place of horror as civil unrest and the Vietnam War are tied together, displaying both as dark threats to America, throwing it in "turmoil."[20] The imagery falls in line with Glenn W. Richardson Jr.'s understanding of how campaign ads evoke the horror genre by using "black-and-white film clips" and "rolling black clouds of smoke."[21] All of the videos filling the early part of this ad are in black and white and the first shows riot police amid rolling smoke, presumably tear gas. This sets the horrific tone early. The audio of the ad does its part just as well, using a "deep and serious" narrator just as Richardson suggests.[22] However, in the grand message of this advertisement, the horror framing is not primarily used as a fear appeal. Rather, it is used to give Gore credibility as a savior of sorts. Other potentially fear-inducing issues are listed later in the commercial, including the environment, health care, and issues relating to economic well-being. No audiovisual tropes of horror are used when discussing these. Rather, the upbeat message of the commercial is meant to reassure audience members that Al Gore will protect them from these potential threats.

"Ian," which initially aired on September 9, 2000, delivers a similar message as that of "Bean Counter," but gives the issue a real story and uses subtle horror framing to bring immediacy to health care issues. "Ian" opens with an infant sleeping. The camera then pans to a nurse fiddling with an IV setup. The narrator says, "Medical errors at birth left Ian Malone needing constant care. But the HMO began cutting them off, against doctor's orders."[23] The narrator's tone is serious, and there is ambiguity as to whether the nurse is connecting more fluids for the infant Ian or cutting him off. From here, Ian's mother joins the serious-toned masculine narrator in explaining the situation. She says, "We had gotten to a point of complete desperation."[24] The mother is shown talking into the camera with candor while sitting in a living room. The narrator, now with a more optimistic tone, comes back and claims, "Al Gore heard their story and fought back."[25] Images of Gore seeing the baby and speaking to a crowd are presented. The mother, Christine Malone, explains how he told the insurance company, "don't cut this child's coverage."[26] After establishing that Gore helped the Malone family, the narrator then suggests, "But knowing that all families need protection from HMO abuses, he's fighting for a real patient's bill of rights."[27] The ad concludes with Christine claiming, "Even if he fought half as hard for the people of our country as he did for my son, nobody loses."[28]

The "Ian" advertisement discusses the same issue as "Bean Counter," while using a real example of a past success to make the issue more tangible. This is the type of self-praise of past actions that Pomper believes Gore did not utilize enough.[29] "Bean Counter" leaves the issue abstract, as might happen from time to time. "Ian" makes the issue immediate, and subtle horror framing is used to achieve this. The advertisement starts with the deep and serious narrator suggesting that Ian's life might be at risk. This is combined with a video that could be interpreted as a nurse taking Ian off of critical life assistance. Medical practice has a deep tie with horror, with many of the most recognizable horror films including medical horrors of some variety. Some notable examples include *Frankenstein* (1931), *The Body Snatcher* (1945), and *The Exorcist* (1973), each of which shows the monstrosities of medical practices in unique ways (see figure 2.1).[30] In fact, "the force of *The Exorcist*'s critique is aimed at scientific and medical technologies."[31] "Ian" plays on this connection by showing a sleeping, helpless infant whose life is being used as experimentation for the best bottom line for the insurance company. This casts insurance companies and HMOs as horrific villains, willing to kill the most vulnerable in society, who can only be put in check by Al Gore and his proposed patient's bill of rights. While the rest of the advertisement does not rely heavily upon horror tropes, the initial framing of horror does its job and promotes Al Gore as the audience's choice for efficacy in battling the inhuman(e) insurance companies. Indeed, the metaphor of violence is used

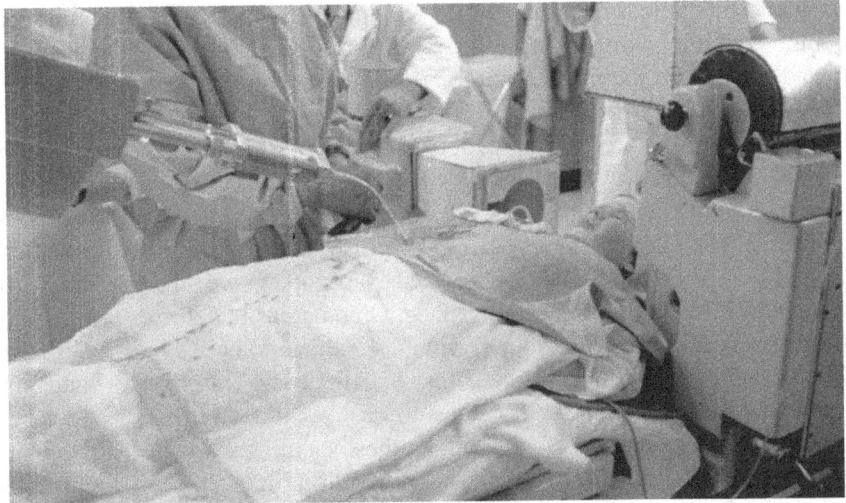

Figure 2.1 *The Exorcist* (1973). Screenshot captured by author.

by Christine when she suggests everyone would win "Even if he fought half as hard for the people of our country as he did for my son."[32]

"Down" frames Bush's tax cuts in a classically horrific way through audiovisual tropes of decay and corrosion. This commercial was first televised on October 7, 2000. "Down" begins by displaying the words "The Facts on George W. Bush's $1.6 TRILLION Tax Cut Promise" on the screen over a darkened $100 bill.[33] The narrator reads this text just before the $100 bill is shown and acid begins to drop on it. As the audience hears the bill disintegrating and sees it melt away, the serious-toned narrator claims, "Almost half goes to the richest one percent."[34] The narrator then asks and answers, "What trickles down? An average of 62 cents a day for most taxpayers."[35] As this is asked and answered, the $100 bill fully withers away to reveal 62 cents in coins. The narrator again repeats that almost half of the tax cut goes to the richest one percent before quickly giving a list of Gore's proposed economic policies. The narrator ends by arguing that "the middle classes earn more than trickle down."[36]

This ad uses the classic horror frame to make Bush's tax cut plan and trickle-down economics monstrous. The use of acidic decay is a classic horror trope, often resulting in a rapid breakdown of whatever encounters the acid. While horror films tend to use this to gruesomely kill or deform human characters, this advertisement deforms a $100 bill into a mere 62 cents. Thus, the argument is that trickle-down economics is not nearly as neutral as it sounds. What really trickles down is acid that eats away at what is, according to Gore, truly owed to the middle class. The serious tone of the narrator also plays into this horror framing. While no images of Bush are shown, his plan and the economics of the Republican Party writ large are cast as evil. Since this ad focuses on the monstrosity of Bush's policy creation, it relies heavily upon the classic horror frame.

"Morph" is an interesting ad, targeted at Ohio, that plays on classic tropes of body horror and possession. The ad, which first reached the public on October 10, 2000, begins with a map of Ohio and a picture of George W. Bush up in the corner. The narrator says, "George W. Bush wants to bring his Texas ideas to Ohio."[37] The narrator then claims that Texas workers are "the 8th worst paid in the nation."[38] As this assertion is made, Ohio begins to deform. The narrator contrasts Texas's pay with Ohio's, which is claimed to be the fourth best. The Ohio border continues to deform as Bush and Texas are criticized for state minimum wages, its low ranking for states to raise a child, and Bush's opposition to health care coverage for children. As these charges are levied, it becomes more and more clear that Ohio's border is shifting into Texas's. Finally, the transformation is complete and the only thing that identifies that the state was once Ohio is the label "OHIO."[39] With this morph complete, the narrator asks, "On November 7, is that the change we really want for Ohio?"[40]

Clearly, "Morph" attempts to position Texas as an evil entity that is going to possess and deform Ohio. Even though Ohio maintains the label "OHIO" throughout the entire ad, the shape of Ohio quickly begins changing into Texas.[41] First, this advertisement evokes body horror tropes of mutation and deformation. A classic, cinematic example of this horror subgenre is *The Fly* (1958) and its remake, *The Fly* (1986).[42] In both versions of *The Fly*, a scientist is slowly transformed into a fly after an experiment goes wrong and the scientist's DNA is mixed with a fly's. The 1986 remake, directed by David Cronenberg, is particularly visceral in its depiction of gory body transformations. In "Morph," Bush is the scientist who will conduct dastardly experiments on Ohio, merging the "DNA" of Ohio with Texas.

"Morph" also plays on tropes of possession. While Ohio is physically deformed, it is also spiritually/politically warped into Texas, which is more or less a demonic entity for the purposes of this advertisement. The narrator gives the facts of how Texas under Bush has fallen horrendously in a number of metrics. The ad then makes the connection that Bush will spread this possession to Ohio, negatively changing its policies toward workers, children, and health care. Such a transformative possession is evocative of films like *The Exorcist*, where a young girl named Regan becomes both spiritually and physically deformed as the demon possessing her achieves a stronger and stronger hold. Since Bush himself is the one pushing this possession and transformation, he is set up as the inhuman agent of possession. Thus, Bush is classically framed in this ad as an evil, inhuman other who will monstrously transform Ohio.

"Word," while mostly a positive ad, has a couple of brief moments of classic horror framing that deserve mention. This ad had an initial airdate of October 18, 2000. "Word" starts in a dark place, with a black-and-white image of a "FOR SALE" sign shown behind chain-link fence.[43] The narrator notes, "From high unemployment and record deficits, the hard work of all Americans turned our economy around."[44] As the second half of that sentence begins, the video immediately gains color and various workers are presented. The ad cuts back from this positive tone to a colored image of Bush. Text reads "George W. Bush gives away almost half the surplus to the wealthiest 1%."[45] Shadowed dollar bills are shown flipping and a shaded video of a Mercedes-Benz driving is displayed. The music becomes dark and dire during this portion discussing Bush. The music lightens up as Al Gore and his policy proposals are juxtaposed against Bush. While these policies are listed, videos of Americans hard at work are presented. The narrator ends by saying "Al Gore. America's prosperity working for all."[46]

"Word" uses classic horror framing in a couple of key instances. First, the high unemployment and deficits of the past are framed through classic images of economic decay. Economic decay and decline is a key theme in horror films such as *The Exorcist* and *The Texas Chainsaw Massacre* (1974).[47] In *The Exorcist*, Chris and Reagan's luxurious lifestyle is juxtaposed with "Father Karras's struggle to find appropriate health care for his ailing and indigent mother."[48] Similarly, in *"Texas Chainsaw*, the psychotic family is destitute after losing their jobs at the local slaughterhouse as a result of mechanization."[49] As such, the "FOR SALE" sign behind chain link fence in "Word" demonstrably elicits notions of economic decline, leading to the closing and shutting down of businesses and factories. Thus, economic decline is framed as a monstrously corrupting specter. However, the first instance is a past horror, temporally separated from the present. This temporal separation is again brought to the fore when Bush's economic plan is criticized. The advertisement clearly attempts to show that Bush's plan will bring the woes of the past into the future, throwing America back into economic decline. The image of Bush is classically framed through ominous music, and the montage of darkly shaded dollar bills and a fancy car that follow. Bush is made out to be an inhuman agent of corruption that wants to bring the evils of the past back into the present. Once again, this ad also relies on a deliberative presentation of future policy proposals.

Gore's Conflicted Question

Gore hardly used the conflicted horror frame, however, there are hints of it in "Question," which aired in 2000. The advertisement visually relies upon newspaper clippings and the narrator asks, "Question. In politics, what happens when you promise the same money to two different groups of people?"⁵⁰ The ad then provides evidence that Bush promised a trillion dollars from Social Security to both young workers and seniors. The narrator reiterates the initial question, as an image of Bush looking suspicious is shown, before saying, "Answer: one promise gets broken. Next question: which one?"⁵¹

"Question" does not classically frame Bush, but rather plays on notions of conflicted horror framing. Bush's tactics are positioned as mundane, setting them up as something that happens "[i]n politics."⁵² However, the misguided monstrosity of the situation is still apparent. Bush is offering a massive amount of money to both young and old people. He is deceiving one of those groups for his own gain. The image of Bush looking suspicious and disingenuous is clearly meant to show that his intentions are to deceive for self-gain. The narrator does not take on the dark tone of Al Gore's classically framed advertisements, but the voice is still serious and accusatory, clearly showing how Bush is misleading and mundanely monstrous within the context of politics.

Al Gore's campaign relied heavily on deliberative, self-positive advertisements that portrayed Gore as a future defender of the vulnerable. His classic horror framing targeted everything from HMOs and insurance companies to Bush and his uniquely Texan economic policies. "Question" is the one ad that used the conflicted horror frame, attacking Bush for promising more than he can fulfill.

BUSH'S HEROIC NARRATIVE

Similar to Gore, Bush relied heavily on positive campaign ads and specific policies. However, whereas Gore relied mostly on deliberative, future-oriented advertisements, Bush depended on a narrative of defending the nation from too much government, anchored in past, praiseworthy achievements. Bush's horrific advertisements often articulate threats created either by a lack of government where it should be doing its job or too much government where it does not have any business. Bush's conflicted horror ads get aimed directly at Gore and his future policies.

As Pomper notes, "Rhetorically and politically, Gore conceded the issue of prosperity to Bush. The Texas governor, too, saw both a good present economy and a challenge for future improvement."⁵³ Bush leveled with Gore's future policies, proposing his own. This created a situation where "If the campaign were to be only a choice of future programs, with their great uncertainties, a Bush program might be as convincing to the voters as a Gore program."⁵⁴ However, Bush's heavier usage of epideictic self-praise meant that "If the election were to be only a choice of the manager of a consensual agenda, Bush's individual qualities might well be more attractive."[55] Thus, Bush used similar levels of horror framing and positive advertising as Gore. However, his roughly equal focus on both past achievements and future policy seemed to help craft a potentially persuasive message. These positive appeals set Bush up as the better hero in the horror narrative of the campaign.

Bush: A Proven Texas Hero

"Successful Leader" is a purely self-positive advertisement for Bush, which first aired on October 25, 1999. Soft, inspirational piano music plays as an upbeat narrator says, "He's been hailed as the Republican Party's best hope to win the White House."[56] As the narrator speaks, both color and black-and-white videos of Bush interplay, showing him speaking, shaking hands, and talking to children. The narrator continues by listing Bush's achievements in Texas, including economic gains, improved education, and lower crime rates.[57] The narrator ends by stating, "George W. Bush. A compassionate conservative leader. A fresh start for America."[58]

This ad is a heavily epideictic ad, positioning Bush as the candidate to which voters should turn. Richardson highlights black-and-white images as a hallmark of horror framing.[59] However, even though these are used in this ad, they are clearly not meant to be horrific in context. If anything, they seem to give the effect that Bush has plenty of experience to his name. Every part of the ad is meant to be positive and set Bush apart as a heroic individual, proven through past accomplishments.

"Hopeful" is another self-positive campaign ad which aims to show how Bush's campaign will be different from others. This ad was first televised on October 25, 1999. Bush himself narrates, claiming, "I think there's a lot of cynicism today in America because of broken promises."[60] Bush is shown saying this to the camera as upbeat piano music plays. After a title card that reads "Governor George W. Bush," Bush continues speaking to the camera, "I believe most people expect the best out of elected officials and when elected officials disappoint them it creates a cynical environment."[61] He continues, "Secondly, I believe oftentimes campaigns resort to mud-throwing and name-calling, and Americans are sick of that kind of campaigning."[62] A young woman is shown in deep thought near the end of this statement, before switching to a group seemingly in deep discussion. A video of Bush hugging his wife in front of colorful, red and blue balloons is played as Bush concludes, "What they want to hear is what's on people's minds, and where the candidates' hearts are. I'd like to run a positive campaign that is hopeful and optimistic and very positive."[63]

The ad "Hopeful" attempts to show how the Bush campaign will be different from those of other candidates and reasons through why that should be the case. Bush seems to be directly shooting down the possibility of using negative campaign tactics, which would include horror framing. A campaign that is "hopeful and optimistic and very positive" would seem to be in direct opposition to fear appeals and horror framing.[64] However, as is well known, candidates do not necessarily stick to the promises of early campaign ads.

"Priorities," which was first released to the public on October 25, 2000, is an advertisement designed to give a brief overview of some of Bush's major policy positions. The ad starts with Bush speaking in front of a white background, saying, "I believe that government should do a few things and do them well."[65] Upbeat piano music plays, as Bush lists his "top priorities," which include Social Security, Medicare, education, and the military.[66] As these priorities are enumerated, colorful videos of smiling senior citizens, kids, and a father and daughter are displayed. Bush's face reappears on the white background again, where he says, "I believe that once priorities have been funded we should pass money back to the taxpayers."[67] Bush then talks about his tax cuts in Texas, as more happy families are shown. He returns in front of the white background one last time to deliver the final summation of his position, where he states, "I believe we ought to cut tax rates to continue economic growth and to broaden prosperity."[68]

This ad is an entirely deliberative one with no mention of Gore or anything negative. The imagery and music are positive and uplifting, with Bush simply giving his policy positions on a number of issues. This advertisement is meant to set Bush apart as a calm, rational choice for audience efficacy in the face of threats mentioned in other ads throughout the campaign.

"Muchas Gracias," which initially aired on November 1, 2000, is different from every other ad listed here, in that it is entirely in Spanish. I will quote what is said in English for the purposes of this chapter, using the translations provided by *The Living Room Candidate*. A white text appears on a blue backdrop that reads "It's a New Day."[69] Chanting is heard, and a crowd is shown watching Bush speak. The narrator says, "George W. Bush's plan deposits trust in you: the people. Democrats trust only bigger government. With Bush's plan, no one will be left behind."[70] Videos of happy people and Bush shaking hands are then displayed, before the ad cuts back to Bush speaking in front of the audience again, saying in Spanish that the "dream is for everyone that lives in this country. Thank you for everything!"[71]

"Muchas Gracias" is a purely positive ad targeted at Spanish-speaking voters. The ad speaks in broad generalities, praising Bush's future plans and having Bush himself thank the viewer. The ad's upbeat and vivid tone makes Bush out as a method of audience efficacy not just for English-speaking voters, but Spanish speakers as well.

Classic Monstrosities: Terror, Prescriptions, and Decrepit Education

"Dangerous World" relies heavily on fear appeals and classic horror tropes. The advertisement, which was first released on November 16, 1999, opens with an image of a young girl standing outside of a fenced off gate, which looks like the entrance to a military facility. Bush is heard saying, "Today we live in a world of terror, madmen and missiles."[72] Bush's voice is distorted with a slight echo to sound more urgent, like an important presidential address or emergency broadcast. Ominous music plays in the background. As Bush lists the threats of the world, the video of the young girl quickly cuts to a video of munitions being fired into the night sky and a black-and-white video of a missile launching. Both videos of weaponry are very darkly shaded, a staple of the horror genre.[73] Bush then appears in front of a white background, claiming, "Our military is challenged by aging weapons and low morale. Because a dangerous world still requires a sharpened sword. . . . I will rebuild our military. I will move quickly to defend our country and allies against blackmail . . . by building missile defense systems."[74] As Bush lists these defense objectives, the young girl is shown again moving around the seemingly shutdown military facility. She goes down a set of stairs, walks along the fence, and puts a traffic cone back up. Bush comes back on the screen, concluding by saying, "As President, I will have a foreign policy with a touch of iron, driven by American interests and American values."[75] The music lightens as the girl is seen reaching up to hold the hand of a uniformed military member. The camera then pans up toward the sky. The words "George W. Bush: a fresh start" are displayed in front of the sky.[76]

Clearly, this advertisement plays on public fears of terrorism, rogue nations, and missiles. The opening contrasts the stakes of such violence with the means of the violence. The young girl is juxtaposed with munitions and missiles lighting up the night sky. Through montage, the connection between violence and a threat to our children is made. Both the imagery and Bush's words make clear that with an aging and demoralized military, the threats from "terror, madmen and missiles" are becoming more and more real.[77] These are the inhuman threats facing the United States, classic monstrosities that threaten our young children. The way to fight these monstrosities, for Bush, is through a rebuilt military and improved missile defense system. This is the "touch of iron" Bush promises to bring to foreign policy.[78] Thus, while monstrosities clearly lurk outside the city walls of the United States, Bush sets himself as the man who can keep those monsters at bay, away from the innocents of the country. He does this through future policy proposals.

"Priority MD RNC" plays on medical fears and is aimed at primarily older voters. The ad, which was first televised on August 28, 2000, begins with ominous music, distorted images of prescription pill bottles, and a rising red bar graph over a large number "8."[79] A serious toned feminine narrator says, "Under Clinton/Gore, prescription drug prices have skyrocketed and nothing's been done."[80] The music lightens some as Bush is shown and the narrator claims, "George Bush has a plan. Add a prescription drug benefit to Medicare."[81] Bush is shown shaking hands with happy, elderly individuals. Then, a video of Bush speaking to an audience is displayed, where he declares, "Every senior will have access to prescription drug benefits."[82] A distorted video of Gore, framed within a countertop television, then appears. The narrator says, "Gore opposed bipartisan reform."[83] This video cuts to an image of pill bottles in the background with a big cutout of the Capitol Building covering most of them. The words "INTERFERE WITH DOCTORS" are shown as the narrator says, "He's pushing a big government plan that lets Washington bureaucrats interfere with what your doctors prescribe."[84] White words on a black screen then show, as the narrator also reads them, "THE GORE PRESCRIPTION PLAN: BUREAUCRATS DECIDE."[85] The screen then lightens up with a colorful image of Bush shaking more hands as the text and narrator read, "The Bush Prescription Plan: Seniors Choose."[86]

The "Priority MD RNC" ad is clearly meant to frighten elderly voters by playing on fears of government and bureaucrats interfering with their prescription medications. The horror tropes are heavy and constant, starting with distorted pill bottles, deep, blood-red lines, and a distorted Al Gore. These all are examples of various horror elements. Distortions have been a particularly strong element of the horror genre, drawing its roots in early proto-horrors such as *The Cabinet of Dr. Caligari* (1920) and German Expressionism more broadly.[87] The Capitol Building is also visually portrayed as monstrous, looming eerily between audience members and prescription medications. Decrepit manors and buildings, like the U.S. Capitol, are mainstays of the horror genre, drawing their roots from gothic horror like *The Castle of Otranto*.[88] Kendall R. Phillips describes how the "old dark houses were almost always rumored to be haunted" in horror cinema.[89] Thus, bureaucrats are framed as "dangerous men lurking in shadows often appear[ing] monstrous."[90] Even Gore's plan is horrifically framed through the choice of font. White, slightly distorted text over a black background gives a clearly negative depiction of Gore's policies toward prescription medications. This visual framing—juxtaposed against Bush's plan, which is depicted with a jovial, colorful background—makes the distinction clear. Thus, Bush frames bureaucrats, Washington, and Gore's policies as monstrous toward senior citizens. Only Bush's plan and leadership give audience efficacy in stopping this monstrosity.

"Education Recession," which was first broadcast on September 25, 2000, again uses the classic horror frame, here to attack the "Clinton/Gore education recession."[91] The ad starts with a very shadowed, black-and-white image of a student sitting on the stairs of a school. The masculine narrator, with a serious tone, says, "America's having a recession. An educational recession, that's hurting our children."[92] While the narrator says this, more black-and-white, shadowed images of students in schools are shown. Supposed educational facts and statistics are read aloud and displayed on the screen, with the words "Education Recession" encasing each claim on top and bottom.[93] "Education Recession" is in a partially translucent white text that floats along each claim with a ghostly presence.[94] These include low math and physics rankings and low literacy. The narrator takes these claims and ties them together with the statement, "The Clinton/Gore education recession. It's failing our kids."[95] The music swings more positively and the ad gains color as Bush is then shown. The narrator contrasts, saying, "But in Texas, George Bush raised standards, and test scores soared."[96] More fact claims are provided over images of happy students graduating and Bush reading to young, elementary-aged students. The narrator concludes, "Learn more about the Bush Blueprint for accountability, high standards, and local control."[97] The URL "www.EducationBlueprint.com" is provided at the bottom of the screen.[98]

Classic horror framing is used here to portray the Clinton/Gore education recession as an inhuman phantom presence that is possessing and negatively affecting the youth of the country. The very dimly lit, black-and-white images of students in school buildings immediately evoke horror.[99] In addition, the setting of these images inside an older-looking school building draws associations with gothic manors, a dominant setting in gothic ghost stories.[100] The ghostly text that reads "Education Recession" makes the connection clear, advocating that the education recession is haunting and hurting the vulnerable youth of the United States.[101] Many horror films, especially those about hauntings and possession, portray a youthful victim. This trend has been argued as an extension of anxiety about young voters not displaying "enough agency."[102] Clearly, the students in this ad are not old enough to vote. However, in the not so far off future, they will be old enough. And, more importantly, they will be the future economic drivers of the United States. Lagging education makes voters anxious about the future. This ad uses classic horror framing to show how failing education is an inhuman specter that will haunt and possess the youth of America into the future. Thus, the failings of Gore's past are tied to his potential future policies, where only Bush can save America's youth.

Conflicted Framing of Gore and his Misguided Policies

"Really MD" is a strong attack ad aimed directly at Gore, which initially aired on August 31, 2000. The advertisement opens by slowly panning in on a countertop television that shows Gore speaking. The feminine narrator says, "Well, there's Al Gore, reinventing himself on television again."[103] The video changes to a close-up of Gore on the television, with prominent horizontal lines distorting his image. The narrator continues, "Like I'm not going to notice? Who's he going to be today?"[104] TV static is then used as the image cuts to Gore at a Buddhist temple. The narrator asks, "The Al Gore who raises campaign money at a Buddhist temple? Or the one who now promises campaign finance reform?"[105] Another static transition is displayed, then Gore is seen in a sit-down interview as the narrator says, "Really. Al Gore, claiming credit for things he didn't even do."[106] Then, Gore says one of the most infamous lines of the campaign, "I took the initiative, in creating the internet."[107] The narrator scoffs, saying, "Yeah, and I invented the remote control, too."[108] Static is once again used to transition and the shot returns to the wider shot of the television in the kitchen with Gore once again giving a press conference. The narrator, in apparent frustration, claims, "Another round of this and I'll sell my television."[109] A URL then comes onto the screen, reading, "gorewillsayanything.com."[110]

This ad relies heavily on conflicted horror framing to portray Gore as unreliable, inconsistent, and absurd. Clearly, Gore is not made out to be a classic, inhumane horror villain. But his overly flawed human traits become apparent as the advertisement progresses. The spot claims that Gore flips on his policy positions for the sake of political expediency. It also claims that he comes up with bogus falsehoods like his internet claims. These are meant to show that the horror of Gore is mundane, to the point that the narrator will sell her television if he keeps it up. The distortion and static effects also play into the broad genre of horror. However, the lack of dark shading and the mocking tone this advertisement takes firmly places it in the conflicted horror camp as opposed to the classic one. This ad shows that Gore's past actions are so inconsistent, that any future policy proposals made by Gore should be viewed with skepticism.

"$2.2 Trillion" is a 2000 ad that, while at first glance seems devoid of horror, is horrific through a conflicted frame thanks to its overwhelming banality. The ad is almost entirely just a plain white background with black font. The masculine narrator sounds almost bored as he utters, "2.2 trillion dollars. That's a lot of money."[111] The text "$2.2 trillion dollars" is shown, which transitions to "$8,000 per American" as the narrator reads that text. The narrator then explains that the figure is "our government's projected surplus for the next ten years."[112] Here, the narrator begins to attack Gore, claiming, "Al

Gore plans to spend it all. And more."[113] After this, the only non-black-and-white color of the ad—red—comes in. Text on the screen reads, "Al Gore's Spending Plan: 3 times the new spending Clinton proposed."[114] The "3" is in red font and under this text, a graph shows in red Clinton's new spending and Gore's new spending, with Gore's vastly outweighing Clinton's. The narrator argues that Gore's plan will wipe out the surplus and create a deficit again. The narrator concludes by saying, "Al Gore's big-government spending plan threatens America's prosperity."[115]

While this ad is very simplistic and seemingly devoid of energy, let alone horror, it is that same minimalistic approach that frames Al Gore and his plan through a conflicted horror lens. The mundaneness of Gore's big-government spending plan, one that "threatens America's prosperity" is an example of the merging of the sphere of normalcy and the sphere of the fantastic.[116] The ad and the narrator are both unrelentingly dull and mundane. But the amount of money that is purported to be spent is a fantastical number to almost anyone: $2.2 trillion. Thus, the spheres collide here and create the basis of the threat to the United States. Further, the fact that the only color used is red and it is only used in the context of Gore's plan provides further evidence of the subtle conflicted frame placed upon Gore and his future plan.

The Bush campaign relied on a heavy dosage of self-positive advertising, while interspersing conflicted and classic horror frames. The classic horror frame was generally used against policy threats such as terrorism, rogue nations, prescription costs, and education. The conflicted frame was used to show how flawed and misguided Gore and his policies were.

CONCLUSION

In the end, Gore and Bush used very similar amounts and methods of horror framing in their televised campaign advertisements. Both Bush and Gore used a heavy dose of purely positive ads in an attempt to instill voter efficacy and set themselves apart as the "good guy" of the narrative. Both also used classic and conflicted horror frames, with Bush relying on the conflicted horror frame a little more than Gore. The main areas of differentiation are how each candidate attacked the other and how they praised themselves. With the exception of "Question," Gore typically attacked Bush using the classic horror frame. Bush, on the other hand, attacked Gore using the conflicted horror frame. Gore leaned very heavily on future-based policy—likely trying to move on from his past with Clinton so as to turn a page on the presidency—whereas Bush balanced future policy with past accomplishments.

The threats and enemies that each candidate tried to persuade the public they could defeat were slightly different as well. Gore positioned himself as a defender of the vulnerable, such as sick children, poor people, and the environment. He demonized HMOs, insurance companies, and conservative stances toward the economy and the environment. Bush, on the other hand, positioned himself as a proven hero that could actively defeat threats from both outside and within the country. External threats were terrorists and rogue nations, internal threats were an overrun economy, high costs of prescriptions, big government, and a decrepit education system.

Bush went on to secure the presidency by the narrowest margin in U.S. history, winning the deciding state of Florida by only 537 votes.[117] Ultimately, a 5–4 Supreme Court decision was required to stop recounts and award Bush the presidency.[118] While an extremely narrow win, experts agreed that Gore should have won the election in "a runaway" based on various election indicators.[119] Clearly, horror framing played a central role in both candidates' televised campaigns. However, as will be seen in the following chapters, both the number of ads directly using horror framing and the magnitude of that horror framing would ratchet up significantly in coming years. The things Americans had to fear grew exponentially with a terror attack on domestic soil, multiple wars, an economic recession, and a pandemic. This chapter demonstrates that horror framing is nothing unique to subsequent elections; its omnipresence had already been established. Yet, the normative element of its narrative usage has increased significantly with the passage of time, moving from one rhetorical tool to a cornerstone of contemporary campaign advertising.

NOTES

1. Chris Matthews and Stephen Gandel, "Is the Economy Partying Like It's 1999?" *Fortune*, December 5, 2014, http://fortune.com/2014/12/05/us-economy-growth-1999-vs-2014/.

2. Pew Research Center, "IV. What the Voters Want," *Pew Research Center*, July 13, 2000, http://www.people-press.org/2000/07/13/iv-what-the-voters-want/.

3. Pew Research Center, "IV. What the Voters Want."

4. Gerald M. Pomper, "The 2000 Presidential Election: Why Gore Lost," *Political Science Quarterly* 116, no. 2 (2001): 210.

5. Pomper, "The 2000 Presidential Election," 210–11.

6. Pomper, "The 2000 Presidential Election," 211–12.

7. Gore/Liberman, Inc., "Bean Counter," *The Living Room Candidate: Presidential Campaign Commercials 1952–2020*, August 31, 2000, http://www.livingroomcandidate.org/commercials/2000/bean-counter.

8. Gore/Liberman, "Bean Counter."

9. Gore/Liberman, "Bean Counter."

10. Democratic National Committee, "Accountability," *The Living Room Candidate: Presidential Campaign Commercials 1952–2020*, September 16, 2000, http://www.livingroomcandidate.org/commercials/2000/accountability.

11. Democratic National Committee, "Accountability."

12. *The Living Room Candidate* did not provide a specific airdate, simply the year. Democratic National Committee, "Matters," *The Living Room Candidate: Presidential Campaign Commercials 1952–2020*, 2000, http://www.livingroomcandidate.org/commercials/2000/matters.

13. Democratic National Committee, "Matters."

14. Democratic National Committee, "Matters."

15. Gore/Liberman, Inc., "1969," *The Living Room Candidate: Presidential Campaign Commercials 1952–2020*, August 22, 2000, http://www.livingroomcandidate.org/commercials/2000/1969.

16. Gore/Liberman, "1969."

17. Gore/Liberman, "1969."

18. Gore/Liberman, "1969."

19. Gore/Liberman, "1969."

20. Gore/Liberman, "1969."

21. Glenn W. Richardson Jr., *Pulp Politics: How Political Advertising Tells the Stories of American Politics* (Lanham, MD: Rowman & Littlefield, 2008), 39.

22. Richardson, *Pulp Politics*, 39.

23. Gore/Liberman, Inc., "Ian," *The Living Room Candidate: Presidential Campaign Commercials 1952–2020*, September 9, 2000, http://www.livingroomcandidate.org/commercials/2000/ian.

24. Gore/Liberman, Inc., "Ian."

25. Gore/Liberman, Inc., "Ian."

26. Gore/Liberman, Inc., "Ian."

27. Gore/Liberman, Inc., "Ian."

28. Gore/Liberman, Inc., "Ian."

29. Pomper, "The 2000 Presidential Election," 211–12.

30. *Frankenstein*, directed by James Whale (1931; Universal Studios Home Entertainment, 2016), DVD; *The Body Snatcher*, directed by Robert Wise (1945; Google Play, 2009), Digital; *The Exorcist*, directed by William Friedkin (1973; Warner Bros., 2011), DVD.

31. Kendall R. Phillips, *Projected Fears: Horror Films and American Culture* (Westport, CT: Praeger, 2005), 115.

32. Gore/Liberman, Inc., "Ian."

33. Gore/Liberman, Inc., "Down," *The Living Room Candidate: Presidential Campaign Commercials 1952–2020*, October 7, 2000, http://www.livingroomcandidate.org/commercials/2000/down.

34. Gore/Liberman, "Down."

35. Gore/Liberman, "Down."

36. Gore/Liberman, "Down."

37. Gore/Liberman, Inc., "Morph," *The Living Room Candidate: Presidential Campaign Commercials 1952–2020*, October 10, 2000, http://www.livingroomcandidate.org/commercials/2000/morph.

38. Gore/Liberman, "Morph."

39. Gore/Liberman, "Morph."

40. Gore/Liberman, "Morph."

41. Gore/Liberman, "Morph."

42. *The Fly*, directed by Kurt Neumann (1958; 20th Century Fox), Digital; *The Fly*, directed by David Cronenberg (1986; 20th Century Fox), Digital.

43. Democratic National Committee, "Word," *The Living Room Candidate: Presidential Campaign Commercials 1952–2020*, October 18, 2000, http://www.livingroomcandidate.org/commercials/2000/word.

44. Democratic National Committee, "Word."

45. Democratic National Committee, "Word."

46. Democratic National Committee, "Word."

47. *The Exorcist*, Friedkin; *The Texas Chainsaw Massacre*, directed by Tobe Hooper (1974; Dark Sky, 2014), DVD.

48. Phillips, *Projected Fears*, 114.

49. Phillips, *Projected Fears*, 114.

50. *The Living Room Candidate* did not provide a specific airdate, simply the year. Democratic National Committee, "Question," *The Living Room Candidate: Presidential Campaign Commercials 1852–2020*, 2000, http://www.livingroomcandidate.org/commercials/2000/question.

51. Democratic National Committee, "Question."

52. Democratic National Committee, "Question."

53. Pomper, "The 2000 Presidential Election," 211.

54. Pomper, "The 2000 Presidential Election," 212.

55. Pomper, "The 2000 Presidential Election," 212.

56. Bush for President, Inc., "Successful Leader," *The Living Room Candidate: Presidential Campaign Commercials 1952–2020*, October 25, 1999, http://www.livingroomcandidate.org/commercials/2000/successful-leader.

57. Bush, "Successful Leader."

58. Bush, "Successful Leader."

59. Richardson, *Pulp Politics*, 39.

60. Bush for President, Inc., "Hopeful," *The Living Room Candidate: Presidential Campaign Commercials 1952–2020*, October 25, 1999, http://www.livingroomcandidate.org/commercials/2000/hopeful.

61. Bush, "Hopeful."

62. Bush, "Hopeful."

63. Bush, "Hopeful."

64. Bush, "Hopeful."

65. Bush for President, Inc., "Priorities," *The Living Room Candidate: Presidential Campaign Commercials 1952–2020*, October 25, 2000, http://www.livingroomcandidate.org/commercials/2000/priorities.

66. Bush, "Priorities."

67. Bush, "Priorities."
68. Bush, "Priorities."
69. Republican National Committee, "Muchas Gracias," *The Living Room Candidate: Presidential Campaign Commercials 1952–2020*, November 1, 2000, http://www.livingroomcandidate.org/commercials/2000/muchas-gracias.
70. Bush, "Muchas Gracias."
71. Bush, "Muchas Gracias."
72. Bush for President, Inc., "Dangerous World," *The Living Room Candidate: Presidential Campaign Commercials 1952–2020*, November 16, 1999, http://www.livingroomcandidate.org/commercials/2000/dangerous-world.
73. Richardson, *Pulp Politics*, 39.
74. Bush, "Dangerous World."
75. Bush, "Dangerous World."
76. Bush, "Dangerous World."
77. Bush, "Dangerous World."
78. Bush, "Dangerous World."
79. Republican National Committee, "Priority MD RNC," *The Living Room Candidate: Presidential Campaign Commercials 1952–2020*, August 28, 2000, http://www.livingroomcandidate.org/commercials/2000/priority-md-rnc.
80. Republican National Committee, "Priority MD RNC."
81. Republican National Committee, "Priority MD RNC."
82. Republican National Committee, "Priority MD RNC."
83. Republican National Committee, "Priority MD RNC."
84. Republican National Committee, "Priority MD RNC."
85. Republican National Committee, "Priority MD RNC."
86. Republican National Committee, "Priority MD RNC."
87. *The Cabinet of Dr. Caligari*, directed by Robert Wiene (1920; Horrortheque, 2010), Digital; Harry M. Benshoff, "Horror Before 'The Horror Film,'" in *A Companion to the Horror Film*, ed. Harry M. Benshoff (New York: Wiley Blackwell, 2014), 216.
88. See Rosemary Jackson, *Fantasy: The Literature of Subversion* (London: Methuen, 1981), 179 and Horace Walpole, *The Castle of Otranto* (Edinburgh: James Ballantyne & Co., 1811). Walpole's *The Castle of Otranto* is widely considered the literary foundation of the gothic horror genre, using a gothic castle as its primary setting. This trope, a decrepit castle or manor, became a foundational setting element of classic horror. See David Punter and Glennis Byron, *The Gothic* (Malden, MA: Blackwell, 2004) and "The Castle of Otranto: The Creepy Tale that Launched Gothic Fiction," *BBC News*, December 13, 2014, https://www.bbc.com/news/magazine-30313775.
89. Kendall R. Phillips, *A Place of Darkness: The Rhetoric of Horror in Early American Cinema* (Austin: University of Texas Press, 2018), 149.
90. Phillips, *A Place of Darkness*, 149.
91. Republican National Committee, "Education Recession," *The Living Room Candidate: Presidential Campaign Commercials 1952–2020*, September 25, 2000, http://www.livingroomcandidate.org/commercials/2000/education-recession.

92. Republican National Committee, "Education Recession."
93. Republican National Committee, "Education Recession."
94. Republican National Committee, "Education Recession."
95. Republican National Committee, "Education Recession."
96. Republican National Committee, "Education Recession."
97. Republican National Committee, "Education Recession."
98. Republican National Committee, "Education Recession."
99. Richardson, *Pulp Politics*, 39.
100. See Jackson, *Fantasy*, 179; Walpole, *The Castle of Otranto*; Punter and Byron, *The Gothic*; and "The Castle of Otranto: The Creepy Tale."
101. Republican National Committee, "Education Recession."
102. Derek Lewis, "Voting Horrors: Youthful, Monstrous, and Worrying Agency in American Film," *The Popular Culture Studies Journal* 6, no. 2–3 (2018): 315.
103. Republican National Committee, "Really MD," *The Living Room Candidate: Presidential Campaign Commercials 1952–2020*, August 31, 2000, http://www.livingroomcandidate.org/commercials/2000/really-md.
104. Republican National Committee, "Really MD."
105. Republican National Committee, "Really MD."
106. Republican National Committee, "Really MD."
107. Republican National Committee, "Really MD."
108. Republican National Committee, "Really MD."
109. Republican National Committee, "Really MD."
110. Republican National Committee, "Really MD."
111. *The Living Room Candidate* did not provide a specific airdate, simply the year. Republican National Committee, "$2.2 Trillion," *The Living Room Candidate: Presidential Campaign Commercials 1952–2020*, 2000, http://www.livingroomcandidate.org/commercials/2000/22-trillion.
112. Republican National Committee, "$2.2 Trillion."
113. Republican National Committee, "$2.2 Trillion."
114. Republican National Committee, "$2.2 Trillion."
115. Republican National Committee, "$2.2 Trillion."
116. Republican National Committee, "$2.2 Trillion." See Steffen Hantke, "The Kingdom of the Unimaginable: The Construction of Social Space and the Fantasy of Privacy in Serial Killers Narratives," *Literature/Film Quarterly* 26, no. 3 (1998): 178–95.
117. Michael Levy, "United States Presidential Election of 2000," *Encyclopedia Britannica*, https://www.britannica.com/event/United-States-presidential-election-of-2000.
118. Levy, "United States Presidential."
119. Pomper, "The 2000 Presidential Election," 210.

Chapter 3

John Kerry versus George W. Bush in the 2004 Election

The 2004 election was President George W. Bush's attempt at a second term in office. The political landscape changed drastically in just four years: the attacks of September 11, 2001, were still fresh in voters' minds, the War on Terror in Afghanistan and Iraq was still slugging along, and the economic boom of the late 1990s had slipped into recession. In the wake of these pressing problems, the Democrats nominated Senator John Kerry (D-MA), a Vietnam War veteran, to take on Bush in the general election.

A wide array of issues was pressing to the American public in the lead up to the 2004 election. Among swing voters, the top three issues that were "very important to their vote" included the economy (83%), education (80%), and jobs (78%).[1] Somewhat surprisingly, terrorism (72%) and Iraq (68%) ranked relatively low for swing voters, at seventh and eighth, respectively.[2] Still, over half of swing voters found these issues important. However, when looking at certain Bush voters (as in, those voters who were almost guaranteed to vote for Bush), terrorism and Iraq became much more prominent issues. Terrorism was the top issue for certain Bush voters at 88 percent and Iraq was second at 74 percent. Certain Kerry voters were far more interested in economic and health care issues, placing Iraq sixth at 77 percent and terrorism eighth at 70 percent.[3]

Given this knowledge of policy areas that were important to voters, this chapter explores how Bush used horror framing in his televised reelection campaign and how Kerry attempted to use these frames as a challenger (see table 3.1). Bush was quick to unleash a campaign of horror, using the classic frame to portray the reasons Americans should still be frightened of foreign threats and vote for a strong leader. This was combined with the use of the conflicted frame to attack Kerry and portray him as a weak leader. Kerry, on the other hand, tried to avoid horror framing early in the campaign. His ads

Table 3.1 John Kerry and George W. Bush Campaign Advertisements' Airdates

John Kerry		George W. Bush	
Airdate	Title	Airdate	Title
April 21, 2004	Risk	March 3, 2004	Safer, Stronger
May 3, 2004	Heart	March 18, 2004	Troops
June 1, 2004	Optimists	March 30, 2004	Wacky
July 10, 2004	Three Minutes	April 26, 2004	Weapons (Florida)
July 30, 2004	Strength	June 4, 2004	Pessimism
August 18, 2004	Rassman	July 6, 2004	First Choice
September 23, 2004	Juvenile	July 30, 2004	Changing World
October 2, 2004	He's Lost, He's Desperate	August 13, 2004	Victory
October 26, 2004	Obligation	September 23, 2004	Windsurfing
October 27, 2004	Heroes	October 22, 2004	Wolves
		October 26, 2004	Whatever It Takes

initially did not portray war as horrifically as Bush, but this strategy shifted later in the campaign.

KERRY'S RESTRAINED APPROACH

For the Kerry campaign, there were two very clear issues that posed "potential threats to President Bush's prospects for re-election: the economy and the Iraq war."[4] Both of these issues were extraordinarily ripe for fear appeals made through horror framing, as few things tend to scare people more than violence and their financial well-being. Further, these problems were well founded in the electorate.

In voters' eyes, the economy had gotten much worse. "In the 2000 election, only 13 percent of voters leaving the polls said that the nation's economy was not good or poor. In 2004, more than half of voters (52 percent) rated the economy not good or poor, giving the Kerry campaign an important opening."[5] Further, "Mr. Bush's decision in March 2003 to go to war in Iraq placed on the public agenda a brand new issue that had not even been on the radar screen in 2000."[6] The war certainly seemed ripe for attack, since although "initial public support for the war was relatively broad, the continued resilience of the insurgency . . . led to increasing public disenchantment."[7] Accordingly, it makes sense that Kerry would focus his televised campaign advertisements on the war and the economy. However, "Exit poll results suggest that these issues were not the clear-cut silver bullet the Kerry campaign had hoped they would be."[8]

In line with these positions, the Kerry campaign made a concerted effort to position him as someone who has enough experience with warfare to make the correct and humane decisions regarding the war in Iraq. The Kerry campaign was hesitant early on to use horror framing in relation to warfare, likely to avoid scaring the public into thinking the war was necessary. However, later campaign advertisements used the classic horror frame to encapsulate Kerry's Vietnam experience, the Iraq War, and Bush. Most of the discussion of the economy was tied to the costs of the war in Iraq.

Self-Positive and Policy Advertisements

"Heart," which originally aired on May 3, 2004, is an entirely positive advertisement about the character of Kerry. This ad resists the temptation to go horrific in a couple of key moments. "Heart" focuses heavily on Kerry's army service and military lineage. It opens with him speaking into the camera, informing the audience that he was born in an army hospital while his father was in the Army Air Corps. A black-and-white image of Kerry's father in front of an aircraft is shown, before switching to a close-up picture of his mother. The text "mother was a community leader" is presented with this photo. Kerry explains how his parents taught him about public service, leading him to enlist during the Vietnam War. A color photograph of Kerry in Vietnam airs as he advocates that service to country is important. Optimistic music continues to play as a video of Kerry walking in full army gear is shown. Two of his fellow veterans speak into the camera, claiming that "The decisions that he made saved our lives."[9] Kerry's daughter, Vanessa Kerry, explicitly ties his military service to his public service, highlighting that throughout all of these experiences, "he has shown an ability to fight for things that matter."[10] His wife, Teresa Heinz-Kerry, testifies that Kerry is hopeful and generous. Finally, Kerry closes by arguing the United States is "a country of optimists" and that "we just need to believe in ourselves again."[11]

This ad has plenty of moments in which horror imagery could have been interjected but was not. This type of restraint is apparent throughout much of the Kerry campaign. The first half of the ad focuses almost exclusively on Kerry's service in the Vietnam War. There is plenty of horrific imagery that can go along with war, as is seen in numerous advertisements throughout the twenty-first century. However, the campaign never frames it horrifically in this advertisement. Instead, Kerry is purely propped up as a generous hero. Both of the veterans that speak in this advertisement talk about Kerry saving their lives, but they give no detail on the kinds of horrors that were threatening their lives. Certainly, much of the public has sufficient context to understand the horrors of war—specifically the Vietnam War. Yet, the campaign leaves that part of the equation up to the audience, putting no effort into horrifically framing it in this advertisement.

"Risk," released on April 21, 2004, is another example of the Kerry campaign showing restraint when dealing with the horrors of war. This ad is almost entirely Kerry speaking into the camera, presenting "exactly what I would do to change the situation in Iraq."[12] White text on a black screen reads, "LEARN MORE ABOUT JOHN KERRY'S PLAN FOR IRAQ: JohnKerry.com," before reverting back to Kerry talking to the camera for the remainder of the advertisement.[13] He claims that he would "immediately reach out to the international community in sharing the burden, the risk, because they also have a stake in the outcome . . . in Iraq."[14] Kerry argues that the United States is paying a high cost both financially and "in the loss of the lives of our young soldiers."[15]

Clearly, the content of this ad presents plenty of opportunities for horror framing. The loss of young lives through gruesome warfare is not a pleasant notion. However, there is nothing done audiovisually to horrifically frame the war in Iraq. Kerry simply continues speaking to the camera in a matter-of-fact policy discussion. Thus, once again, restraint is shown by the Kerry campaign in its decision not to horrifically frame a horrifying situation.

Originally televised on June 1, 2004, "Optimists" expands on Kerry's claim that the United States is "a country of optimists" from "Heart."[16] Images of a young girl and an American saluting are shown as Kerry reiterates the optimism of the country. Then, an upbeat narrator argues that "For John Kerry, a stronger America begins at home."[17] A montage of Kerry interacting with different people, from young children to manufacturers, plays as upbeat music continues. A number of domestic policy proposals are given before the narrator asserts that Kerry will create "a strong military and strong alliances to defeat terror."[18] Immediately after this claim, a young girl with a soccer ball is shown happily running through a field. The advertisement finishes with shots of Kerry talking individually with constituents as the text reads, "Stronger at home. Respected in the world."[19]

Once again, the Kerry campaign turns to strong positive advertising, avoiding horror framing even when issues of terrorism are mentioned. This entire advertisement is exceedingly upbeat and positive, trying to present Americans with a bright future under a Kerry presidency. Most of this advertisement deals with jobs and domestic issues, but it turns toward international issues when it argues for a robust military and alliances to takedown terror. However, horror is never instilled audiovisually with these themes. This is clearly evidenced by the imagery of a happy young girl running with a soccer ball at the same moment terrorism is introduced. There is an apparent hesitancy by the Kerry campaign to use horror framing when discussing terrorism, a notion that clearly scared Americans in the wake of September 11.

"Strength" is an advertisement that, while exceedingly positive, fits into larger horror themes by positioning Kerry as an excellent defender of the

United States. This advertisement, which originally aired on July 30, 2004, is entirely made up of Kerry giving a speech at one of his rallies. He claims, "I defended this country as a young man and I will defend it as President."[20] The crowd, holding Kerry signs, cheers him on as he continues with his defense policy proposals. He argues that with a "strong military" and strong alliance network, "we will be able to tell the terrorists: 'You will lose, and we will win.'"[21] He concludes, "The future doesn't belong to fear; it belongs to freedom."[22]

Once again, the Kerry campaign discusses at length issues of defense and terror without horrifically framing them. The music of this advertisement is upbeat as Kerry speaks to an excited crowd. There appears to be an overt rejection of fear campaigning as Kerry claims that "The future doesn't belong to fear."[23] Thus, instead of playing on people's fears, Kerry takes this for granted and positions himself as the hero that can vanquish the people's fears. Ostensibly, the Kerry campaign seems to recognize that horror does not need to be narrativized heavily in this campaign since it is already present in the minds of U.S. citizens. Rather, the campaign relies heavily on the hero and defender aspects of a typical horror plot. Thus, Kerry's opening statement, "I defended this country as a young man and I will defend it as President," makes a strong claim to Kerry's position as the real hero America needs.[24]

"Three Minutes" again draws on Kerry's experience in the Vietnam War, but has his valor retold by his running mate, John Edwards. With an original release of July 10, 2004, "Three Minutes" begins with Edwards passionately speaking to a crowd, arguing, "There is no one better prepared to keep the American people safe than this man."[25] Edwards then issues a stark challenge, "[I]f you have any question about what John Kerry's made of, just spend three minutes with the men who served with him thirty years ago, who still stand by his side."[26] The image of Kerry in Vietnam from "Heart" is shown again alongside images of three veterans that served with Kerry. These images are displayed over the backdrop of an American patrol boat. The ad cuts back to Edwards, who claims Kerry "has courage, determination, and he would never leave any American behind."[27]

This advertisement works as yet another non-horrific retelling of Kerry's past efforts of valor. Kerry's war achievements are praised and used as a litmus test for his ability to defend the nation as a whole. Even though Kerry is positioned as a hero and there is mention of his Vietnam service, none of that is framed in opposition to an outright horror. Rather, like many of the advertisements before it, the horrors faced by the United States are left implied rather than presented.

"Heroes," an advertisement that was released on October 27, 2004, is another example of positive framing in the context of the war in Iraq. It uses upbeat music and starts with a flag unfurling. An optimistic narrator says, "Our soldiers fighting in Iraq are heroes."[28] An image of a uniformed soldier is shown with a bride. A calm home and a man and child lifting a flag are presented as the narrator mentions the "deepening crisis and chaos in Iraq."[29] The ad then makes its only mention of the election, stating, "[A]s we choose a new commander-in-chief and a fresh start, we will always support and honor those who serve."[30] The advertisement displays text of "Strength. Courage. Patriotism" over a bald eagle before silently presenting the text "Thank You."[31] The only thing that makes clear this is a Kerry ad is the "Approved by John Kerry" message in small print at the very end of the advertisement.[32]

This commercial is once again a very upbeat account of the war in Iraq. The music and narrator are optimistic in tone. Patriotism abounds with numerous shots of the flag and a bald eagle. However, this ad does not positively frame Kerry other than a very oblique reference to him as a "fresh start."[33] The potentially horrific telling of "crisis and chaos in Iraq" is overshadowed by positive imagery and music, so as to ensure it is not horrifically framed by the audience in this instance. This ad is not about the terrors of the war, but rather to present U.S. soldiers as heroic.

A Shift to Classic Horror Framing

"Rassman" is the first advertisement by the Kerry campaign analyzed here which uses horror framing when discussing the Vietnam War. This ad, which first aired on August 18, 2004, opens with ominous music. A "deep and serious" narrator speaks, the kind of which Glenn W. Richardson Jr. argues is a clear audio marker of the horror genre.[34] Darkly shaded and distorted images of people talking are shown over the backdrop of a black-and-white image of military personnel as bold, black text is displayed, reading, "The Attacks Are Funded By Bush Supporters."[35] The narrator claims that "The people attacking John Kerry's war record are funded by Bush's big money supporters."[36] The advertisement then challenges viewers to listen to someone who was there, Jim Rassman. Rassman is presented on camera and says, "It blew me off the boat."[37] The imagery then shifts to black-and-white patrol boats with a small portion of a distorted, colorized flag flapping over the left corner of the screen. Rassman continues, "All these Viet Cong were shooting at me. I expected I'd be shot. When he pulled me out of the river, he risked his life to save mine."[38] The ad then states Kerry was awarded a Bronze Star for his heroism as a black-and-white photograph of Kerry receiving a medal is shown. The ad concludes with a color video of Kerry walking in Vietnam and the narrator stating, "Today, he still has shrapnel in his leg from his wounds in Vietnam."[39]

This advertisement is unique in that it strays from the precedent set by earlier ads in the Kerry campaign of avoiding horror framing in relation to Vietnam. Rather, this advertisement attempts to frame Kerry's heroism in the context of classic horror. According to Caroline Joan (Kay) S. Picart and David A. Frank, classic horror framing is defined as spatially and temporally separated from normalcy.[40] "Rassman" uses plenty of visual and narrative tools to create this bracketing in relation to the Vietnam War. First, the war is temporally separated not only by its references to the past but also by the old, black-and-white videos of patrol boats as the horrors are discussed. This gives the clear impression of temporal bracketing while using a classic visual horror trope.[41] Spatially, there is an obvious bracket with Vietnam itself. There is a long tradition of horror films depicting monsters coming from the east (whether it be Eastern Europe or Asia), including *Dracula* (1931), *The Wolf Man* (1941), *The Ring* (2002), and *The Grudge* (2004), to name a few (see figure 3.1).[42] Kendall R. Phillips confirms this foreignness in *Dracula* where, "Dracula himself, of course, is dramatically foreign. His accent is extreme and his mannerisms peculiar."[43] Thus, monstrosity being completely isolated within Vietnam fits well with this genre trope of foreignness.

Additionally, the Viet Cong mentioned in this advertisement are otherized as only killers. Rassman thought for sure he would be shot and killed by them. However, this ad's main purpose is to respond to those who question Kerry's war record. The individuals who question his record are themselves framed horrifically through dark shading and distortions, as well as the ominous music and serious narrator. Yet, since this ad is designed to make sure the viewer understands Kerry's war record is true, it ends on an abrupt and gruesome

Figure 3.1 *The Grudge* **(2004).** Screenshot captured by author.

note, mentioning Kerry still carries shrapnel with him from Vietnam. Thus, even though the horrors of the war are spatially and temporally separated from modern, normal American life, it makes clear the events did occur. Kerry still literally holds some of the horror within him, much like the heroes who fight monstrosity in horror films are often physically or emotionally scarred.

"Juvenile" continues the theme of using classic horror framing to depict warfare. However, this ad, which was released on September 23, 2004, in response to the Bush campaign's "Windsurfing" ad, now frames the war in Iraq through the classic horror frame. The commercial opens with the same ominous music used in "Rassman." The deep and serious narrator says, "One thousand U.S. casualties" while a very darkly shadowed U.S. flag unfurls.[44] Gruesome details are then further given as the narrator informs the audience that there were "[t]wo Americans beheaded just this week."[45] White text reading "Kidnappings and murders" is displayed over the flag.[46] The ad then further claims, "The Pentagon admits terrorists are pouring into Iraq."[47] Here, the advertisement lambasts Bush for his choice of using a comedic attack ad against Kerry, asserting, "In the face of the Iraq quagmire, George Bush runs a juvenile and tasteless attack ad."[48] With this attack established, the TV spot pivots to Kerry's plans for Iraq before advocating, "On Iraq, it's time for a new direction."[49]

Expanding on the strategic shift in "Rassman," "Juvenile" clearly uses classic horror framing to depict the atrocities of the war in Iraq. While the imagery of a shadowy flag is simple, it effectively utilizes the dark shading typical of the horror genre.[50] The details are just as horrifying, as beheadings, kidnappings, and warfare are rapidly described to the audience. Just like "Rassman," these horrors are kept strategically isolated in Iraq. The Kerry campaign wants voters to realize there are real horrors of war occurring and that Bush running a comedic ad is distasteful. However, the campaign clearly does not want voters overly fearful about their own domestic safety, since Bush polled better with those concerned about such issues.[51] Thus, the temporal and spatial bracketing of classic horror framing is an effective tool in this instance for a moderate fear appeal. The verbal imagery of terrorists pouring into Iraq, plays on similar notions of otherization often levied against immigrants, where they are not humans but rather environmental pollutants.[52] Further, the horror framing is isolated to the war in Iraq and not levied against Bush, even though he is attacked in this ad. Rather, Bush is simply chastised as being juvenile.

"He's Lost, He's Desperate," first televised on October 2, 2004, moves beyond "Juvenile" by framing Bush himself with classic horror. The ad shows a very shadowed speaker at a podium, presumably Bush at the presidential debate, as the narrator says, "George Bush lost the debate. Now he's lying about it."[53] From here, the ad clarifies the statement Kerry made in the debate about preemptive strikes and terrorists before offering "something new about George Bush."[54] The serious narrator claims, "newspapers report [Bush] withheld key intelligence information from the American public so he could overstate the threat Iraq posed."[55] While this information is revealed, an image of Bush with shadowy borders transitions to darkly filtered newspapers. Then, the image reverts back to Bush as the narrator and the text on screen say, "Bush rushed us into war."[56] The word "war" is displayed in blood-red text as the background image of Bush transitions to a distorted video of U.S. soldiers milling around. This transition is accompanied by additional text, reading, "Now we're paying the price."[57]

This ad, while trying to defend Kerry, goes on the offensive against Bush by framing him through the classic frame. The dark lighting of Bush at the debate podium adds the initial visual component of horror to this advertisement, but the themes of horror ratchet up with the description of the exceptional lengths Bush went to in order to rush the United States into war. The blood-red text of "war," coupled with a shadowy Bush and distorted soldiers makes clear that Bush's supposedly malicious intent is costing thousands of young lives.[58] This advertisement uses the classic frame against Bush, and not the conflicted, because it argues that this information is "new" and extraordinary, moving far beyond some of the more mundane horrors of politics that would fall within the conflicted frame.[59]

"Obligation" is an attack ad that uses a limited amount of classic horror framing to attack Bush's Iraqi policies. This advertisement, which originally aired on October 26, 2004, relies heavily on Kerry speaking directly into the camera. Kerry claims, "The obligation of a Commander in Chief is to keep our country safe. In Iraq, George Bush has overextended our troops."[60] Then, Kerry brings up a new failure, where Bush has "now failed to secure 380 tons of deadly explosives."[61] A shadowed newspaper clipping shows up on the screen, corroborating this claim. Kerry asserts that Bush's "Iraq misjudgments put our soldiers at risk, and make our country less secure. And all he offers is more of the same."[62] Kerry then stakes his position of defender, saying, "As President, I'll bring a fresh start to protect our troops and our nation."[63]

This advertisement does just enough to be included in this section on classic horror framing. The framing is mainly done through Kerry's language, stirring up fear that Bush is no longer the hero of America, but possibly the villain. While Bush the person is not horrifically framed, his policies are—they directly cost people their lives, allowed the spread of explosives, and made the country less safe. Most of this is spatially bracketed to the soldiers in the Middle East and the loss of explosives is temporally framed as an oddity not fitting with the normal flow of a presidency. The shading of the newspaper clipping brings some visual horror to this advertisement as well.

The Kerry campaign was sharply divided in how it treated the very overwhelming presence of fear among voters about various wars. Early in the campaign, both the war in Iraq and the Vietnam War, which Kerry served in, were framed non-horrifically. The horror was presumed to be known by the audience, likely through daily news briefings and the like. Rather, the campaign focused on the positive aspects of Kerry and how he could be the hero needed for these implied, but not overtly framed, horrors. However, later advertisements flipped this notion and began horrifically framing both Vietnam and Iraq. Imagery became darker, the music melancholier, and the narrator more dire. The framing of Bush in relation to these wars was done inconsistently. "He's Lost, He's Desperate" framed Bush himself through the classic horror frame, while the other ads only framed his policy or the war classically. Regardless, the Kerry campaign was noticeably positive and upbeat, only diverging to the classic frame in a few select instances. The conflicted frame was rarely used, likely because the Kerry campaign did not want the horrors of war to breach the sphere of normalcy and come to the American home front.

BUSH'S BALANCED HORROR OFFENSIVE

For the Bush campaign, two main issues stood between the president and reelection: the Iraq War and the economy. However, the Bush campaign was able to successfully counter these potential "silver bullet" issues with two issues of their own: "terrorism and moral values."[64] "The primary goal for Mr. Bush was to emphasize another major new issue arising from the events of 9/11—the issue of the war on terrorism."[65] Indeed, Bush wanted to convince the public that he possessed the "strength and decisiveness" to win the fight against terrorism and that Kerry did not.[66] This was combined with the argument that Bush was stronger on traditional moral issues than Kerry. "CBS News Exit Poll results suggest that the Bush campaign strategy was relatively effective in blunting the potential damage of the issues of the economy and Iraq."[67]

In order to establish counters to Kerry's positions, the Bush campaign deployed a mixture of classic and conflicted horror frames. The classic frames were directed at terrorists and other threats to U.S. well-being, establishing that there are still threats facing the American people. This is an essential component of Bush's strategy to make terrorism a key voting issue. The Bush campaign then deployed the conflicted frame against Kerry himself, setting him up as a misguided fool. This, when combined with a heavy dose of self-positive advertising, helped establish the narrative that Bush was the only candidate strong enough and consistent enough to win the War on Terror.

Bush's Classic Horror Framing of Threats

"Safer, Stronger" attempts to use classic horror framing to establish what threats still face the United States. This advertisement, released on March 3, 2004, opens with Bush swearing his oath to office and lists the challenges he has faced since then. The first is the economy, as shaded numbers whizz by on the screen. A clearly disgruntled man rests his head in anguish as text reads, "A stock market in decline."[68] Somber music continues as another challenge appears over a shaded computer browser, "A dot com boom . . . gone bust."[69] The ad then pivots to September 11, with text reading, "Then . . . a day of tragedy."[70] Images of a shaded U.S. flag in front of the wreckage of the World Trade Center and firefighters carrying a body wrapped in the flag are presented. The music lightens here a touch, as an American is shown raising a flag before Bush speaking in front of a podium. The music eases further as the text reads, "Today, America is turning the corner. Rising to the challenge."[71] Bush is again shown speaking in front of images fading in and out of workers, a business with an "open" sign, smiling people, and a fighter jet.[72] The advertisement ends with a piano crescendo as the text, "PRESIDENT BUSH. Steady leadership in times of change" is displayed over a waving U.S. flag.[73]

"Safer, Stronger" is clearly meant to set up the horrors America faced during Bush's time in office and to show how he has been able to effectively meet those challenges. The economy is presented first through a classic horror frame, spatially separated as something that occurred not physically but digitally with the "dot com" bust and stock markets. Fears of technology and the digital age have a storied tradition in the horror genre, especially where the genre crosses over with science fiction. *Demon Seed* (1977), *The Fly* (1986), and *The Ring* (2002) are all great examples of horror based on technological innovation.[74] Thus, while the economy collapsed during the Bush presidency, he shifts blame from himself and hardworking Americans to the horror of inhuman technology through the internet and the digitized stock markets. Terrorism is also clearly framed through a classic lens, although not directly. Terrorism is never specifically mentioned but the events of September 11 are assumed as part of the public memory. The ad ends on a positive note, asserting Bush is the hero strong enough to continue defeating these foes.

"Weapons (Florida)," which first aired on April 26, 2004, continues to frame the threats of the War on Terror through a classic horror lens. The ad opens with soldiers running across a desert field as the narrator claims, "As our troops defend America in the War on Terror . . . they must have what it takes to win."[75] A foreboding bell tolls as the narrator argues that "John Kerry has repeatedly opposed weapons vital to winning the War on Terror."[76] A shaded video of soldiers milling around a desert field as ominous smoke lightly blows by is presented along with various images of military equipment. These military supplies, such as fighter jets, missiles, and tanks disappear as the narrator lists the equipment Kerry has voted against. The ominous bell tolls once again as the shot moves to a scared soldier and the narrator says, "Kerry even voted against body armor for our troops on the front line of the War on Terror."[77] The ad concludes with the text, "John Kerry's record on National Security: Troubling."[78]

This advertisement uses classic horror framing to present the threat to American troops in the face of a lack of supplies. The shading, smoke, and terrified expression of soldiers all point toward the ominous threats that face them in the spatially bracketed Middle East. The ad sets this up as a dangerous theater of war for U.S. troops, who require both advanced military technology and basic supplies like body armor. Kerry's plans get swept into this framing as a bell—presumably a funeral bell—tolls when the narrator argues that Kerry is denying basic supplies to U.S. soldiers. Thus, while Kerry himself is not framed as monstrous, his policies are sending troops undersupplied into a distant land of terror.

"Victory," which was first broadcast on August 13, 2004, uses subtle classic horror framing to juxtapose the horror of the past with the optimism of the present. This spot opens with a distorted, clearly dated video of an Olympics gathering. The narrator says, "In 1972, there were 40 democracies in the world."[79] The shot shifts to a shaded crowd as the text reads "40 democracies."[80] The music lightens up and the image immediately shifts from shaded to brightly lit Olympic swimmers. Text then reads "120 democracies" as the narrator makes note of this increase in the present day.[81] The swimmers dive in the pool as a flare of sun hits the camera and the narrator claims, "Freedom is spreading throughout the world like a sunrise. And this Olympics, there will be two more free nations. And two fewer terrorist regimes."[82] The flags of Afghanistan and Iraq are presented as a swimmer celebrates and the narrator argues that "With strength, resolve and courage, democracy will triumph over terror. And, hope will defeat hatred."[83]

While this ad is mostly positive, classic horror framing is used to show why the present is so positively framed in juxtaposition to the horrors of the undemocratic past. All undemocratic regimes are clumped together as relics of the past: temporally bracketed evils fighting against the conservative notion of history's march toward democracy. Afghanistan and Iraq are presented as examples of democracy's continued expansion. Not only are undemocratic regimes framed through old, distorted videos and temporality, but also through base notions of hatred and terror.

"Changing World," originally televised on July 30, 2004, juxtaposes an optimistic future with classically framed threats. The central visual tool of this advertisement is a young boy who is looking through an open door at an image of the Earth, which has various videos overlaid on it. The music is used to create a sense of awe as images of scientists, world leaders, and athletes flash by. The narrator claims, "The world is changing. Sometimes in ways that astound."[84] A deep drum beats as the camera abruptly zooms in and the video filter changes to a crimson red. Tanks and a man shooting in front of Arabic graffiti are presented as the narrator notes that other changes "terrify."[85] The mood abruptly lightens again as images of Bush are intercut with happy firefighters and families. A soldier is shown hugging his family as the camera zooms back out to the child looking through his door frame. The narrator argues, "We need a sense of purpose, a vision for the future, the conviction to do what's right."[86] Bush concludes by saying, "Together, we're moving America forward."[87]

"Changing World," while mostly positive, makes an abrupt turn to strong classic horror framing midway through the advertisement. The use of a red filter to distort images is a strong, classic horror trope. The horrors are spatially separated by their clear placement in the Middle East, indicated by the Arabic graffiti, desert climate, and tanks rolling through city streets. The person shown up close in this advertisement firing an assault rifle, presumably a terrorist, is facing away from the camera with a head covering. This tactic of hiding a subject's face is a common dehumanization tactic used in visual rhetoric deployed against various groups of people.[88] Thus, this portrayal of the terrorist as completely other helps to amplify the classic horror framing in this advertisement. This section gets juxtaposed against very positive segments of the advertisement both before and after. Thus, this ad sets up the terrors of the world and appeals to audience efficacy through Bush.

"First Choice" uses the classic horror frame to position Bush as the hero who can defeat the horrors of terrorism. This ad, which first aired on July 6, 2004, uses a speech by John McCain in favor of Bush as the main narrative thrust of the advertisement. McCain speaking about the War on Terror claims, "It's a fight between right and wrong, good and evil. And should our enemies acquire for their arsenal the chemical, biological and nuclear weapons they seek, this war will become an even bigger thing. It will become a fight for our survival."[89] Shots of McCain speaking are cut with images of black-and-white U.S. soldiers, terrorists, and Osama bin Laden. McCain argues that Bush "has led with great moral clarity and firm resolve."[90] Full-color videos of Bush smiling play as McCain heaps praise upon him, concluding that "He deserves not only our support but our admiration."[91] The crowd cheers as he introduces Bush.

"First Choice" continues the trend of juxtaposing the horrors of the world with Bush's leadership. The black-and-white filter placed on images of terrorists, bin Laden, and anxious soldiers highlights the monstrous otherness of the terrorists and the Middle East in the Bush campaign's eyes. In the face of this threat, McCain vouches for Bush's ability to be a great defender of the United States. Further, McCain carries the moral argument forward for the Bush campaign by arguing that through all this evil, President Bush has maintained "great moral clarity."[92]

"Wolves" is the strongest classic horror advertisement analyzed from the 2004 election. This ad, which was broadcast on October 22, 2004, relies heavily on the imagery of wolves stalking prey in the wilderness. Dark, cloudy woods are shown with very brief glimpses of wolves as the serious narrator claims, "In an increasingly dangerous world, even after the first terrorist attack on America, John Kerry and the liberals in Congress voted to slash America's intelligence operations by six billion dollars."[93] Ominous music continues as the narrator asserts these cuts would have weakened America. A final shot of a full pack of wolves is then revealed as the narrator threateningly notes, "And weakness attracts those who are waiting to do America harm."[94] As the narrator makes this claim, the wolves begin charging toward the camera and the shot fades out.

This advertisement relies almost exclusively on classic horror framing, using metaphorical wolves to represent the monstrous threats facing the United States. This seems to be a spiritual successor to Ronald Reagan's famous "Bear" advertisement, which uses a bear in a similar nature-horror role as these wolves.[95] Early in "Wolves," it is unclear what the wolves are supposed to represent. Nevertheless, wolves have a storied tradition in horror dating back to the genre's literary roots and popping up in the cast of classic Universal Studios horror monsters through *The Wolf Man*.[96] Much like *The Wolf Man* where the monster is only seen in glimpses early and there is some ambiguity as to what the monster really is, it is unclear if the wolves represent "John Kerry and the liberals in Congress" or something else.[97] However, as the advertisement progresses, it becomes clear that the wolves are terrorists and enemy nations of the world, waiting for a weakness in the United States to strike. The ad posits that John Kerry will open up this weakness, allowing the wolves of the world to leave the spatial separation of the woods and launch a direct attack on the United States. Even the use of the verb "slash" helps amplify the gruesome horror of those violently threatening America.[98] "Wolves" is certainly an advertisement dripping with classic horror elements.

"Whatever It Takes" mixes classic horror narrative framing with patriotic visuals to instill a message of strength and resiliency in the audience. This TV spot, which first aired on October 26, 2004, focuses on a speech given by Bush. He says that over his four years as president he has "learned first hand that ordering Americans into battle is the hardest decision, even when it is right."[99] Bush describes meeting with wounded soldiers and "the children of the fallen."[100] The music swells as the background behind Bush is replaced by smiling, waving people and stoic soldiers. He claims that "in those military families, I have seen the character of a great nation."[101] He further argues that because of those sacrifices, America is "defeating the terrorists where they live and plan."[102] Finally, Bush tells the audience that he will "never relent in defending America" and the crowd releases a roaring cheer.

This advertisement uses no visual horror tropes, relying rather on Bush's narrative speech to instill these elements. Bush's discussion of wounded and slain soldiers sets the horror elements in place by giving a sense of reality to the horrors of war. Bush uses this horror to justify why he is the only choice for audience efficacy with voters, since he will not relent in defending the United States. Further, terrorists are framed through the classic horror lens as Bush talks about their spatial separation, attacking them where they live rather than letting them come to the U.S. homeland. This stark division between the horrific narrative and positive imagery helps to sell Bush as a leader who has the resolve to vanquish the fears troubling Americans.

Conflicted Horror Framing of Kerry

"Troops" uses the conflicted horror frame to indict Kerry's voting record in Congress. This commercial, released on March 18, 2004, begins with an image of the Capitol as the narrator claims, "Few votes in Congress are as important as funding our troops at war."[103] A distorted video of Kerry is shown beside an aircraft carrier runway as the narrator says, "Though John Kerry voted in October, 2002 for military action in Iraq, he later voted against funding our soldiers."[104] The image transitions to a split between a woman soldier walking with her back to the camera and a military helicopter, before getting transitioned to a shaded image of the Senate voting floor. An echoing voice is heard asking, "Mr. Kerry?" before the narrator fills the role of Kerry and exclaims, "No."[105] The vote count totals are presented, with far more voting for than against. This pattern is repeated exactly, cutting between images of soldiers happily returning home and votes on the Senate floor pertaining to body armor, higher pay, and better health care for troops. The narrator then retorts, "And what does Kerry say now?"[106] Kerry himself is then shown claiming that he did vote for the funding before he voted against it. The narrator concludes by stating that Kerry is "Wrong on defense."[107]

"Troops" uses the conflicted frame to tie the domestic actions of Kerry to the horrors faced by U.S. soldiers. The imagery of soldiers used throughout this ad is either clearly of a happy homecoming or vague enough to be construed as either at home or abroad. There is no clear visual imagery of foreignness. Further, the monotonous repetition of an issue being voted on, Kerry being asked to vote, and the narrator filling in his vote of no works to weave Kerry's horrifying policies into the sphere of normalcy. Kerry is not made out to be an inhuman entity, but rather a lying, uncaring politician. The slight distortions placed on Kerry when he first appears in this attack ad help cement that he is the aim of this conflicted horror frame.

"Wacky," which was originally televised on March 30, 2004, again attacks Kerry's policies using the conflicted horror frame, this time focusing on Kerry's gas tax. The ad is shot entirely in old-timey black and white. A startled and terrified man is shown staring into the camera as the narrator says, "Some people have wacky ideas."[108] Kerry's wacky idea is "taxing gasoline more so people drive less."[109] With this accusation, a gasoline price meter starts rocketing up before a video of roughly ten people riding a long bicycle is presented. John Kerry is then shown sped up, distorted, and still in black and white as the narrator claims, "That's John Kerry. He supported a 50 cent a gallon gas tax."[110] The narrator asserts that the average family would end up paying "$657 more a year" as a man checks his pockets and finds that they are empty.[111] The next shot is split between three different videos. On the left, Kerry is again shown speaking. In the middle, a gas meter rising in price is depicted. On the right, a woman is turning to look back toward the prices and Kerry and horrified by what she sees (see figure 3.2). The ad concludes with a man pushing a car up the road as the text reads, "John Kerry: Wrong On Taxes."[112]

Figure 3.2 Bush, "Wacky." Screenshot captured by author.

Wacky combines the conflicted horror frame with a comedic edge to levy a strong attack on Kerry. Horror and comedy have a long tradition of fitting together, with *Evil Dead II* (1987) serving as an excellent exemplar.[113] The black-and-white filter placed on the entirety of this advertisement fits within the conventions of horror framing as described by Richardson.[114] Additionally, there are various shots of individuals looking horrified at the premise of rising gasoline taxes. However, this falls within the realm of conflicted horror framing because of the imminently relatable, normalcy of the horror: rising gas prices. Further, Kerry is not portrayed as outright monstrous, but rather misguided and "wacky."[115] The comedic tones of this ad also help to soften the attack on Kerry from outright monster to foolishly human.

"Pessimism," released on June 4, 2004, uses the conflicted horror frame in combination with many positive messages to juxtapose Bush with a misguided Kerry. Upbeat piano music plays as Bush comes on screen, stating, "I'm optimistic about America because I believe in the people of America."[116] The ad notes that "after recession, 9/11, and war" the American economy has rebounded in a number of key indicators. Happy people are shown working in stores, on construction sites, and in an office. The narrator then asks, "John Kerry's response? He's talking about the Great Depression."[117] A video of Kerry speaking fades to black and white as the narrator concludes, "One thing's sure.... Pessimism never created a job."[118]

This spot is split down the middle between strongly positive messages and a conflicted horror framing of Kerry. The positive aspects of the advertisement show how the United States has persevered through tragedy and hardship. Bush speaks overtly about his optimism. This contrasts with Kerry, who is shown as out-of-touch talking about classic horrors of the past. However, this ad does not frame those past horrors, only Kerry, who is misguided and visually framed using black-and-white video filters.

A Strictly Comedic Attack

"Windsurfing" is a unique advertisement in that it is a rare example of a negative attack ad that does not use any horror framing and rather relies solely on comedy, a move criticized by the Kerry campaign in the "Juvenile" advertisement. This ad, first broadcast on September 23, 2004, relies entirely on video of Kerry windsurfing. Fanciful music plays in the background as the narrator asks, "In which direction would John Kerry lead?"[119] The video of Kerry is then flipped back and forth as he seems to jaunt between text saying "Supported" and "Opposed."[120] The narrator highlights this further by saying, "Kerry voted for the Iraq war, opposed it, supported it and now opposes it again."[121] The scope of Kerry's flip-flopping then expands to other issues like education reform and Medicare. The narrator ends with a final jab, "John

Kerry: whichever way the wind blows."[122] Even though this ad is in and of itself non-horrific, it plays into the Bush campaign's larger narrative of Kerry as a fool.

The Bush campaign relied heavily on both the classic and conflicted horror frames to establish Bush as the continued hero the United States needs. Typically, the Bush campaign used the classic horror frame to demonize threats to the country from terrorists and rogue factions and even classically framed technological advances as worthy of blame for the economic recession. The conflicted frame was used against Kerry himself, depicting him as misguided, foolish, and dangerous to American troops. These horrific fear appeals were often combined with positive parts of advertisements, making sure to remind the viewer that while the world is filled with monsters, President Bush has the country on the path to a brighter future.

CONCLUSION

Ultimately, incumbent George W. Bush defeated challenger John Kerry by a margin of thirty-five electoral votes and over three million popular votes.[123] Throughout the lead up to the election, both campaigns deployed vastly different strategies in their usage of televised horror framing. The Bush campaign upped its usage of horror from the 2000 election while the Kerry campaign resisted using it at first before eventually deploying classic horror framing in specific instances.

The Bush campaign used horror framing early and often, relying on the classic frame to demonize threats to America from terrorists, enemy nations, and even technology. This helped to amplify the threats still facing the United States in voters' minds. Bush then used the conflicted frame to attack Kerry himself, portraying him as a misguided, insidiously flawed human. This plays into the demonic theming of contemporary campaign advertising, which casts opponents into polarizing, us vs. them binaries. Kerry's weak fortitude was juxtaposed with Bush's resilient resolve, a positive refrain sprinkled throughout many of Bush's advertisements.

The Kerry campaign took a different approach, attempting to avoid using horror framing for as long as possible. Kerry likely knew that he was viewed as the weaker candidate on defense issues, so the campaign tried to emphasize his credentials as a veteran, while downplaying the threats facing America. It seems obvious in many ads that the audience can fill in the horrors facing the United States for themselves, and Kerry would not have wanted to scare people further and drive them toward Bush. As such, Kerry resisted the normative and omnipresent dynamics of horrific campaign advertising. However, later in the campaign there is a shift and the Kerry campaign begins using gruesome details to horrifically frame the Vietnam and Iraq wars. This strategy is used less to scare the public into wanting to fight terrorists, but more so to convince people that war is horrific and sending young Americans to face such terror is immoral. However, this is a difficult line to walk as too strong of a fear appeal would likely reinforce a knee-jerk reaction to continue fighting the war on the other side of the world as opposed to it leaking into the American home front. As exit polls indicate, Bush seemed to convince voters that terrorism was a threat worth fighting, and Bush had the strength and moral convictions to accomplish that task.[124] It is unclear what role Bush's campaign advertising had in convincing voters of this narrative, but one way or another that is the narrative that seemed to resonate with voters and secure Bush a second term.

NOTES

1. Pew Research Center, "Race Tightens Again, Kerry's Image Improves," *Pew Research Center*, October 20, 2004, https://www.people-press.org/2004/10/20/race-tightens-again-kerrys-image-improves/.
2. Pew Research Center, "Race Tightens Again."
3. Pew Research Center, "Race Tightens Again."
4. David R. Jones, "Why Bush Won," *CBS News*, November 3, 2004, https://www.cbsnews.com/news/why-bush-won-02-11-2004/.
5. Jones, "Why Bush Won."
6. Jones, "Why Bush Won."
7. Jones, "Why Bush Won."
8. Jones, "Why Bush Won."
9. John Kerry for President, Inc., "Heart," *The Living Room Candidate: Presidential Campaign Commercials 1952–2020*, May 3, 2004, http://www.livingroomcandidate.org/commercials/2004/heart.
10. Kerry, "Heart."
11. Kerry, "Heart."
12. John Kerry for President, Inc., "Risk," *The Living Room Candidate: Presidential Campaign Commercials 1952–2020*, April 21, 2004, http://www.livingroomcandidate.org/commercials/2004/risk.
13. Kerry, "Risk."
14. Kerry, "Risk."
15. Kerry, "Risk."
16. John Kerry for President, Inc., "Optimists," *The Living Room Candidate: Presidential Campaign Commercials 1952-2020*, June 1, 2004, http://www.livingroomcandidate.org/commercials/2004/optimists.
17. Kerry, "Optimists."
18. Kerry, "Optimists."
19. Kerry, "Optimists."

20. Democratic National Committee, "Strength," *The Living Room Candidate: Presidential Campaign Commercials 1952–2020*, July 30, 2004, http://livingroomcandidate.org/commercials/2004/filter/party.

21. Democratic National Committee, "Strength."
22. Democratic National Committee, "Strength."
23. Democratic National Committee, "Strength."
24. Democratic National Committee, "Strength."
25. John Kerry for President, Inc., "Three Minutes," *The Living Room Candidate: Presidential Campaign Commercials 1952–2020*, July 10, 2004, http://www.livingroomcandidate.org/commercials/2004/three-minutes.
26. Kerry, "Three Minutes."
27. Kerry, "Three Minutes."
28. Kerry-Edwards 2004, Inc., "Heroes," *The Living Room Candidate: Presidential Campaign Commercials 1952–2020*, October 27, 2004, http://www.livingroomcandidate.org/commercials/2004/heroes.
29. Kerry-Edwards, "Heroes."
30. Kerry-Edwards, "Heroes."
31. Kerry-Edwards, "Heroes."
32. Kerry-Edwards, "Heroes."
33. Kerry-Edwards, "Heroes."
34. Glenn W. Richardson Jr., *Pulp Politics: How Political Advertising Tells the Stories of American Politics* (Lanham, MD: Rowman & Littlefield, 2008), 39.
35. John Kerry for President, Inc., "Rassman," *The Living Room Candidate: Presidential Campaign Commercials 1952–2020*, August 18, 2004, http://www.livingroomcandidate.org/commercials/2004/rassman.
36. Kerry, "Rassman."
37. Kerry, "Rassman."
38. Kerry, "Rassman."
39. Kerry, "Rassman."
40. Caroline Joan (Kay) S. Picart and David A. Frank, *Frames of Evil: The Holocaust as Horror in American Film* (Carbondale: Southern Illinois University Press, 2006), 6–7.
41. Richardson, *Pulp Politics*, 39.
42. *Dracula*, directed by Tod Browning (1931; Peacock TV), Digital; *The Wolf Man*, directed by George Waggner (1941; Universal Studios Home Entertainment, 2016), DVD; *The Ring*, directed by Gore Verbinski (2002; Paramount Pictures, 2012), DVD; *The Grudge*, directed by Takashi Shimizu (2004; Sony Pictures, 2009), DVD.
43. Kendall R. Phillips, *Projected Fears: Horror Films and American Culture* (Westport, CT: Praeger, 2005), 23.
44. Kerry-Edwards 2004, Inc., "Juvenile," *The Living Room Candidate: Presidential Campaign Commercials 1952–2020*, September 23, 2004, http://www.livingroomcandidate.org/commercials/2004/juvenile.
45. Kerry-Edwards, "Juvenile."
46. Kerry-Edwards, "Juvenile."
47. Kerry-Edwards, "Juvenile."
48. Kerry-Edwards, "Juvenile."

49. Kerry-Edwards, "Juvenile."
50. Richardson, *Pulp Politics*, 39.
51. Pew Research Center, "Race Tightens Again."
52. J. David Cisneros, "Contaminated Communities: The Metaphor of 'Immigrant as Pollutant' in Media Representations of Immigration," *Rhetoric & Public Affairs* 11, no. 4 (2008): 570.
53. Kerry-Edwards 2004, Inc., "He's Lost, He's Desperate," *The Living Room Candidate: Presidential Campaign Commercials 1952–2020*, October 2, 2004, http://www.livingroomcandidate.org/commercials/2004/hes-lost-hes-desperate.
54. Kerry-Edwards, "He's Lost."
55. Kerry-Edwards, "He's Lost."
56. Kerry-Edwards, "He's Lost."
57. Kerry-Edwards, "He's Lost."
58. Kerry-Edwards, "He's Lost."
59. Kerry-Edwards, "He's Lost."
60. Kerry-Edwards 2004, Inc., "Obligation," *The Living Room Candidate: Presidential Campaign Commercials 1952–2020*, October 26, 2004, http://www.livingroomcandidate.org/commercials/2004/obligation.
61. Kerry-Edwards, "Obligation."
62. Kerry-Edwards, "Obligation."
63. Kerry-Edwards, "Obligation."
64. Jones, "Why Bush Won."
65. Jones, "Why Bush Won."
66. Jones, "Why Bush Won."
67. Jones, "Why Bush Won."
68. Bush-Cheney '04, Inc., "Safer, Stronger," *The Living Room Candidate: Presidential Campaign Commercials 1952–2020*, March 3, 2004, http://www.livingroomcandidate.org/commercials/2004/safer-stronger.
69. Bush-Cheney, "Safer, Stronger."
70. Bush-Cheney, "Safer, Stronger."
71. Bush-Cheney, "Safer, Stronger."
72. Bush-Cheney, "Safer, Stronger."
73. Bush-Cheney, "Safer, Stronger."
74. *Demon Seed*, directed by Donald Cammell (1977; Warner Archive Collection, 2017), DVD; *The Fly*, directed by David Cronenberg (1986, 20th Century Fox), Digital; *The Ring*, Verbinski.
75. Bush-Cheney, '04, Inc., "Weapons (Florida)," *The Living Room Candidate: Presidential Campaign Commercials 1952–2020*, April 26, 2004, http://www.livingroomcandidate.org/commercials/2004/weapons-florida.
76. Bush-Cheney, "Weapons."
77. Bush-Cheney, "Weapons."
78. Bush-Cheney, "Weapons."
79. Bush-Cheney '04, Inc., "Victory," *The Living Room Candidate: Presidential Campaign Commercials 1952–2012*, August 13, 2004, http://www.livingroomcandidate.org/commercials/2004/victory.
80. Bush-Cheney, "Victory."

81. Bush-Cheney, "Victory."
82. Bush-Cheney, "Victory."
83. Bush-Cheney, "Victory."
84. Bush-Cheney '04, Inc., "Changing World," *The Living Room Candidate: Presidential Campaign Commercials 1952–2020*, July 30, 2004, http://www.livingroomcandidate.org/commercials/2004/changing-world.
85. Bush-Cheney, "Changing World."
86. Bush-Cheney, "Changing World."
87. Bush-Cheney, "Changing World."
88. Cisneros, "Contaminated Communities," 588.
89. Bush-Cheney '04, Inc., "First Choice," *The Living Room Candidate: Presidential Campaign Commercials 1952–2020*, July 6, 2004, http://www.livingroomcandidate.org/commercials/2004/first-choice.
90. Bush-Cheney, "First Choice."
91. Bush-Cheney, "First Choice."
92. Bush-Cheney, "First Choice."
93. Bush-Cheney '04, Inc., "Wolves," *The Living Room Candidate: Presidential Campaign Commercials 1952–2020*, October 22, 2004, http://www.livingroomcandidate.org/commercials/2004/wolves.
94. Bush-Cheney, "Wolves."
95. Reagan-Bush '84, "Bear," *The Living Room Candidate: Presidential Campaign Commercials 1952–2020*, October 2, 1984, http://www.livingroomcandidate.org/commercials/1984/bear.
96. *The Wolf Man*, Waggner.
97. Bush-Cheney, "Wolves."
98. Bush-Cheney, "Wolves."
99. Bush-Cheney '04, Inc., "Whatever It Takes," *The Living Room Candidate: Presidential Campaign Commercials 1952–2020*, October 26, 2004, http://www.livingroomcandidate.org/commercials/2004/whatever-it-takes.
100. Bush-Cheney, "Whatever It Takes."
101. Bush-Cheney, "Whatever It Takes."
102. Bush-Cheney, "Whatever It Takes."
103. Bush, "Troops," *The Living Room Candidate: Presidential Campaign Commercials 1952–2020*, March 18, 2004, http://www.livingroomcandidate.org/commercials/2004/troops.
104. Bush, "Troops."
105. Bush, "Troops."
106. Bush, "Troops."
107. Bush, "Troops."
108. Bush-Cheney '04, Inc., "Wacky," *The Living Room Candidate: Presidential Campaign Commercials 1952–2020*, March 30, 2004, http://www.livingroomcandidate.org/commercials/2004/wacky.
109. Bush-Cheney, "Wacky."
110. Bush-Cheney, "Wacky."
111. Bush-Cheney, "Wacky."

112. Bush-Cheney, "Wacky."
113. *Evil Dead II*, directed by Sam Raimi (1987; Lionsgate, 2018), DVD.
114. Richardson, *Pulp Politics*, 39.
115. Bush-Cheney, "Wacky."
116. Bush-Cheney '04, Inc., "Pessimism," *The Living Room Candidate: Presidential Campaign Commercials 1952–2020*, June 4, 2004, http://www.livingroomcandidate.org/commercials/2004/pessimism.
117. Bush-Cheney, "Pessimism."
118. Bush-Cheney, "Pessimism."
119. Bush-Cheney '04, Inc., "Windsurfing," *The Living Room Candidate: Presidential Campaign Commercials 1952–2020*, September 23, 2004, http://www.livingroomcandidate.org/commercials/2004/windsurfing.
120. Bush-Cheney, "Windsurfing."
121. Bush-Cheney, "Windsurfing."
122. Bush-Cheney, "Windsurfing."
123. "2004 Presidential Election," *270 to Win*, https://www.270towin.com/2004_Election/.
124. Jones, "Why Bush Won."

Chapter 4

John McCain versus Barack Obama in the 2008 Election

The 2008 election came on the heels of George W. Bush's two terms as president. The American political landscape shifted dramatically over the preceding eight years, with the attacks of September 11, the War on Terror, and the economic collapse of 2008 that happened in the middle of the campaign. With this, the Republicans nominated Senator John McCain (R-AZ) and the Democrats chose Senator Barack Obama (D-IL), a surprise as many believed Hillary Clinton would be the nominee.

The top issues for voters in the 2008 election, according to the Pew Research Center, were the economy and energy.[1] 87 percent of voters said the economy would be very important to their vote and 77 percent said that energy policy would be very important to their vote. Beyond the economy and the environment, "Four other issues cluster just below, with 72%–73% mentioning health care, education, the war in Iraq and terrorism."[2] Immigration settled in at 52 percent, while abortion was only mentioned by 39 percent of respondents and gay marriage by 28 percent.

With the issues of the time in view, this chapter examines how the 2008 presidential election ads of John McCain and Barack Obama used horror framing to make fear appeals to voters (see table 4.1). McCain and Obama diverged significantly in how they deployed elements of the horror genre in their campaign ads. McCain used both the classic and conflicted horror frames consistently depending on the threats being expressed. Conversely, Obama slowly evolved his ads from a conflicted frame to a classic one, with the financial crisis of 2008 seemingly providing the impetus for a final pivot toward the classic frame. Additionally, Obama's late, self-positive appeals to audience efficacy allowed these increasingly frightening threats to have a narrative solution. On the other hand, McCain's attempts at audience efficacy were too little and too contradictory to his self-proclaimed status as a "maverick."

Table 4.1 John McCain and Barack Obama Campaign Advertisements' Airdates

John McCain		Barack Obama	
Airdate	Title	Airdate	Title
May 18, 2008	2013	June 20, 2008	Country I Love
July 31, 2008	Celeb	August 11, 2008	Embrace
August 5, 2008	Broken	September 8, 2008	No Maverick
September 8, 2008	Original Mavericks	September 10, 2008	What Kind
September 10, 2008	Education	September 15, 2008	Honor
September 12, 2008	Disrespectful	September 16, 2008	Fundamentals
September 15, 2008	Crisis	September 19, 2008	Need Education
September 18, 2008	Dome	October 1, 2008	Spending Spree
October 6, 2008	Dangerous	October 5, 2008	This Year
October 22, 2008	Sweat Equity	October 9, 2008	Country I Believe In
October 25, 2008	Storm	October 25, 2008	Defining Moment
October 28, 2008	Compare (R)	October 30, 2008	Rearview Mirror
October 29, 2008	Special	October 30, 2008	Something
October 31, 2008	Freedom		

MCCAIN'S CONSISTENT MONSTERS

According to Charles Prysby and Carmine Scavo, McCain's campaign strategy relied on distancing himself from President Bush and emphasizing "his credentials as someone who would change Washington."[3] With this, he tried to emphasize his status "as a Republican maverick to argue that he could work with members of both parties in Congress."[4] Possibly as an attempt to confirm this bipartisan potential, McCain never framed Obama through a classic horror frame. In fact, McCain demonized Bush and Establishment Republicans far more than he did Obama. Instead, McCain simply claimed that "he had the experience and maturity to be president, and that Obama did not. This strategy involved contrasting his own lengthy record of military and public service with Obama's short resume."[5] These themes became extremely apparent throughout McCain's campaign ads, where he classically framed threats to America, including from his own party, but only ever framed Obama through a conflicted horror frame, casting him as unprepared. This unpreparedness draws deep connections with racist tropes of the horror genre.

Washington, Bush, and Crisis: Classic Monstrosities

John McCain's first television ad, "2013," initially aired on May 18, 2008, and it showed what the world would look like in the year 2013 under McCain's leadership.[6] The ad claims that the Middle East will be "stabilized," the threat of nuclear terror will be "reduced," border security will be "strengthened," energy independence will be "advanced," wasteful spending will be "reformed," healthcare choice will be "delivered," and economic confidence will be "restored."[7] This advertisement, accordingly, highlights some of the threats to the United States as John McCain sees them, but inverts them. Instead of listing the issues faced by the nation in 2008, it jumps to how these issues will be overcome by 2013. This logic is expressed visually when the advertisement argues that the nuclear terror threat will be "reduced," showing an image of a nuclear blast but in reverse. Thus, horrifying images like nuclear blasts and disturbing threats, like nuclear terror, instability in the Middle East, unsecure borders, wasteful spending, and more are shown, but these various monsters have been slain in the hypothetical future. Accordingly, this advertisement sets up the temporal bracketing of classic horror, arguing that normalcy and peace will return with a John McCain presidency where he fights the external, monstrous threats to the United States. Efficacy is shown to the audience in what America will look like if they elect John McCain.

"Broken," originally televised on August 5, 2008, takes up classic horror framing once again, using distortions and unsettling music to frame monstrous corruption.[8] The advertisement starts with two quick shots of the Capitol and the White House, shot in black and white with shading distortions over both, as the narrator says, "Washington's broken."[9] The shading distortions are reminiscent of the German Expressionism in *The Cabinet of Dr. Caligari* (1920),[10] showing the internal corruption of Washington. Eerie music, vaguely reminiscent of the main theme from *The Exorcist* (1973),[11] plays in the background.[12] The advertisement admits, "We're worse off than we were four years ago" before shifting to color when depicting McCain smiling, talking with potential voters, and shaking hands with a businessman.[13] The narrator notes that McCain has "taken on big tobacco, drug companies, [and] fought corruption in both parties" and he will "reform Wall Street, battle Big Oil, [and] make America prosper again."[14] Within this segment, multiple elements of classic horror framing are present. First, it sets up the monstrous other that is draining America: Big Tobacco, Washington politicians, Wall Street, and Big Oil. Then, it highlights how McCain will battle those monsters, much like a protagonist such as Van Helsing in *Dracula* (1931).[15] Finally, it again brackets time, arguing that the United States is presently corrupt and decaying. But once the monsters are defeated, America will "prosper again," returning to the normalcy of the past.[16]

This ad, accordingly, uses a classic horror framing to depict monstrous others, but has no mention of Obama. Further, this advertisement inherently admits that President Bush, a fellow Republican, was a failed president through the mention of being "worse off than we were four years ago" and the depiction of a distorted White House.[17] This synergizes with McCain's strategy of distancing himself from the Republican Party and Bush.[18] Thus,

McCain positions himself as the only one able to battle all of these monsters in Washington since he is "The Original Maverick."[19] Audience efficacy in the face of these threats is lacking, as they can only be dealt with by the maverick McCain.

"Original Mavericks" is ostensibly an epideictic self-praise ad for the McCain campaign, highlighting the battles McCain and Sarah Palin have won, which still fits within the larger horror narrative.[20] This commercial had an initial airdate of September 8, 2008. The metaphorical language of conflict and combat is heavy throughout this ad, with the narrator and text saying, "fights," "stopped," "took on," "battled," and "fought" throughout in relation to Bush, Big Oil, Washington, the GOP, and the drug industry.[21] Once again, this advertisement carries on the notion of McCain being the only one who can fight the monstrous threats to the country, adding Sarah Palin to the team. Notably, many of these threats are coming from their own party. The campaign attempts to position McCain and Palin as redeemed heroes, breaking away from the monstrous GOP.

Initially aired on September 15, 2008, in the immediate wake of the 2008 economic crash, "Crisis" continues to classically frame a horrific threat to America, the economic crisis.[22] A dimly lit foreclosure sign, distorted images of the New York Stock Exchange and Lehman Brothers, and a sad, defeated man in a tie are all shown. These images depict three elements of classic horror. The foreclosure sign alludes to the decay of the home, a gothic theme common in classic horror films.[23] The distorted images of the stock exchange and Lehman Brothers show the monstrous other, Wall Street and the current American economy. The distraught businessman shows the devastation that monsters create. The advertisement then pivots to specific policies McCain will implement to fight the monster such as "Tougher rules on Wall Street," "No special interest giveaways," "Lower taxes," and "Offshore drilling."[24] Thus, the audience is given a specific method for slaying the monster through these policy proposals.

"Dome" is the most classically horrific advertisement, at least in imagery, that McCain released.[25] The advertisement, which was first broadcast on September 18, 2008, opens by saying, "When our economy is in crisis, a Big Government casts a big shadow on us all. Obama and his liberal congressional allies want a massive government."[26] While this is being said by the narrator, the U.S. Capitol Building is shown growing larger, covering most of the east coast.[27] Then, an image of the Capitol colored blood red is displayed next to a black-and-white picture of Obama, before images of the shadow of the Capitol growing over buildings and neighborhoods are presented. As this shadow continues to grow, it starts to overtake a sleeping baby.[28] This imagery is evocative of horrific framings of alien invasions, where their huge ships cast shadows on the defenseless human race, such as *Independence*

Day (1996).²⁹ It is also reminiscent of movies that make children the target of monstrous attacks, such as *The Exorcist*.³⁰ Clearly, the government is depicted as a completely inhuman, monstrous threat. This threat is linked to Obama, but Obama himself is not this inhuman monster. In line with the conflicted framing in the next subsection, Obama is cast more as a gatekeeper or a creator than a monster himself.

"Special," which was initially aired on October 29, 2008, again deploys a heavy dosage of classic horror imagery, while still maintaining that Obama himself is not explicitly monstrous but just unfit.³¹ Images of Obama are shown as the narrator says that "Behind the fancy speeches, grand promises, and TV specials, lies the truth. With crises at home and abroad, Barack Obama lacks the experience America needs."³² After this foreword, classic horror audiovisuals are montaged. Images of a foreclosure sign, a chain locking a fence in front of a closed down building, terrorists, a fully armed American soldier, and boarded-up houses are all shown in rapid succession. This imagery frames the classically horrific threats looming over America. But Obama is not himself one of these monstrosities. Rather, he "lacks the experience" and is "not ready . . . yet."³³ This last quote is particularly interesting because it even leaves open the possibility that Obama could one day become ready and fit to be president. Clearly, a classic horror monster could never become fit for this position given its complete inhuman ontology. Accordingly, Obama is once again not a classically framed monster. But the threats facing America, particularly terrorists, most certainly are monstrosities within this advertisement.

"Freedom," which was first aired on October 31, 2008, as McCain's final televised advertisement, uses the classic horror frame that has been constructed throughout the campaign to firmly position McCain as the savior.³⁴ The ad opens with images of McCain recovering from injuries he sustained in Vietnam while he says, "I've served my country since I was 17 years old and spent five years longing for her shores."³⁵ Then, images of McCain returning home and saluting are shown while he says, "I came home dedicated to a cause greater than my own."³⁶ These images of McCain from the time of his service in Vietnam illustrate that McCain has literally fought the "evil other" on behalf of America. Contemporary images of McCain are then presented while McCain asserts, "We can grow our economy. We will cut government waste."³⁷ The usage of inclusive "we" language attempts to provide the audience a sense of efficacy in fighting the monstrous threats looming together. This continues when McCain implores, "Don't hope for a stronger America. Vote for one. Join me," as large rally crowds are seen.³⁸ While not nearly as classically horrific as many of the other ads in this section, "Freedom" clearly plays on the classic horror narrative trope of the hero leading the masses. These inclusive calls for action against monstrosity remind one of mob justice found in classic horror films—where the many defeat the monstrous—like the ending of *Frankenstein* (1931).³⁹

A Consistently Conflicted Candidate: Unprepared Obama

McCain's campaign was extremely consistent in its framing of candidate Obama. The campaign went out of its way to depict Obama as completely unprepared to lead, but also completely human/non-monstrous. This was clearly exemplified in the ad "Special" which was included in the previous section. Even though the advertisement delves heavily into classic horror imagery, it completely removes Obama from that visceral imagery by saying he is "not ready . . . yet."⁴⁰

While this movement of Obama from the classic to the conflicted may seem almost altruistic on the surface, there is a far more insidious message when examined through the horror genre and its relationship to Black actors and filmmakers. Indeed, Robin R. Means Coleman argues, "For most of film history, black actors have appeared in horror films in supporting roles. Many were deeply problematic."⁴¹ However, Coleman, who writes in 2019, claims the horror genre has reached a golden age, "becoming more imaginative and inclusive—in who can play hero and antihero, and who gets to be the monster and savior."⁴² However, in the context of the 2008 election, inclusive "glimpses of blackness faded as many horror films in the 1980s, 1990s and 2000s reverted to well-worn tropes."⁴³ Thus, while McCain's argument that Obama isn't ready for the presidency yet may seem, on the surface, to be an indictment of Obama's lack of experience, when read through the horror genre a more insidious argument is made. Obama is not ready for the presidency because a Black man, according to much of horror cinema up until the 2000s, can't be the hero (see figure 4.1 for a notable exception in *Night of the Living Dead* (1968) with protagonist Ben).⁴⁴ Obama isn't the one unprepared to be the hero, rather McCain's version of America is unprepared for a Black protagonist.

McCain's second TV spot, "Celeb," which was released on July 31, 2008, takes the chronologically first shot at Obama by using the conflicted frame to highlight his human flaws and portray him as too hypnotic.⁴⁵ People chanting "Obama" are heard, while videos of Obama rallies and camera flashes are mixed with images of Britney Spears and Paris Hilton. The ad then says, "He's the biggest celebrity in the world. But is he ready to lead?"⁴⁶ The advertisement attacks his policies, concluding "Higher taxes. More foreign oil. That's the real Obama."⁴⁷ Thus, "gas prices soaring" and other threats are slightly construed through a classic frame.⁴⁸

However, Obama himself is not framed as classically horrific. Instead, he is framed through a conflicted lens, at worst creating monstrosity rather than being himself monstrous. One is reminded of the character Murder Legendre in *White Zombie* (1932), who uses Haitian voodoo to turn people

Figure 4.1 *Night of the Living Dead* (1968). Screenshot captured by author.

into monstrous zombies.[49] Similarly, Barack Obama is not a true monster. He is a celebrity, a cult of personality. He is misguided and villainous in a conflicted framing sense. But not classically horrific. The classically horrific threats are those to the economy, and those to the safety of America. This fits with Coleman's assessment of horror-influenced, right-wing attacks on Obama and his campaign which portray him as an exotic "hypnotist," using "Voodoo power" in order to "dupe masses of young people."[50] Indeed, it is the "shininess of it all" that allows Obama to hypnotize the youth into accepting his "message of hope and change."[51] This shininess and elevated status are clearly reflected in "Celeb," quite literally through the use of bright, flashing camera effects. Thus, racist horror tropes again seep into McCain's attacks.

While not a television ad, it is worth mentioning here the sarcastically toned "The One" advertisement that played on the internet at nearly the same time as "Celeb." This advertisement, following a similar tact as "Celeb," showed Obama talking about himself as if he was a divine savior.[52] The ad ends with "Barack Obama may be the one. But is he ready to lead?"[53] Clearly, McCain is depicting Obama as comically misguided in his belief that he can be a hero, but not a monstrous other.

"Education" again uses the conflicted frame to carry forward the theme of Obama being ineffectual, with an explicit attack on Obama's record on education.[54] This ad, which was originally aired on September 10, 2008, argues that Obama "hasn't made a significant mark on education" and that he is a "defender of the existing public school monopoly."[55] The one accomplishment Obama has made, as the ad notes, is "Legislation to teach comprehensive sex education to kindergarteners."[56] The ad ends by saying Obama is "Wrong on education. Wrong for your family."[57] Throughout the advertisement, nursery room–type music is playing in the background. This fits with the theme of education but also continues the message that Obama is not a monstrous other. Rather, he is completely unqualified to fight real monsters like the "public school monopoly."[58]

This advertisement plays on similar horror tropes as *The Exorcist*. Derek Lewis argues that "anxieties about youth voters who do not display enough agency also permeated films" like *The Exorcist*.[59] While *The Exorcist* is the most widely recognized exemplar of this anxiety in film, there are countless other films that use the trope of childhood possession. Even though kindergarteners are clearly too young to be voters, this ad speaks to larger anxieties among Republican voters that the education system is brainwashing and liberalizing the youth, who will eventually be of voting age. This fear of manipulation and even possession is very analogous to *The Exorcist*. Given the charge of Obama's almost absurd devotion to science through early sex education, one thinks of the doctors in *The Exorcist* who are unable to cure the possessed Regan with established medical practices.[60] Rather, it is only the priestly duo that is able to fight and ultimately remove the demon from Regan.[61] Clearly, the doctors are not monstrous. They are just completely inept. In a similar way, McCain is constructing a dual narrative argument. At best Obama may have good intentions, but he is too unqualified to fight the kinds of monsters the American education system is facing. At worst, Obama himself is brainwashing the youth of America through his alluring charm. In either case, the only efficacy the American people have according to the ad is to vote for the duo of McCain and Palin.

"Dangerous," which was first broadcast on October 6, 2008, is another conflicted attack ad on Obama that largely hinges on associating him with congressional Democrats.[62] This ad has two parts: in the first half, it attacks Obama directly through his saying troops in Afghanistan are "Just air-raiding villages and killing civilians," to which the narrator calls Obama "dishonorable."[63] Obama is not framed as a monster here. Just inconsiderate, unpatriotic, and dishonorable. Conversely, the second half of the ad frames congressional liberals as "dangerous" in their military spending cuts, which the ad argues "increases the risk on [troops] lives."[64] Here, Congress is the real threat monstrously imperiling American lives. Thus, once again, the government is made classically monstrous. Yet, the narrative thrust of the ad ultimately positions Obama as a conflicted antagonist.

Another example of a conflicted advertisement came on October 22, 2008, with "Sweat Equity," which plays on the sound bite that swept the election when "Joe the plumber" was told by Obama that "I think when you spread the wealth around, it's good for everybody."[65] The ad uses this clip of Obama, then pivots to a group of people who say "I'm Joe the plumber" and explain why they do not want the wealth spread around.[66] Finally, the advertisement ends with the narrator and text saying, "Barack Obama. Higher taxes, more spending, not ready."[67] Once again, the notion of Obama not being ready or fit for office is elicited. Obama is not a monster, but he is unable to defeat the real monsters facing America.

"Storm," which was released on October 25, 2008, relies heavily on disaster film tropes, arguing that America is currently in a terrible "storm" that some say "cannot get worse."[68] The advertisement deploys a metaphor of the president being the captain of the ship that is America, using images of increasingly choppy and stormy water to visually make this connection.[69] The commercial further suggests "What if the storm does get worse? With someone who's untested at the helm?"[70] The advertisement ends with the text "Barack Obama. Untested."[71] As other ads have made clear; the narrative is clearly not that Obama is a monster. He is just incapable of navigating and defeating the issues threatening America. With him at the helm, it can be inferred that the ship that is America will wreck similar to the more horrific moments of the ship sinking in movies such as *Titanic* (1997) or *Poseidon* (2006).[72] The captain is clearly no monster, but there is certainly blame to assign when the ship crashes.

"Compare (R)," which was first aired on October 28, 2008, uses the conflicted frame to highlight the differences in policy between John McCain and Barack Obama in the context of "Your choice."[73] McCain is shown looking happy and heroic with Republican-red backlighting, as he is associated with "Workin' Joes," "Keep what's yours," "Freeze spending," "Eliminate waste," "Economic growth," and "Proven."[74] Obama, on the other hand, is shown looking upset and angry with Democratic-blue backlighting and is associated with "Higher taxes," "Spread your income," "New spending," "Pain for small business," and "risky."[75] While the commercial looks like it might stray into classic framing by making Obama himself a potential threat to America through his policies, the ad comes back to the narrative of Obama as unproven and "risky" at the end, framing him again ultimately through a conflicted lens.[76] Thus, change from the status quo of white presidents and white heroes is a potential threat with Obama's bid for the presidency.

John McCain's televised campaign was nothing if not narratively consistent. Throughout the entirety of his ad campaign, he classically framed existential threats to America as horrific, such as Washington, the economy, terrorism, and many others. He also never framed Obama in a way as to cast him as a monstrous threat. Rather, he repeatedly referred to him as unfit, unprepared, and risky. McCain's campaign even went as far as to say that

Obama could potentially be fit in the future with more experience. However, these somewhat positive assessments come loaded with racist baggage when examined through the horror genre. Thus, these ads positioned McCain as the only candidate with enough monster-slaying experience (and whiteness) to defeat the new monstrosities facing America. Accordingly, while classic horror elements were certainly a central element of the McCain campaign, they were never focused at candidate Barack Obama. Rather, a more insidious use of the conflicted frame was launched at Obama.

OBAMA'S EVOLVING HORROR TALE

Obama's advertisements followed a horror frame progression throughout the campaign. The advertisements started with heavy usage of the conflicted frame, but evolved with the campaign and the external circumstances, primarily the financial crash of 2008. Prysby and Scavo argue that Obama's campaign hinged on the theme of change. "For this theme to be effective, Obama had to link McCain to the failures of the Bush administration. The link was based in part on the simple fact that McCain was the Republican nominee."[77] Indeed, "Even though he was not part of the Bush White House, and even though he did not always support the Bush administration, McCain nevertheless would be linked in the eyes of many voters because he represented the same party as the president."[78] This began through a conflicted frame, merely associating the two. However, as the campaign continued to develop this association, it turned to the classic frame, arguing that McCain would become his own inhuman agent of Republican monstrosity.

Conflicted Roots: Obama's Initial Framing of McCain

Obama's first televised ad, released on June 20, 2008, was "Country I Love," which is almost completely unhorrific.[79] Its purpose is to show what characteristics make up Barack Obama the candidate. Images of Obama as a child play as he talks about his values of "Accountability," "self-reliance," "Love of country," "Working hard," and "Treating your neighbor as you'd like to be treated."[80] He then lists the things he's done which include putting people to work, cutting taxes, and extending veteran health care.[81] The only horrific elements of the ad are distorted images of run-down homes as he talks about the things he has fixed. Thus, Obama's first ad sets an extremely positive tone for what he would do if elected president. He is the protagonist, the hero.

Obama's second ad was "Embrace," which was aired on August 11, 2008, and mirrors McCain's "Celeb" advertisement to a high level, seeming to act as a response.[82] "Embrace" shows McCain walking out onto a late-night show with camera bulbs flashing and ritzy music playing as the narrator says, "For decades, he's been Washington's biggest celebrity."[83] The lightbulb flash effect is almost identical to the one used in McCain's "Celeb" commercial.[84] The ad then shows McCain hugging President George W. Bush, as the narrator says, "And as Washington embraced him, John McCain hugged right back."[85] Then, it associates McCain with tax breaks for drug and oil companies leaving "almost nothing for families like yours."[86] However, McCain is ultimately framed here through a conflicted lens, not a classic one. He is part of the merging of the spheres of the fantastic/horrific and the normal/mundane as the ad says he is "a Washington celebrity playing the same old Washington games."[87] While these games clearly have horrific effects on the American public, McCain himself is portrayed more as a celebrity who is just insincerely playing the game. The responsiveness of this ad also shows at an early stage that the Obama campaign is willing to shift its messages in order to meet changing exigencies, a direct contrast to the almost stubborn consistency of the McCain campaign.

"No Maverick" is the next ad for the Obama campaign, which initially aired on September 8, 2008. This commercial highlights how McCain and Palin's claims of being "mavericks" are wrong.[88] The advertisement argues that "Seven of [McCain's] top campaign advisors are Washington lobbyists" and that he "votes with Bush 90 percent of the time."[89] The advertisement then argues that Palin was "for the bridge to nowhere before she was against it," concluding that "Politicians lying about their records? You don't call that maverick. You call it more of the same."[90] Thus, this advertisement is again trying to tie McCain to the Washington Establishment. Obama seemingly concedes the arguments that McCain makes when impacting the Washington Establishment as corrupt and monstrous. With the monster being defined by his opponent, Obama is then able to focus on proving that McCain is really the one with stronger ties to the Washington Establishment. This can be seen through the responsiveness of both this ad and his last one to the advertisements McCain was running.

"What Kind," which was first televised on September 10, 2008, continues the trend of tying McCain to Washington, while also giving specific, disastrous policies that he has supported.[91] The ad starts by framing the issues through the American youth, with an image of children in school shown as the narrator asks, "When they grow up, will the economy be strong enough?"[92] Here, classic horror framing begins to seep in. The narrator then positions the hero, saying, "Barack Obama understands what it takes: make America number one in education again."[93]

Four classic horror elements are all at play in this advertisement. First, the victims are highlighted as being American children. Second, the threat of a bad economy is monstrously framed as an existential threat to these children. Third, the method for slaying this monster is given: better education. And fourth, time is bracketed with this methodology as the present aberration of poor American education will be returned to normalcy by making America "number one in education again."[94] With the monster, victims, monster-slaying weapon, and bracketed time all laid out, the ad then argues that "John McCain doesn't understand"[95] this horror slaying formula. McCain is shown as harmful toward education through specific policies he implemented.[96] At the same time, these indictments against McCain are listed, unflattering, menacing pictures of McCain are shown in black and white.[97] The big twist at the end is when this picture of McCain smiling is revealed to be a picture of him standing with President Bush as the narrator concludes that "We can't afford more of the same."[98] Thus, McCain is once again tied to the Establishment, almost trying to merge him into the monstrous other. However, the advertisement never explicitly frames McCain himself through classic horror. Rather, it frames McCain as someone who "doesn't understand"[99] and will, intentionally or not, break the weapon necessary for defeating American's economic demons: education.

"Honor" calls out McCain for supposedly running a deceitful, dirty campaign.[100] The ad, which was originally broadcast on September 15, 2008, opens with McCain saying, "I will not take the low road to the highest office in this land."[101] The narrator then asks, "What's happened to John McCain?" before reading numerous excerpts from news outlets calling McCain's campaign "dishonest," "one of the sleaziest," and "disgraceful and dishonorable."[102] Then, the ad reiterates that McCain voted with Bush "90% of the time, proposing the same disastrous economic policies."[103] Thus, Obama seems to be making a trend of associating McCain not as the villainous other himself (that role is left to Bush and the Establishment), but rather the henchman of the monster.

"Fundamentals," which was released on September 16, 2008, jumped on the news that Lehman Brothers filed for bankruptcy, creating a financial crisis.[104] This news is played with foreboding music, as images of foreclosure signs and chain link fences indicate classically horrific financial decay, both literally and metaphorically related to the decaying manor.[105] All of these problems are then juxtaposed with McCain saying that same morning, "The fundamentals of our economy are strong" with an image of the stock market at the time of his speech shown in the bottom corner of the frame.[106] This sound bite is played two more times, with the last time featuring a video of McCain happily embracing and waving with Bush.[107] Thus, the financial crisis is blamed on Bush and the Establishment, but henchman McCain would continue those same policies that created and let loose the monstrous financial collapse.

"Need Education," which was initially aired on September 19, 2008, is a personal testimony ad, utilizing a woman who was a former employee of Goodyear.[108] "[P]ersonal testimony ads consist of actual individuals reporting their opinions of the opposing candidate's performance"[109] and are deemed fair game because "we are taught that everyone is entitled to express his or her opinion."[110] In this commercial, Lilly Ledbetter explains how she was "paid 40 percent less than men doing the same work" and that "John McCain opposed a law to give women equal pay for equal work."[111] Lilly concludes that "On the economy, it's John McCain who needs an education."[112] Thus, McCain is again framed through a conflicted frame as someone misguided, in need of proper education.

No Longer a Henchman: Obama's Pivot to Classically Framing McCain

Up until this point, Obama has reserved classic horror framing primarily for President Bush. However, the campaign has moved McCain closer and closer to Bush, even using a surprise visual twist in "What Kind."[113] As the full extent of the 2008 financial crisis became clearer, the Obama campaign pivoted in how it portrayed McCain. Instead of McCain being a henchman of President Bush, supporting his policies, the campaign focused on McCain's own policies and own monstrosity. Thus, both narratively and visually, McCain is moved into the realm of a classic horror monster. He is no longer a henchman, but an heir or potential equal of Bush. This move becomes clearer and more effective as the campaign inches toward the election and McCain's reaction to the financial crisis becomes more apparent. As Prysby and Scavo indicate, McCain's "reaction to this financial crisis raised doubts about his ability to handle economic matters. He initially responded to the Lehman Brothers failure by saying that the economy was fundamentally sound, words that the Obama campaign was happy to use against him."[114] This allowed the Obama campaign to ramp up its horror appeals, moving from the conflicted frame to the classic frame. Additionally, the campaign balanced these darker messages with highly self-positive ads, firmly positioning Obama as the heroic protagonist, evoking audience efficacy.

"Spending Spree," which was released on October 1, 2008, again tries to lump McCain in with the monstrous Washington Establishment, with this ad making a more explicit push toward McCain being a fundamental part of this Establishment rather than only a henchman.[115] The ad opens by arguing that McCain is one of the "BIG SPENDERS in Washington D.C."[116] This point is made by showing how McCain's plan would create "over $3 Trillion in Debt," "privatize Social Security," and give tax credits "to insurance companies."[117] All of this is articulated over distorted, darkly shaded images of McCain, evoking classic horror. Then, a foreign threat is introduced as images of Chinese people appear with the narrator saying, "So as we borrow from China to fund his spending spree, ask yourself: can we afford John McCain?"[118] Thus, McCain is seen as welcoming a foreign, monstrous other into the U.S. economy, similar to foreign infections like in *The Wolf Man* (1941) or demonic possession through the use of a tool like a Ouija Board.[119] The ad ends with an image of Bush smiling and putting his hand on McCain's back.[120] This conjures up earlier messages of McCain as a henchman. However, this ad takes that notion and creates more of an apprentice relationship between the monstrous Bush and McCain. The difference in this ad is that it shows specific policies that McCain *will* implement, not policies that *were* implemented by the Establishment and that there is an intentionality behind it, not just a lack of understanding. Accordingly, McCain is moved from the conflicted horror framing to the classical.

"This Year," first televised on October 5, 2008, continues to push the demonization of McCain, opening up with an image of a rusted, padlocked fence.[121] This classically horrific image of decay is then tied to distorted images of McCain which have the corners shaded. McCain is articulated as "erratic" and looking to lead "dishonest, dishonorable 'assaults' against Barack Obama."[122] Thus, the increasingly monstrous McCain is now viewed as erratic, similar in a way to the erratic nature of monsters like Frankenstein's creature, in that they can be content at one moment then violent the next.[123] In McCain's case, this violence is vented through "assaults" against Obama.[124] The commercial ends with, you guessed it, an image of master Bush and apprentice McCain.[125]

"Country I Believe In," which was originally broadcast on October 9, 2008, recalls Obama's first campaign television ad, "Country I Love," by focusing on Obama's youth and American upbringing and avoiding any horror framing.[126] The commercial has Obama talking about his youth, watching astronauts return home, waving an American flag, and reciting the lessons of his grandfather. The narrator then tells how "His grandfather fought in Patton's Army. His grandmother worked on a bomber assembly line."[127] Then, the narrative shifts to the mentoring relationship his mother had with him, and how she instilled in him the values of "Hard work. Honesty. Self-reliance. Respect for other people. Kindness. Faith."[128] Obama closes by saying, "That's the country I believe in."[129] While horror imagery is not used in this advertisement, in the larger narrative, this ad depicts Obama as an all-American protagonist able to defeat the monstrous with strong values. As the prior ads made clear, both Bush and McCain are monsters that must be defeated.

"Defining Moment," an ad released on October 25, 2008, uses no overt horror imagery, but functions within the emerging classic frame to provide audience efficacy and a bracketing of time. This commercial is two minutes long and makes the positive case for an Obama presidency.[130] Instead of explicit horror framing, Obama supplies a detailed plan to fix the economy.[131] These specific proposals show his readiness and ability to slay the monsters articulated in his earlier ads. As Prysby and Scavo argue, "The fact that Obama had not been part of the Congress for many years made it easier for him to present himself as an agent of change. However, it also left him open to the criticism that he lacked the experience to be president. Therefore, part of his campaign strategy was to assure voters that he was capable of handling the job."[132] This commercial attempts that persuasive task. Obama ends the advertisement with a call for inclusive audience efficacy, saying, "I approve this message and ask for your vote because if we stand together, we can meet our challenges and ensure that there are better days ahead."[133] This serves two purposes. First, to show the audience how they can respond to the daunting threats facing America. Second, it again brackets time through a classic horror framing by arguing that voting for Obama ensures "better days ahead."[134]

"Something" explicitly continues this message of audience efficacy, furthering a late game correction for the lack of such notions throughout earlier campaign ads.[135] This advertisement first aired on October 30, 2008 and shows crowds of happy people waving American flags as the narrator notes that "Something's happening in America. In small towns and big cities. People from every walk of life . . . uniting in common purpose."[136] The narrator then, with images of Obama speaking to a large crowd, calls him "A leader who'll bring us together."[137] Obama is created as the heroic leader of the mob, who will defeat the monstrous. Obama voices over the images, "We can choose hope over fear."[138] He implores his audience to overcome the fear they hold through the hope of his campaign. This fear of the monstrous other can be defeated by hope embodied in Obama. The ad concludes with Obama claiming that emerging from this crisis will make the nation stronger "as one people."[139] Thus, a very strong appeal to audience efficacy is made.

"Rearview Mirror" aired on the same day as "Something," making them the final one-two punch of the Obama televised campaign. While "Something" was a positive ad, developing the hero of this classic horror narrative, "Rearview Mirror" is a robust negative attack ad on John McCain, evoking classic horror elements that explicitly link Bush and McCain.[140] The ad shows a man driving in a car, seemingly unable to escape images of Bush and McCain.[141] Bush's face is shown in the car's rearview and side mirrors, and McCain's face is shown all over road signs with his policies.[142]

The seeming inability to escape Bush and McCain as they stalk the driver is reminiscent of horror movies like *Halloween* (1978), where dehumanized/ seemingly supernatural serial killer Michael Myers continually shows up wherever characters go, especially behind them.[143] Further, a key theme to

Halloween is the concept of cultural returns, stepping back to conservative values.[144] These slasher themes classically frame McCain as horrific not only because of the inability of America to escape him, but also because of how he is temporally bracketed by the end of the ad when he is placed in the rearview mirror with Bush.[145] Thus, with McCain moved from the signs to the rearview mirror at the end of the ad, an avenue for escape is opened up by speeding forward into the future of President Obama. Thus, a horrific framing that denies efficacy to the one trying to escape the murderer, is saved at the last moment. This, in combination with the "Something" ad, finishes Obama's televised campaign with a high priority on audience efficacy being needed to defeat the spawn (McCain) of the monstrous other (Bush).

The Obama campaign started positive, moved to responsive ads that took conflicted framing elements from the McCain ads, continued these elements for a time, then shifted toward casting McCain through a classic horror lens, before ending with positive calls for efficacy. This narrative progression never made leaps that were large enough to create "plot holes," allowing the campaign to be adaptive and evolutionary. As Kathleen Hall Jamieson notes, consistent and coherent messages are of the utmost importance in television advertising.[146] Obama's messages were consistent and coherent, it was simply the way that he framed these messages and his opponent that changed throughout the campaign, creating a compelling, dynamic narrative.

CONCLUSION

Ultimately, McCain and Obama used very different horror framing methods in their televised campaign ads. McCain, with undying consistency, used both classic and conflicted horror frames depending on the target of his attacks. He classically framed the threats to America: the economy, foreign threats, and the Washington Establishment (including Bush and the GOP). However, he always framed Obama through a conflicted lens, showing him as unfit and not ready rather than monstrous. This certainly carried racist connotations with it given the relationship of Black folks to the horror genre. The insidious racism this narrative tactic brought with it shows the demonic tendency of contemporary campaign advertising. Further, John McCain's calls to efficacy were largely premised on him being a "maverick," meaning that he did not need anyone but himself, and later Palin, to defeat these monsters. This messaging left the American people out of the solution. Only very late in the campaign does he subtly invite the American people to join him.

Obama, on the other hand, developed his campaign like the ongoing plot of a movie. Initially, one was led to believe that McCain was a misguided tool of the Establishment. At worst, he was Bush's henchman, voting with him on many issues. However, as the campaign progressed, McCain started getting framed less as conflicted and more classically as the apprentice and/or spawn of the evil Bush. This movement rhetorically constructed McCain as the new threat facing America, which McCain would devastate in the form of disastrous economic policies formed in cooperation with the Washington Establishment. Further, Obama made strong late game pushes for audience efficacy by using inclusive rhetoric that explained how, as a group, he and the electorate could defeat the monster. This established both a demonic and polarizing campaign narrative.

Obama went on to win the 2008 election in a landslide.[147] Obama's hyper-focused advertising campaign was extremely flexible. It responded to attacks from McCain and shifted horror frames entirely from the conflicted to the classic as the campaign progressed. This shift by Obama seemed to articulate that voting for McCain was equitable to voting for the devil, or at least the devil's heir. McCain, on the other hand, only ever argued that voting for Obama was a vote for an underprepared Black celebrity. As this and the 2016 election might show, America is seemingly unfazed by the idea of electing potentially underprepared celebrities.

NOTES

1. Pew Research Center, "Section 3: Issues and the 2008 Election," *Pew Research Center*, August 21, 2008, http://www.people-press.org/2008/08/21/section-3-issues-and-the-2008-election/.
2. Pew Research Center, "Section 3: Issues."
3. Charles Prysby and Carmine Scavo, "Campaign Themes, Strategies, and Developments," in *American Political Science Association, and Inter-university Consortium for Political and Social Research. SETUPS: Voting Behavior: The 2008 Election* (Ann Arbor, MI: Inter-university Consortium for Political and Social Research, 2009).
4. Prysby and Scavo, "Campaign Themes."
5. Prysby and Scavo, "Campaign Themes."
6. John McCain 2008, "2013," *The Living Room Candidate: Presidential Campaign Commercials 1952–2020*, May 18, 2008, http://livingroomcandidate.org/commercials/2008/2013.
7. McCain, "2013."
8. John McCain 2008, "Broken," *The Living Room Candidate: Presidential Campaign Commercials 1952–2020*, August 5, 2008, http://www.livingroomcandidate.org/commercials/2008/broken.
9. McCain, "Broken."
10. *The Cabinet of Dr. Caligari*, directed by Robert Wiene (1920; Horrortheque, 2010), Digital.
11. *The Exorcist*, directed by William Friedkin (1973; Warner Bros., 2011), DVD.

12. McCain, "Broken."
13. McCain, "Broken."
14. McCain, "Broken."
15. *Dracula*, directed by Tod Browning (1931; Peacock TV), Digital.
16. McCain, "Broken."
17. McCain, "Broken."
18. Prysby and Scavo, "Campaign Themes."
19. McCain, "Broken."
20. John McCain 2008, "Original Mavericks," *The Living Room Candidate: Presidential Campaign Commercials 1952–2020*, September 8, 2008, http://www.livingroomcandidate.org/commercials/2008/original-mavericks.
21. McCain, "Original Mavericks."
22. McCain-Palin 2008, "Crisis," *The Living Room Candidate: Presidential Campaign Commercials 1952–2020*, September 8, 2008, http://www.livingroomcandidate.org/commercials/2008/original-mavericks.
23. See *Dracula*, Browning and *Frankenstein*, directed by James Whale (1931; Universal Studios Home Entertainment, 2016), DVD.
24. McCain-Palin, "Crisis."
25. McCain-Palin 2008, "Dome," *The Living Room Candidate: Presidential Campaign Commercials 1952–2020*, September 18, 2008, http://www.livingroomcandidate.org/commercials/2008/dome.
26. McCain-Palin, "Dome."
27. McCain-Palin, "Dome."
28. McCain-Palin, "Dome."
29. See *War of the Worlds,* directed by Byron Haskin (1953; Paramount Pictures, 1999), DVD; *War of the Worlds*, directed by Steven Spielberg (2005; Paramount Home Entertainment, 2005), DVD; and *Independence Day*, directed by Roland Emmerich (1996; 20th Century Fox Home Entertainment, 2016), DVD.
30. *The Exorcist*, Friedkin.
31. McCain-Palin 2008, "Special," *The Living Room Candidate: Presidential Campaign Commercials 1952–2020*, October 29, 2008, http://www.livingroomcandidate.org/commercials/2008/special.
32. McCain-Palin, "Special."
33. McCain-Palin, "Special."
34. McCain-Palin 2008, "Freedom," *The Living Room Candidate: Presidential Campaign Commercials 1952–2020*, October 31, 2008, http://www.livingroomcandidate.org/commercials/2008/freedom.
35. McCain-Palin, "Freedom."
36. McCain-Palin, "Freedom."
37. McCain-Palin, "Freedom."
38. McCain-Palin, "Freedom."
39. McCain-Palin, "Freedom."
40. McCain-Palin, "Special."
41. Robin R. Means Coleman, "We're in a Golden Age of Black Horror Films," *The Conversation*, May 29, 2019, http://theconversation.com/were-in-a-golden-age-of-black-horror-films-116648?utm.

42. Coleman, "We're in a Golden Age."
43. Coleman, "We're in a Golden Age."
44. For a notable exception, see *Night of the Living Dead*, directed by George A. Romero (1968; Film Detective, 2018), DVD.
45. John McCain 2008, "Celeb," *The Living Room Candidate: Presidential Campaign Commercials 1952–2020*, July 31, 2008, http://www.livingroomcandidate.org/commercials/2008/celeb.
46. McCain, "Celeb."
47. McCain, "Celeb."
48. McCain, "Celeb."
49. *White Zombie*, directed by Victor Halperin (1932; Music Video Dist., 2014), DVD.
50. Robin R. Means Coleman, *Horror Noire: Blacks in American Horror Films from the 1890s to Present* (New York: Routledge, 2011), 211.
51. Coleman, *Horror Noire*, 211.
52. John McCain 2008, "The One (Web)," *The Living Room Candidate: Presidential Campaign Commercials 1952–2020*, August 1, 2008, http://www.livingroomcandidate.org/commercials/2008/the-one-web.
53. McCain, "The One."
54. John McCain 2008, "Education," *The Living Room Candidate: Presidential Campaign Commercials 1952–2020*, September 10, 2008, http://www.livingroomcandidate.org/commercials/2008/education.
55. McCain, "Education."
56. McCain, "Education."
57. McCain, "Education."
58. McCain, "Education."
59. Derek Lewis, "Voting Horrors: Youthful, Monstrous, and Worrying Agency in American Film," *The Popular Culture Studies Journal* 6, no. 2–3 (2018): 315.
60. *The Exorcist*, Friedkin.
61. *The Exorcist*, Friedkin.
62. McCain-Palin 2008, "Dangerous," *The Living Room Candidate: Presidential Campaign Commercials 1952–2020*, October 6, 2008, http://www.livingroomcandidate.org/commercials/2008/dangerous.
63. McCain-Palin, "Dangerous."
64. McCain-Palin, "Dangerous."
65. McCain-Palin, "Sweat Equity," *The Living Room Candidate: Presidential Campaign Commercials 1952–2020*, October 22, 2008, http://www.livingroomcandidate.org/commercials/2008/sweat-equity.
66. McCain-Palin, "Sweat Equity."
67. McCain-Palin, "Sweat Equity."
68. Republican National Committee, "Storm," *The Living Room Candidate: Presidential Campaign Commercials 1952–2020*, October 25, 2008, http://www.livingroomcandidate.org/commercials/2008/storm.
69. Republican National Committee, "Storm."
70. Republican National Committee, "Storm."
71. Republican National Committee, "Storm."

72. *Titanic*, directed by James Cameron (1997; Paramount Home Video, 2012), DVD. *Poseidon*, directed by Wolfgang Peterson (2006; Warner Home Video, 2010), DVD.

73. John McCain 2008, "Compare (R)," *The Living Room Candidate: Presidential Campaign Commercials 1952–2020*, October 28, 2008, http://www.livingroomcandidate.org/commercials/2008/compare-r. Note: the transcript for this ad is in all caps for an unapparent reason. I have fixed the capitalization for easier readability.

74. McCain, "Compare (R)."
75. McCain, "Compare (R)."
76. McCain, "Compare (R)."
77. Prysby and Scavo, "Campaign Themes."
78. Prysby and Scavo, "Campaign Themes."
79. Obama for America, "Country I Love," *The Living Room Candidate: Presidential Campaign Commercials 1952–2020*, June 20, 2008, http://www.livingroomcandidate.org/commercials/2008/country-i-love.
80. Obama, "Country I Love."
81. Obama, "Country I Love."
82. Obama for America, "Embrace," *The Living Room Candidate: Presidential Campaign Commercials 1952–2016*, August 11, 2008, http://www.livingroomcandidate.org/commercials/2008/embrace.
83. Obama, "Embrace."
84. McCain, "Celeb."
85. Obama, "Embrace."
86. Obama, "Embrace."
87. Obama, "Embrace."
88. Obama for America, "No Maverick," *The Living Room Candidate: Presidential Campaign Commercials 1952–2020*, September 8, 2008, http://www.livingroomcandidate.org/commercials/2008/no-maverick.
89. Obama, "No Maverick."
90. Obama, "No Maverick."
91. Obama for America, "What Kind," *The Living Room Candidate: Presidential Campaign Commercials 1952–2020*, September 10, 2008, http://www.livingroomcandidate.org/commercials/2008/what-kind.
92. Obama, "What Kind."
93. Obama, "What Kind."
94. Obama, "What Kind."
95. Obama, "What Kind."
96. Obama, "What Kind."
97. Obama, "What Kind."
98. Obama, "What Kind."
99. Obama, "What Kind."
100. Obama for America, "Honor," *The Living Room Candidate: Presidential Campaign Commercials 1952–2020*, September 15, 2008, http://www.livingroomcandidate.org/commercials/2008/honor.

101. Obama, "Honor."
102. Obama, "Honor."
103. Obama, "Honor."
104. Obama for America, "Fundamentals," *The Living Room Candidate: Presidential Campaign Commercials 1952–2020*, September 16, 2008, http://www.livingroomcandidate.org/commercials/2008/fundamentals.
105. See *Dracula*, Browning and *Frankenstein*, Whale.
106. Obama, "Fundamentals."
107. Obama, "Fundamentals."
108. Obama for America, "Need Education," *The Living Room Candidate: Presidential Campaign Commercials 1952–2020*, September 19, 2008, http://www.livingroomcandidate.org/commercials/2008/need-education.
109. Kathleen Hall Jamieson, *Packaging the Presidency: A History and Criticism of Presidential Campaign Advertising* (New York: Oxford University Press, 1984): 450.
110. Jamieson, *Packaging the Presidency*, 450.
111. Obama, "Need Education."
112. Obama, "Need Education."
113. Obama, "What Kind."
114. Prysby and Scavo, "Campaign Themes."
115. Obama for America, "Spending Spree," *The Living Room Candidate: Presidential Campaign Commercials 1952–2020*, October 1, 2008, http://www.livingroomcandidate.org/commercials/2008/spending-spree.
116. Obama, "Spending Spree."
117. Obama, "Spending Spree."
118. Obama, "Spending Spree."
119. *The Wolf Man*, directed by George Waggner (1941; Universal Studios Home Entertainment, 2016), DVD.
120. Obama, "Spending Spree."
121. Obama for America, "This Year," *The Living Room Candidate: Presidential Campaign Commercials 1952–2020*, October 5, 2008, http://www.livingroomcandidate.org/commercials/2008/this-year.
122. Obama, "This Year."
123. *Frankenstein*, Whale.
124. Obama, "This Year."
125. Obama, "This Year."
126. Obama for America, "Country I Believe In," *The Living Room Candidate: Presidential Campaign Commercials 1952–2020*, October 9, 2008, http:/www.livingroomcandidate.org/commercials/2008/country-i-believe-in.
127. Obama, "Country I Believe In."
128. Obama, "Country I Believe In."
129. Obama, "Country I Believe In."
130. Obama for America, "Defining Moment," *The Living Room Candidate: Presidential Campaign Commercials 1952–2020*, October 25, 2008, http://www.livingroomcandidate.org/commercials/2008/defining-moment.

131. Obama, "Defining Moment."
132. Prysby and Scavo, "Campaign Themes."
133. Obama, "Defining Moment."
134. Obama, "Defining Moment."
135. Obama for America, "Something," *The Living Room Candidate: Presidential Campaign Commercials 1952–2020*, October 30, 2008, http://www.livingroomcandidate.org/commercials/2008/something.
136. Obama, "Something."
137. Obama, "Something."
138. Obama, "Something."
139. Obama, "Something."
140. Obama for America, "Rearview Mirror," *The Living Room Candidate: Presidential Campaign Commercials 1952–2020*, October 30, 2008, http://www.livingroomcandidate.org/commercials/2008/rearview-mirror.
141. Obama, "Rearview Mirror."
142. Obama, "Rearview Mirror."
143. *Halloween*, directed by John Carpenter (1978; Lionsgate Home Entertainment, 2007), DVD.
144. Kendall R. Phillips, *Projected Fears: Horror Films and American Culture* (Westport, CT: Praeger, 2005), 132, 137–40.
145. Obama, "Rearview Mirror."
146. Jamieson, *Packaging the Presidency*, 447.
147. "Election Results 2008," *New York Times*, 2008, https://www.nytimes.com/elections/2008/results/president/map.html.

Chapter 5

Mitt Romney versus Barack Obama in the 2012 Election

The 2012 election pit President Barack Obama, a Democrat, against challenger Mitt Romney (R-UT), a Republican governor. Obama ran on the notions of hope and change in his first election and now faced the challenge of defending his first term in the presidency. Mitt Romney opposed him as a moderate conservative, known for economic turnarounds. The economy was beginning to show signs of recovery after the 2008 economic collapse, but the nation's financial well-being still weighed heavily in the political arena.

Among voters, it is unsurprising that monetary issues were widely deemed "very important."[1] The top issue was the economy at 86 percent.[2] Jobs trailed just behind at 84 percent, with the budget deficit filling the third position at 74 percent.[3] Other issues were also on voters' minds with health care at 74 percent, education at 72 percent, and Medicare at 66 percent. Foreign issues were significantly lower on the list, with terrorism (59%), foreign policy (52%), Iran (47%), and Afghanistan (46%) falling into the lower half of the list.[4]

While percentages tell the story of a domestic election, looking at the trends stemming from past years helps illuminate how the voting landscape had shifted. While the economy was still the most important issue, its percentage dropped four points from 2010.[5] Jobs also dropped four points from 2010.[6] On the other hand, the budget deficit had risen five points, while health care dropped four points.[7] Some of the largest drop-offs in a mere two years were terrorism (down twelve points), Afghanistan (down thirteen points), and immigration (down sixteen points).[8] In fact, every issue declined in percentage or remained the same with the sole exception of the budget deficit. Nevertheless, domestic issues seemed to be at the forefront of voters' minds.

The Obama and Romney campaigns took nearly opposite approaches in their usage of horror framing in their campaign ads (see table 5.1). Romney

Table 5.1 Mitt Romney and Barack Obama Campaign Advertisements' Airdates

Mitt Romney		Barack Obama	
Airdate	Title	Airdate	Title
July 16, 2012	Political Payoffs and Middle Class Layoffs	July 14, 2012	Firms
August 10, 2012	Cancer	August 7, 2012	Understands
September 6, 2012	Give Me a Break	August 23, 2012	There Is a Clear Choice
September 13, 2012	Failing American Workers	September 14, 2012	The Cheaters
September 17, 2012	Failing America's Families	September 18, 2012	47 Percent
November 6, 2012	The Moment	October 2, 2012	Mandatory
		October 8, 2012	Policy
		October 9, 2012	Big Bird
		October 18, 2012	Seen
		October 21, 2012	Challenges
		October 23, 2012	Determination
		October 24, 2012	He's Got It Right
		November 3, 2012	Will Ferrell Will Do Anything to Get You To Vote
		November 4, 2012	What We're Fighting For
		2012	Always

relied heavily on the classic horror frame to racistly place Obama amongst a number of other entities threatening the country. The Romney campaign would often incorporate some self-positive messaging within these same horror advertisements. The Obama campaign, on the other hand, used the conflicted horror frame as its primary vector for attack, interweaving ads that are almost entirely self-positive to strike a balance.

ROMNEY'S HORRIFIC OFFENSIVE

Entering the 2012 election, the Romney campaign had to first weather a brutal primary season. After making it through the Republican field, "Romney emerged as the presumptive nominee, [but] he was battered and broke. He had spent most of the roughly $100 million he had raised and would not be able to tap into his general election funds until after the August convention."[9] This funding discrepancy can be seen in the number of advertisements furnished directly by the campaign.[10]

Romney's televised campaign advertisements relied heavily on the classic horror frame. This was used to create monstrosity out of the budget deficit, China, the Obama campaign, and Obama himself. These classic horror attacks on Obama often carried racist baggage. In fact, as Charlton D. McIlwain and Stephen M. Caliendo note, Romney and his allies "sought to frame [Obama's] presidency in implicitly racial terms."[11] The conflicted frame was used as well to show Bill Clinton's inconsistency in supporting Obama. There were a few self-positive messages sprinkled throughout, but the campaign tried to correct for the lack of purely positive messaging late in the campaign with an over five-minute ad reframing Romney's journey in a motivating light. Still, the lack of self-positive ads and, in particular, defensive ads in the face of the Obama campaign's onslaught is particularly noticeable, and likely dampened the potential impact of Romney's horror ads.

Classic Horror: Obama, China, and the Economy

"Political Payoffs and Middle Class Layoffs" heavily uses the classic horror frame against Obama. This ad, first aired on July 16, 2012, opens with a deeply shaded shot of people walking on a crowded sidewalk. Eerie ambient noises play over a mostly silent soundtrack as text reads, "Right now there are 23 million Americans struggling for work. . . . Americans need help."[12] The screen abruptly shifts to a white background and the Obama campaign logo with text asking, "So who is President Obama helping? His friends."[13] Obama is then heard singing as newspaper headlines about him favorably treating donors are presented. This seems to be a direct retaliation to the "Firms" ad released by the Obama campaign only two days earlier, which uses Romney singing as its focal point. There is then a deep, booming noise as the ad transitions back to a darkened background that slowly reveals Obama. There is heavy distortion and the image is shaking as another eerie sound effect grows louder and louder before cutting to a pitch-black screen with text stating, "The Obama Record: Political Payoffs and Middle Class Layoffs."[14] Another deep thud is heard as the ad fades out.

This ad is one of the strongest examples of audio being used to unleash the classic horror frame. If one were to close their eyes and just listen to the sound of the advertisement, many would believe they were listening to a horror movie trailer. The ad uses deep thuds, eerie reverbs, dissonant singing, and silence to instill a sense of foreboding fear. All of this is directed at Obama, who is clearly made out to be the horror of the commercial for his mistreatment of the middle class in favor of the "donor class."[15] Obama's singing is used to cast him as a "Siren," a mainstay "in horror and the supernatural" dating all the way back to Homer, which uses their "extraordinary musical ability" to seduce unsuspecting victims.[16] Thus, the Romney campaign uses a similar racist tactic as the McCain campaign, portraying Obama as "exotic" and able to hypnotize and mislead the masses.[17] However, this racist attack is far more monstrous and otherizing than McCain's ads.

Visual cues help build up the monstrous otherization of Obama as well, especially the distortions and shaking when he is pictured in the advertisement. Further, the dark shot of people walking at the beginning of the ad immediately instills a sense of dread as the nation has been zombified, invoking films like *White Zombie* (1932).[18] The dark shading and distortion are characteristic of the horror genre, as Glenn W. Richardson Jr. notes.[19] Both are mainstays of horror, dating all the way back to the proto-horror days of *The Cabinet of Dr. Caligari* (1920), which also plays on notions of hypnosis.[20]

"Cancer" similarly uses strong classic horror framing to go on the offensive and refute an Obama attack ad. The commercial, which originally aired on August 10, 2012, opens with eerie guitar music and a distorted video of Obama speaking to an audience. Deep thuds then transition the ad to newscasters talking about a new Obama attack advertisement that "basically blames Mitt Romney for a woman's death from cancer."[21] A video then plays of an interview with Stephanie Cutter, Obama's Deputy Campaign Manager, who deflects questions about the advertisement and is repeatedly shown making a strange face. Shaded images then show David Axelrod, Obama's Chief Strategist, and accuse him of meeting with PAC groups. Other key campaign advisors are shown in a similar manner as the ominous music continues to play. The ad then calls for Obama to denounce the advertisement as he is presented in black and white and verbally distorted in the background. The ad claims that anything less than a denouncement would be "BS."[22] The ad ends with a man saying, "We have a cancer within—close to the presidency, that's growing. It's growing daily."[23]

This advertisement is once again heavy with classic horror framing used to attack Obama himself. The commercial uses visual frames to distort and shade Obama and his campaign advisors, accusing them of dishonest attacks and illegal collusion. The music and ambient sound effects help to further frame this ad through a clear horror lens. However, the most direct form of horror framing comes at the end of the advertisement where an anonymous voice makes a direct effort to dehumanize Obama and his campaign and turn them into monstrosity. Obama and his campaign advisors are compared directly to a cancer that is "growing daily."[24] One of the key elements of the classic horror frame is an otherized monster, which this TV spot clearly executes.

"Failing American Workers" uses subtle amounts of the classic horror frame to attack Obama and demonize China while bolstering Romney. This advertisement, released on September 13, 2012, opens with a shaded room with two stacks of boxes, one taller than the other and colored with the U.S. flag. The narrator explains that "This is America's manufacturing when

President Obama took office."[25] The shot zooms out to reveal the Chinese flag on the other boxes, representing Chinese manufacturing. The U.S. boxes slowly disappear as the Chinese boxes grow. The narrator asserts, "Seven times, Obama could have stopped China's cheating. Seven times, he refused."[26] The ad cuts to Romney speaking in a factory, saying, "It's time to stand up to cheaters and make sure we protect jobs for the American people."[27] The ad concludes with the boxes again, but this time a sad Obama is shown over the U.S. boxes instead of the flag.

This advertisement uses the classic horror frame to make China out as a monstrous entity, siphoning U.S. jobs. The shadowy appearance of the room with boxes already sets up this frame. As the shot widens and the viewer sees the bright red Chinese flag boxes absorbing the dusty U.S. flag boxes, a vampiric relationship is created. There is a long-established tradition of vampires in horror films and their ties to eastern geographic locations in movies like *Dracula* (1931).[28] The bright red blood of America—jobs—is being siphoned away by the purportedly unethical cheaters in China. Romney is posited as the candidate who can successfully defeat the parasitic menace from the east. As the economy and jobs stand as top issues in voters' minds,[29] it makes sense that a spatially separated horror was used to attempt to scare voters into finding efficacy in voting for Romney.

"Failing America's Families," which was aired on September 17, 2012, follows almost the exact same formula as "Failing American Workers." The ad opens with the same room of two stacks of boxes. This time, however, the boxes on the right have a typical American home placed over them. The second stack of boxes has dollar bills plastered over them with "$10.6 TRILLION" written on top of that.[30] The same siphoning animation occurs, where boxes are drained from the housing side and added to the debt side. The narrator explains, "Under Obama, families have lost over $4,000 a year in income. And the national debt is now $16 trillion and growing."[31] The ad cuts to Romney speaking at a rally, saying, "We have a moral responsibility not to spend more than we take in. . . . I'll stop it."[32] The ad concludes by switching back to the boxes and replaces the house on the boxes with a saddened Obama.

In almost the same way as "Failing American Workers," which was released four days before "Failing America's Families," the Romney campaign classically frames a vampiric entity that is draining the United States. This time, however, it is the monstrous, inhuman debt that is draining household income. Yet, this ad interestingly also injects elements of possession films, where family decline is intermingled with "the disparity inherent in modern American capitalism."[33] Just like the previous ad, this one also positions Romney as the only defender strong enough to vanquish the horrific debt. The saddened image of Obama does not frame him horrifically, but rather shows that he is supposedly powerless in the face of such adversity. The Romney campaign posits that the fresh, moral energy of Romney would be able to carry out the battle against the national debt.

Conflicted Attack on Bill Clinton

"Give Me a Break," released on September 6, 2012, represents the Romney campaign's foray into using the conflicted horror frame against Obama and his supporters. The advertisement begins with soft piano music and an image of Obama, looking downtrodden behind a bar graph trending downward. The narrator says, "As the economy gets worse, Barack Obama calls on Bill Clinton to help his failing campaign."[34] Clinton is then shown testifying on behalf of Obama, with the narrator noting, "He's a good soldier."[35] However, the ad then jumps to a statically distorted television with the text, "What did Clinton say about Obama in 2008?"[36] Clinton is then seen criticizing Obama's plans as a big "fairytale."[37] Another static distortion is used to transition to a shaded video of people walking down a street while the narrator argues that the middle class is "falling further behind."[38] The ad concludes with Clinton again saying, "Give me a break."[39]

This advertisement uses the conflicted frame to target Clinton and Obama. The ad recognizes that what Clinton is doing is fairly ordinary within the realm of politics, calling him "a good soldier" for "helping his party's president."[40] However, this mundane political campaigning is criticized as an exemplary flipping of positions worthy of notice by the American public. The visual framing of this advertisement, while subtle, also helps to draw out conflicted horror frames. Slight distortions, static transitions, selective shading, and red graphs all help develop the audience's unease with what is going on within the political workings of the Obama campaign.

Self-Positive Patriotism

"The Moment," which was televised on November 6, 2012, is an interesting entry in this analysis due to its 5:17 run time and near-complete lack of horror framing. The Romney campaign admitted that, in hindsight, "we should've done more positive ads to get his favorables up."[41] This ad certainly seems like a too little too late attempt at fixing that mistake in the final hours of the campaign. "The Moment" follows the narrative timeline of Romney and his campaign, starting at his decision to run and winding through the key moments of the campaign from Romney's perspective. Romney narrates over the advertisement, speaking generally in clichés about the United States, conservatism, and values. The first third of the advertisement is labeled as "The Journey" and includes Romney announcing his candidacy and videos of historic American moments.[42] Romney is then seen speaking to a crowd about freedom, as videos intercut of individuals doing everyday tasks and working. Romney argues, "We have a moral responsibility to keep America the strongest nation on earth."[43] Romney's selection of Paul Ryan as his running mate is memorialized next. The middle of the advertisement is labeled "The Turning Point" and focuses on the success Romney had in the first presidential debate. Romney argues that the deficit could "crush the future generations" and that developments in the Middle East are of "real concern."[44] Romney ensures the audience that Democrats and Republicans both "love America," but that leadership should be the deciding factor.[45] "The Moment" is the final third of the advertisement and depicts one of Romney's largest rallies in the closing days of the campaign. Romney discusses his successes in business and how that translated to effective governing practices. Crowds cheer as he continues talking about what he will accomplish with the help of voters. The ad ends with text saying, "We're doing this for something bigger than ourselves" before a montage of children closes out the advertisement.[46]

"The Moment" relies on self-positive messages that reframe the entire campaign in a favorable light for Romney. Calls to voter efficacy are made throughout, in a clear attempt to right the ship in the final hours. The only horror even remotely present is when Romney talks about the deficit crushing people and concern with the Middle East. However, these are not framed through horrific audiovisuals and are so light that it would be foolish to claim they have any significant narrative impact. However, in the larger horror narrative, the claim that Romney is the savior the United States needs places him as the protagonist in opposition to the monstrosities framed by the campaign: Obama, his campaign staff, China, and the deficit.

The Romney campaign, in the limited advertisements they released directly, used the classic and conflicted horror frames to create monstrosity to scare audiences into voting for him. The classic horror ads are exemplars of the use of ominous, ambient noises and silence to instill a sense of distress. They take aim at Obama and issues that the campaign clearly thought were in favor of Romney. Some of the ads combine this with epideictic appeals, but many just go on the attack. "The Moment" attempts to correct the attack-heavy campaign strategy with a long, positive narrative about Romney and his journey. However, this ad seemed to come far too late in the campaign.

OBAMA'S FOCUSED CHARACTER ASSASSINATION

The Obama campaign team had a decision to make as the Republican nominee became clear: What was the best plan of attack against Romney? Two options seemed particularly salient. The first was to "campaign against Romney as a flip-flopper—a former centrist governor of Massachusetts who turned conservative to win his party's nomination."[47] The second was to "use his career as the head of Bain Capital to cast him as a protector of the privileged at the expense of the middle class."[48] It should come as little surprise that the highly analytic Obama campaign turned to polling to find their answer.

A senior White House official described that "The most striking data we saw early on was on the 'understands problems of people like me' question. . . . 'Into the summer, Romney was in the teens in this category.'"[49] Given this data, the Obama campaign made its choice to go after Romney's career. "The onetime campaign of hope and change soon began a sustained advertising assault that cast Romney as a heartless executive, a man who willingly fires people and is disconnected from how average Americans live their lives."[50] Thus, a tone of anger and blame settled into both campaigns quickly, as issues such as the economy, Obama's auto bailout, and character moved to the political fore.

Two Classic Horrors with a Touch of Comedy

"Firms," released on July 14, 2012, uses Romney singing as the focal point of a classic horror attack. The ad opens with a distorted video of Romney singing "America the Beautiful" at a campaign rally. The audio gets distorted as the commercial cuts to a closed factory with a headline reading, "In business, Mitt Romney's firms shipped jobs to Mexico. And China."[51] Romney continues singing as more headlines show Romney's private sector ties to foreign nations. The ad ends with a beach in the background as headlines about his tax havens in Bermuda and the Cayman Islands are presented, before the appearance of the text "MITT ROMNEY'S NOT THE SOLUTION . . . HE'S THE PROBLEM."

Just like Romney's "Political Payoffs and Middle Class Layoffs," a seeming response to this advertisement, "Firms" relies heavily on sound to drive the horror of the ad. Romney's singing frames him as a Siren, ready to lull unsuspecting voters into inhuman, spatially bracketed danger. The distortion added to his song further ramps up the horror. The association with a Siren becomes even clearer as the ad ends with images of a beach, since Sirens are known to lure sailors "deep into Poseidon's watery kingdom," drowning them.[52] Not only is Romney depicted as monstrous, but his horrific deeds are spatially separated in a classic horror manner, all being conducted in foreign countries. Visual distortions and shading on Romney and some of the imagery help cement this horror framing.

"Big Bird" is an extremely noteworthy instance of classic horror and comedy being deployed in equal parts. This ad, released on October 9, 2012, uses over-the-top horror elements to show the disparity between real threats to America and what Romney thinks is threatening America. A deep-voiced narrator reads off a list of names, including, "Bernie Madoff. Ken Lay. Dennis Kozlowski" as images of each are presented and shifted to black and white.[53] The narrator notes that these men are "evil" and "gluttons of greed" before asking who was the "evil genius that towered over them?"[54] The soundtrack builds suspense as the camera zooms in on a skyscraper window with an ominous shadow looming. The ad claims that only "one man has the guts to speak his name" as a compilation of clips of Romney saying, "Big Bird" are strewn together.[55] Big Bird himself is revealed, as the narrator calls him, "Big, yellow, a menace to our economy."[56] The narrator assures the audience that "Romney knows it's not Wall Street you have to worry about, it's Sesame Street" as the Wall Street sign spins into the Sesame Street sign. Romney is then shown saying he will cut the subsidy to PBS. The narrator concludes by saying, "Mitt Romney: Taking on our enemies no matter where they nest" as Big Bird sleeps in the background.

This advertisement uses classic horror framing to such an outrageous degree with such a seemingly non-horrific subject that the ensuing dissonance helps establish who the audience should really be afraid of and how ineffectual Romney would be at dealing with them. The ad clearly frames Wall Street and its cronies, through a roundabout sarcastic way, as a truly monstrous threat facing the country. The black-and-white shading, deep-voiced narrator, and language of "evil" and "gluttons of greed" establish this point.[57] However, the ad strays into extreme satire as it posits that the mastermind above all these monstrous threats is Big Bird, a popular children's television character. This combined with numerous clips of Romney attacking Big Bird and PBS show just how out of touch he is. This combination of horror and comedy is a well-established tradition within the genre, with films such as *Evil Dead II* (1987) and *The Cabin in the Woods* (2011) readily coming to mind.[58] Further, this is an established practice in campaign advertising where the mixing of genres has created "tongue-in-cheek horror ad[s]."[59] The thesis of "Big Bird" is that even if Romney was a capable hero, the things he would try to defend America from are absolutely not threats. The real horrors would be allowed to slip through the gate and pillage the country.

Consistently Conflicted Frame: Removing Romney's Heart

First aired on August 7, 2012, "Understands" uses a former steel factory worker to tie Romney to a woman's death from cancer. Joe Soptic, the factory worker, is the focal point of this ad, talking into the camera about what Romney did to him and his family. He claims, "I don't think Mitt Romney understands what he's done to peoples' lives by closing the plant."[60] The ad transitions to a smug-looking Romney at a boardroom table, with dark shading as the text reads, "Mitt Romney and Bain Capital made millions for themselves and then closed this steel plant."⁶¹ A shot of a closed factory behind barbed wire fencing appears as Soptic begins walking the viewer down the chain of events that led him to losing his job, health care, and his wife to lung cancer. Soptic ends by claiming, "I do not think Mitt Romney realizes what he's done to anyone and furthermore I do not think Mitt Romney is concerned."⁶²

This ad uses heavy conflicted horror framing to cast Romney in a terrible light. The visuals of dark shading and closed factories tie in with mainstays of the horror genre focused on death and decay. The narrative push of this advertisement, a woman's death, also clearly fits this model. The ad does not technically claim that Romney himself killed the woman, but it comes as close to that line as possible. Thus, he is put in a similar vein as an unremorseful killer. Human? At least partially. Evil and horrific? Absolutely. The ad also tries to tie this to the plight of other families across America, where health coverage is too difficult to afford. This takes the horror of death and decay and synchronizes it with the mundane sphere of normalcy in the here and now.

"The Cheaters" frames Romney through a conflicted lens as one who feeds jobs to a real monster, China. Originally broadcast on September 14, 2012, this advertisement opens with a shaded picture of Romney looking at a canted television with his own ad playing. Romney's ad indicates that "It's time to stand up to the cheaters, and make sure we protect jobs for the American people."⁶³ Gloomy music plays as the narrator questions, "Mitt Romney, tough on China?"⁶⁴ A smiling Romney, buttoning up his suit coat, is presented in the background with shading as a headline about Romney moving jobs overseas is presented. A more melancholic Romney is then displayed, looking at Chinese factory workers. The narrator and text claim, "Romney's never stood up to China. All he's done is send them our jobs."⁶⁵ The last bit of text turns red as the ad fades out.

While this TV spot dabbles in both the classic and conflicted horror frame, the conflicted ultimately overwhelms the classic. Romney is the conflicted horror villain; China is the classic horror monster. However, this ad focuses on the actions of Romney and not explicitly China. The ad claims that Romney has been sending jobs to China, making him the human keeper of the monster. One thinks of a character like Victor Frankenstein, not the monster himself but the one who created and nourished the monster in *Frankenstein* (1931).⁶⁶ The shading and blood-red text, along with the melancholic music, further helps to frame this ad through such a horror lens.

"47 Percent" again casts Romney through a conflicted lens, using his infamous 47 percent comment against him. This ad, released on September 18, 2012, focuses on a number of average Americans watching and reacting to Romney's comments at a closed-door donor meeting. The subjects of the ad watch in horror and disgust as Romney says, "There are 47 percent of the people who will vote for the president no matter what. All right, there are 47 percent who are with him, who are dependent upon the government. . . . And they will vote for this president, no matter what. And so, my job is not to worry about those people."[67] The ad ends with some verbal responses to the clip that include: "I actually felt sick to my stomach," "It shows he's out of touch," "I think the fact that Mitt Romney made all these comments behind closed doors really shows his character," and "I think it's not the person I want representing me."[68]

This ad attempts to use the leaked footage of Romney's behind-door comments to attack his character and frame him through a conflicted lens. The first half of the commercial is less like watching a horror movie, but like watching audience reactions to a horror movie. Audience reaction marketing "have become a key marketing tool for horror producers and filmmakers looking to generate viral buzz."[69] This strategy, popularized "by the Paranormal Activity series of found footage horror films" helps cue the audience in that whatever the viewers on camera are watching is worth checking out and being horrified by.[70] Thus, in the wake of the leak of Romney's comments, the Obama campaign certainly suited its advertising strategy to a horror subset particularly useful in getting information to spread organically. While Romney is clearly portrayed as misguided, he is never depicted as outright monstrosity in this ad. Rather, the horrified subjects of the ad prefer to make clear that they do not see him as fit for the presidency.

"Mandatory," originally televised on October 2, 2012, attacks Romney for supposedly coercing mine workers to attend one of his rallies. The ad uses dread-inducing music throughout as an image of Romney speaking in front of coal miners is presented. The narrator details, using headlines, that miners were told "that attendance at Mitt Romney's rally was, quote, mandatory."[71] Black-and-white images of forlorn miners are montaged as the story of them losing pay unfolds and news reporters talk about this scandal. The ad ends with, "MITT ROMNEY. NOT ONE OF US" displayed over a melancholic miner.[72]

Using the conflicted horror frame, "Mandatory" calls out Romney for questionable campaign practices. The heavy use of black-and-white images of disheartened miners helps set the tone of dread consistent with the horror genre. Clearly, Romney is not made out as complete monstrosity. Still, his choice is framed as indecent and not something a working-class citizen would do. The soundtrack helps further establish this sense of dread, attempting to create fear amongst lower- and middle-class Americans that Romney is not looking out for their best interest throughout the normalcy of labor.

"Policy," which first aired on October 8, 2012, uses the conflicted horror frame to undercut Romney's ability to defend the United States in the international realm. The ad opens with a slightly shadowy video of Romney boarding an airplane as news headlines call his foreign tour, "Reckless" and "Amateurish."[73] An image of a mob lighting things on fire fades into a color-washed shot of Romney, while the narrator and text claim his response to recent attacks on diplomats in Libya, "Showed an Extraordinary Lack of Presidential Character."[74] The ad even quotes Republicans, saying his response was "the worst possible."[75] The ad ends with the narrator hypothesizing, "If this is how he handles the world now, just think what Mitt Romney might do as president."[76]

This ad uses the conflicted frame to show how unprepared Romney is for the presidency when it comes to foreign policy. The use of news clippings and reports from both Republicans and Democrats help to cement how disastrous Romney's foreign tour was. Very subtle, somewhat ambient music helps guide the audience to noticing something is off about Romney's foray. Further, a brief shot of riots in combination with the news of an attack on U.S. diplomats in Libya help show just how dangerous and worthy of fear the world is today. The ad posits that Romney, while not a monster himself, did nothing worthwhile in the face of these attacks and, in fact, only hurt the situation.

"Seen" uses the conflicted horror frame to attack Romney's stance on abortion. This ad, released on October 18, 2012, opens with an ad from Romney before the feminine narrator says, "[T]ake a look at this."[77] Melancholic music plays as a distorted clip from a Republican primary debate plays. Debate moderator Anderson Cooper asks Romney, "If *Roe v. Wade* was overturned, Congress passed a federal ban on all abortions and it came to your desk would you sign it?"[78] Romney very enthusiastically responds, "Let me say it, I'd be delighted to sign that bill."[79] The screen cuts to black as white text fades in reading, "banning all abortions" before the Romney quote is repeated.[80] The ad concludes with videos of Romney intercut with videos of disapproving women as the narrator quips, "Trying to mislead us? That's wrong. But ban all abortions? Only if you vote for him."[81]

This ad attacks Romney for being both misleading and malicious in his stance on abortion. Shading and distortions are used to visually frame Romney as someone to be worried about. The ad uses his own quote to stick Romney with the pretty extreme position of banning all abortions. "Seen" uses the conflicted frame to pin this as a direct attack on women, as clearly worried women are shown. While not making Romney out as monstrosity, the ad comes close to that line by indicating Romney is willing to take action beyond what is morally "wrong."[82]

Self-Positive Ads and Celebrity Assistance

"Always" is a positive advertisement meant to defend Obama against criticisms from the opposition. Obama narrates the ad over optimistic music, saying, "Those ads, taking my words about small business out of context, they're flat out wrong."[83] The ad showcases hardworking individuals as Obama notes the work people do every day. He then outlines the policy positions he has taken to support workforce in areas such as education, training, and infrastructure. He concludes by saying, "I believe we're all in this together."[84]

This quick, positive advertisement does a terrific job of quickly answering accusations against Obama before providing reasoning for why he should be the preferred candidate of American workers. While there is no horror in this ad, the greater context of the horror framing from other advertisements makes this ad stand out as an epideictic appeal for Obama's ability to defend the working class against a threatening economy. Having Obama himself narrate the advertisement, along with a fitting soundtrack, help make his claims seem sincere and convincing.

"This Is a Clear Choice," first televised on August 23, 2012, uses former president Bill Clinton as the driving force of an argument in favor of Obama. Clinton is positioned in front of a camera and argues, "This election, to me, is about which candidate is more likely to return us to full employment. This is a clear choice."[85] Clinton condemns Republican policy as ineffective, while Obama will "rebuild America from the ground up."[86] Inspirational music continues as Obama is seen meeting with individuals in the community. Clinton concludes by endorsing Obama's plan.

While this ad does criticize Romney and Republicans, it does not use explicit horror framing to accomplish this goal. Rather, they are criticized in comparison with Obama, who the ad focuses on as an exceptional leader in the economic recovery efforts. This type of positive framing is important in a larger horror narrative to set Obama up as the effective protagonist of the narrative, something Romney could never be.

"Challenges," released on October 21, 2012, highlights the struggles Obama has faced and the successes he has had in spite of them. Narrated by actor Morgan Freeman, the ad starts with a black-and-white image of the Oval Office.[87] Freeman notes, "Every president inherits challenges. Few have faced so many."[88] An image of Obama colorizes as the music swells and Freeman claims, "4 years later, our enemies have been brought to justice."[89] A montage of celebrating firefighters, a happy soldier, cars on an assembly line, workers, and happy families ensues with Freeman highlighting Obama's economic successes. He acknowledges that there are still challenges, "but the last thing we should do is turn back now."[90] The TV spot ends with simply "FORWARD" presented on a black screen."[91]

While there is a slight touch of horror framing at the beginning of this ad through black-and-white image filtering, "Challenges" is ultimately an overwhelmingly self-positive ad for Obama. That being said, the positive theme of the ad has strong ties to the horror genre. The ad frames Obama as a strong leader, able to defend the country from foreign threats and a weakened economy. The ad acknowledges that the country might not be free from threats and challenges, but that Obama is the only reasonable choice for audience efficacy. Voters must not turn backwards, but rather continue forward. This theme of "accomplishing some unfished business" ties in with haunting horror films like *The Sixth Sense* (1999), in that "only by reconciling the past and present" can the characters of the film "achieve some level of peace."[92] Thus, even though this ad carries many positive tones, there is an inherent horror in the alternative to pressing forward—a haunting return of the past.

"Determination" is a purely positive advertisement focused on Obama's policy plan. Originally televised on October 23, 2012, this ad is narrated by Obama and shows Americans at work as he highlights job growth, economic recovery indicators, and soldiers returning home. He acknowledges that "we're not there yet" but says we should keep moving forward with his plan.[93] The ad cuts to Obama speaking directly into the camera, as text reading "The President's Plan" appears.[94] President Obama lists a number of his specific policy proposals as optimistic music continues. He asks viewers to compare his plan with Romney's and "decide which is better for you."[95] The ad concludes with Obama asking for the viewer's vote, saying, "together we can keep moving America forward."[96]

This ad makes a strong, positive appeal to audience efficacy. No horror framing is present, but in the larger narrative Obama positions himself as one with an effective plan to combat the threats facing the country. Optimistic music and very specific policy proposals help guide the viewer toward Obama's stance on a number of key issues. Then, once the viewer has been sold, an appeal to vote is made. However, this appeal runs deeper than a simple call to vote for Obama. Rather, the audience is asked to join together with Obama, making it a group effort to repel the horrors and create a better future for the country, again subtly indicating that the past could continue to haunt Americans if Obama is not reelected.

"He's Got It Right" draws on elements of both "Determination" and "This Is a Clear Choice" to provide a strong positive appeal in favor of Obama. Released on October 24, 2012, this ad once again uses Bill Clinton as a narrator, like "This Is a Clear Choice." Clinton claims that him and Obama have both faced the same criticism about their economic plans. But he answers this criticism by saying, we "turned deficits into surpluses."[97] The ad cuts from Clinton to videos of Obama as the music swells. Clinton outlines Obama's plan, given in the "Determination" advertisement. Happy Americans are intercut with Obama hard at work, before Clinton concludes his list of Obama policies with a smile, "Sound familiar?"[98]

Another example of self-positive advertising, "He's Got It Right" continues the push of Obama's specific policy plan with the help of Clinton. Again, the viewer is meant to see Obama as capable of defeating the horrors facing the country with his specific proposals. Nostalgia is also introduced, as Clinton indicates that his time as president and Obama's are very similar. The ad relies on viewers looking favorably upon the 1990s and Clinton's time in office and a desire to go back to that more prosperous time before September 11 and the 2008 financial crisis. Thus, the Obama campaign makes an attempt to bracket all the horrors of the 2000s, and posit that Obama is the one to defeat these evils and allow for "normal time" to return.[99]

"Will Ferrell Will Do Anything To Get You To Vote," which first aired on November 3, 2012, once again relies on celebrity testimony in favor of Obama to call on audience efficacy. Using heavy doses of comedy, Will Ferrell, a comedic actor, is the focal point of the advertisement. Throughout, he tries to convince the audience to vote through various outrageous promises. Suave music airs as he plays pool in a luxurious game room. Ferrell introduces himself as "comedian, actor, founder of Facebook."[100] He makes various promises like cooking the audience a meal, helping to move a couch, and giving a tattoo even though "I do not know how to draw."[101] He then says he will do a dance and follows through with that to an electric dance soundtrack. Ferrell then goes back to listing promises of things he will do as long as the viewer votes. Up until this point, the commercial seems to be a generic get-out-the-vote appeal. However, it ends with text reading "VOTE OBAMA" and Ferrell saying, "Vote Obama: It's a slam dunk" as he catches a football.

This ad provides yet another example of Obama relying on a celebrity to appeal to audience efficacy. Thick with comedic elements, Ferrell does just that, trying to get viewers to vote. While this appeal is generically funny, it gets slanted in favor of Obama by the end of the advertisement. While there is practically no discussion of Obama's plans or credentials, the ad seems to intentionally stray away from typical campaign advertisements to catch a new audience of potential voters. Ultimately, it still works as an efficacy appeal in favor of Obama.

"What We're Fighting For" is a 2:26 minute advertisement released late in the campaign on November 4, 2012. This purely positive epideictic ad attempts to show voters the work that has gone into the Obama campaign and why they need to go out and vote. Obama himself narrates the ad, starting with a recollection of winning his first term in office. Upbeat music continues as Obama says, "Change doesn't happen in a year, it doesn't happen in one term, but every time we . . . move this country forward a little bit, it expands opportunity for everybody."[102] Images of Obama are intercut with folks hard at work as Obama lists his accomplishments while in office. He claims all those accomplishments were made possible by "mobilizing folks all across the country and that's the thing I'm most proud of."[103] Here the only mention of Romney is made, where Obama says the difference between the two campaigns is the reliance on small donors and typical Americans. A multitude of videos of campaign workers performing various tasks play as Obama explains the importance of this "grassroots" movement.[104] He argues that "This is your campaign" before saying he will continue to work hard to make sure it is successful.[105] He talks about battleground states being close and that change will only happen if people vote on election day, making his strong push for voter efficacy.

This lengthy ad is a late campaign positive efficacy appeal, similar in many ways to Romney's "The Moment." "What We're Fighting For" tries to create a cohesive narrative of what the campaign has meant for Obama and the viewer and asks the viewer to join in the last hour through a vote. He makes a callback to his change slogan from four years ago and makes sure the viewer knows that mantra is still alive. Obama sets himself apart as the one who can make things better for the average American. In the grander narrative of this collection of campaign advertisements, that means Obama posits himself as the one who can defeat the objects of his campaign's fear appeals and keep the country safe.

Throughout Obama's televised campaign, there was a heavy reliance on the conflicted horror frame and positive advertising. While there are two notable examples of the classic horror frame being used—"Firms" and "Big Bird"—the conflicted frame seemed far more fitting for Obama as he tried to cast Romney as an unfeeling, out-of-touch candidate. Most of these attacks used Romney's own words or a conglomeration of newspaper headlines to accuse him of dirty practices that harm working-class Americans in a variety of ways. The campaign balanced this heavy slate of attacks with a number of positive advertisements, interestingly relying quite heavily on celebrity figures such as Will Ferrell, Morgan Freeman, and Bill Clinton. Ultimately, the Obama campaign deployed a relentless and balanced televised campaign against Romney.

CONCLUSION

The Romney campaign and the Obama campaign took nearly opposite approaches in their televised advertising. The Romney campaign relied heavily on the classic horror frame, using it to demonize Obama, as well as various threats to American well-being. Positive appeals were interwoven in a few of these ads, with "The Moment" serving as the only purely positive ad analyzed here. The Obama campaign, on the other hand, used the conflicted frame early and often, with a number of positive ads spread in between.

The Romney strategy made some sense, since a challenger would often want voters to think the world is a scary place and the president is evil, relying on the polarizing and demonic implications of horror framing. Romney's campaign certainly made this attempt, framing Obama as monstrous, alongside China and the deficit. Like in 2008, Obama is cast as a hypnotizer through racist subtexts, but this time with a more monstrous angle, using both the demonic and insidious implications of horror framing. However, in order for such a fear appeal strategy to be effective, "positive efficacy information alone" must be provided to the audience.[106] This was attempted late with the over five-minute ad "The Moment," but as Romney campaign advisors themselves admitted, there needed to be more positive campaigning throughout to defend him against the Obama campaign's accusations.[107]

The Obama campaign knew what it wanted the narrative to be and was laser-focused with that strategy in mind. They knew they wanted to cast Romney as uncaring and heartless from his private business background. The attacks on Romney all followed that guiding principle, using whatever ammunition they could find to paint him as at least uncaring toward the working class, if not outright monstrous. Thus, even though the Obama campaign typically used the conflicted frame over the classic, Romney was nevertheless construed as a threat. Using the demonic dimension of horror campaigning, the Obama campaign argued that Romney was a threat that would return America to the haunted past, a threat that needed to be dealt with through voter efficacy. The appeals to voter efficacy were strong and often tied to celebrity support. This is certainly an interesting shift from 2008, where Obama was specifically attacked on the grounds that he was too much of a celebrity. Four years later, the Obama campaign decided to lean into that and use celebrities to support him. Still, the interweaving of audience efficacy into the horror framing creates an environment where that horror can become invasive and insidious, potentially seeping into everyday beliefs and interactions.

In 2008, the Obama campaign was trying to unseat eight years of Republican presidency which had seen the September 11 incident, the War on Terror, and the financial collapse of 2008. Using the classic frame a fair amount once the campaign settled in made sense to scare voters away from the status quo. Here, however, Obama wanted to scare voters away from the opposition while supporting the status quo. While it is impossible to say in this analysis whether or not that particular strategy was successful, Obama won his second presidential term in a major landslide, 332 electoral votes to 206.[108]

NOTES

1. Pew Research Center, "Section 2: Issues of the 2012 Campaign," *Pew Research Center*, April 17, 2012, https://www.people-press.org/2012/04/17/section-2-issues-of-the-2012-campaign/.

2. Pew Research Center, "Section 2: Issues."
3. Pew Research Center, "Section 2: Issues."
4. Pew Research Center, "Section 2: Issues."
5. Pew Research Center, "Section 2: Issues."
6. Pew Research Center, "Section 2: Issues."
7. Pew Research Center, "Section 2: Issues."
8. Pew Research Center, "Section 2: Issues."
9. Scott Wilson and Philip Rucker, "The Strategy that Paved a Winning Path," *Washington Post*, November 7, 2012, https://www.washingtonpost.com/politics/decision2012/the-strategy-that-paved-a-winning-path/2012/11/07/0a1201c8-2769-11e2-b2a0-ae18d6159439_story.html?noredirect=on&utm_term=.d45faa08d05a.
10. Granted, *The Living Room Candidate* is not an exhaustive list of every campaign advertisement released during the election, however the nearly 2:1 ratio between independent ads and candidate/party ads in favor of Romney is telling of how much Romney needed to lean into super PAC advertising. However, "The Republican super PACs, sitting on millions of dollars, also decided not to defend Romney at a time when the campaign could not afford to defend itself." The PAC ads tended, rather, to focus on "anti-Obama" advertising. There are still horror framing elements present in the ads analyzed here. Thus, for the sake of consistency in method, this section looks only to the candidate and party ads available on *The Living Room Candidate* when examining the Romney campaign. Wilson and Rucker, "The Strategy that Paved."
11. Charlton D. McIlwain and Stephen M. Caliendo, "Mitt Romney's Racist Appeals: How Race Was Played in the 2012 Presidential Election," *American Behavioral Scientist* 58, no. 9 (2014): 1166.
12. Romney, "Political Payoffs and Middle Class Layoffs," *The Living Room Candidate: Presidential Campaign Commercials 1952–2020*, July 16, 2012, http://www.livingroomcandidate.org/commercials/2012/political-payoffs-and-middle-class-layoffs.
13. Romney, "Political Payoffs."
14. Romney, "Political Payoffs."
15. Romney, "Political Payoffs."
16. Melissa Mia Hall, "The Siren," in *Icons of Horror and the Supernatural: An Encyclopedia of Our Worst Nightmares*, ed. S. T. Joshi (Westport, CT: Greenwood Press, 2007), 508.
17. Robin R. Means Coleman, *Horror Noire: Blacks in American Horror Films from the 1890s to Present* (New York: Routledge, 2011), 211.
18. *White Zombie*, directed by Victor Halperin (1932; Music Video Dist., 2014), DVD.
19. Glenn W. Richardson Jr., *Pulp Politics: How Political Advertising Tells the Stories of American Politics* (Lanham, MD: Rowman & Littlefield, 2008), 39.
20. *The Cabinet of Dr. Caligari*, directed by Robert Wiene (1920; Horrortheque, 2010), Digital.
21. Romney, "Cancer," *The Living Room Candidate: Presidential Campaign Commercials 1952–2020*, August 10, 2012, http://www.livingroomcandidate.org/commercials/2012/cancer. Note: it appears to me that this advertisement might be a

PAC ad, but *The Living Room Candidate* has it designated under "Candidate & Party Ads Only." Thus, I have left this advertisement in the analysis for consistency.

22. Romney, "Cancer."
23. Romney, "Cancer."
24. Romney, "Cancer."
25. Romney, "Failing American Workers," *The Living Room Candidate: Presidential Campaign Commercials 1952–2020*, September 13, 2012, http://www.livingroomcandidate.org/commercials/2012/failing-american-workers.
26. Romney, "Failing American Workers."
27. Romney, "Failing American Workers."
28. *Dracula*, directed by Tod Browning (1931; Peacock TV), Digital.
29. Pew Research Center, "Section 2: Issues."
30. Romney, "Failing America's Families," *The Living Room Candidate: Presidential Campaign Commercials 1952–2020*, September 17, 2012, http://www.livingroomcandidate.org/commercials/2012/failing-americas-families.
31. Romney, "Failing America's Families."
32. Romney, "Failing America's Families."
33. Kendall R. Phillips, *Projected Fears: Horror Films and American Culture* (Westport, CT: Praeger, 2005), 109–10, 114.
34. Romney, "Give Me a Break," *The Living Room Candidate: Presidential Campaign Commercials 1952–2020*, September 6, 2012, http://www.livingroomcandidate.org/commercials/2012/give-me-a-break.
35. Romney, "Give Me a Break."
36. Romney, "Give Me a Break."
37. Romney, "Give Me a Break."
38. Romney, "Give Me a Break."
39. Romney, "Give Me a Break."
40. Romney, "Give Me a Break."
41. Wilson and Rucker, "The Strategy."
42. Romney, "The Moment," *The Living Room Candidate: Presidential Campaign Commercials 1952–2020*, November 6, 2012, http://www.livingroomcandidate.org/commercials/2012/the-moment.
43. Romney, "The Moment."
44. Romney, "The Moment."
45. Romney, "The Moment."
46. Romney, "The Moment."
47. Wilson and Rucker, "The Strategy."
48. Wilson and Rucker, "The Strategy."
49. Wilson and Rucker, "The Strategy."
50. Wilson and Rucker, "The Strategy."
51. Obama, "Firms," *The Living Room Candidate: Presidential Campaign Commercials 1952–2020*, July 14, 2012, http://www.livingroomcandidate.org/commercials/2012/firms.
52. Hall, "The Siren," 509.

53. Obama for America, "Big Bird," *The Living Room Candidate: Presidential Campaign Commercials 1952–2020*, October 9, 2012, http://www.livingroomcandidate.org/commercials/2012/big-bird.

54. Obama, "Big Bird."
55. Obama, "Big Bird."
56. Obama, "Big Bird."
57. Obama, "Big Bird."

58. *Evil Dead II*, directed by Sam Raimi (1987; Lionsgate, 2018), DVD; *The Cabin in the Woods*, directed by Drew Goddard (2011; Lionsgate, 2011), DVD.

59. John S. Nelson and G. R. Boynton, *Video Rhetorics: Televised Advertising in American Politics* (Urbana: University of Illinois Press, 1997), 55.

60. Obama, "Understands," *The Living Room Candidate: Presidential Campaign Commercials 1952–2020*, August 7, 2012, http://www.livingroomcandidate.org/commercials/2012/understands. Note: it appears to me that this advertisement might be a PAC ad, similar to "Cancer," but *The Living Room Candidate* has it designated under "Candidate & Party Ads Only." Thus, I have left this advertisement in the analysis for consistency.

61. Obama, "Understands."
62. Obama, "Understands."

63. Obama, "The Cheaters," *The Living Room Candidate: Presidential Campaign Commercials 1952–2020*, September 14, 2012, http://www.livingroomcandidate.org/commercials/2012/the-cheaters.

64. Obama, "The Cheaters."
65. Obama, "The Cheaters."

66. *Frankenstein*, directed by James Whale (1931; Universal Studios Home Entertainment, 2016), DVD.

67. Obama, "47 Percent," *The Living Room Candidate: Presidential Campaign Commercials 1952–2020*, September 18, 2012, http://www.livingroomcandidate.org/commercials/2012/47-percent.

68. Obama, "47 Percent."

69. Alexander Swanson, "Audience Reaction Movie Trailers and the Paranormal Activity Franchise," *Transformative Works and Cultures* 18 (2015).

70. Swanson, "Audience Reaction."

71. Obama for America, "Mandatory," *The Living Room Candidate: Presidential Campaign Commercials 1952–2020*, October 2, 2012, http://www.livingroomcandidate.org/commercials/2012/mandatory.

72. Obama, "Mandatory."

73. Obama for America, "Policy," *The Living Room Candidate: Presidential Campaign Commercials 1952–2020*, October 8, 2012, http://www.livingroomcandidate.org/commercials/2012/policy.

74. Obama, "Policy."
75. Obama, "Policy."
76. Obama, "Policy."

77. Obama for America, "Seen," *The Living Room Candidate: Presidential Campaign Commercials 1952–2020*, October 18, 2012, http://www.livingroomcandidate.org/commercials/2012/seen.

78. Obama, "Seen."
79. Obama, "Seen."
80. Obama, "Seen."
81. Obama, "Seen."
82. Obama, "Seen."
83. Obama, "Always," *The Living Room Candidate: Presidential Campaign Commercials 1952–2020*, 2012, http://www.livingroomcandidate.org/commercials/2012/always.
84. Obama, "Always."
85. Obama, "This Is a Clear Choice," *The Living Room Candidate: Presidential Campaign Commercials 1952–2020*, August 23, 2012, http://www.livingroomcandidate.org/commercials/2012/this-is-a-clear-choice.
86. Obama, "This Is a Clear Choice."
87. David Jackson, "Obama Ad Stresses 'Challenges' He Inherited," *USA Today*, October 13, 2012, https://www.usatoday.com/story/theoval/2012/10/13/obama-ad-morgan-freeman-politics-election-2012-mitt-romney/1631365/.
88. Obama for America, "Challenges," *The Living Room Candidate: Presidential Campaign Commercials 1952–2020*, October 21, 2012, http://www.livingroomcandidate.org/commercials/2012/challenges.
89. Obama, "Challenges."
90. Obama, "Challenges."
91. Obama, "Challenges."
92. *The Sixth Sense*, directed by M. Night Shyamalan (1999; Disney, 2000), DVD; Kendall R. Phillips, *Projected Fears: Horror Films and American Culture* (Westport, CT: Praeger, 2005), 190.
93. Obama for America, "Determination," *The Living Room Candidate: Presidential Campaign Commercials 1952–2020*, October 23, 2012, http://www.livingroomcandidate.org/commercials/2012/determination.
94. Obama, "Determination."
95. Obama, "Determination."
96. Obama, "Determination."
97. Obama for America, "He's Got It Right," *The Living Room Candidate: Presidential Campaign Commercials 1952–2020*, October 24, 2012, http://www.livingroomcandidate.org/commercials/2012/hes-got-it-right.
98. Obama, "He's Got It Right."
99. Caroline Joan (Kay) S. Picart and David A. Frank, *Frames of Evil: The Holocaust as Horror in American Film* (Carbondale: Southern Illinois University Press, 2006), 7.
100. Barack Obama, "Will Ferrell Will Do Anything to Get You to Vote," *The Living Room Candidate: Presidential Campaign Commercials 1952–2016*, November 3, 2012, http://www.livingroomcandidate.org/commercials/2012/will-ferrell-will-do-anything-to-get-you-to-vote.
101. Obama, "Will Ferrell."
102. Obama for America, "What We're Fighting For," *The Living Room Candidate: Presidential Campaign Commercials 1952–2020*, November 4, 2012, http://www.livingroomcandidate.org/commercials/2012/what-were-fighting-for.

103. Obama, "What We're Fighting For."
104. Obama, "What We're Fighting For."
105. Obama, "What We're Fighting For."
106. P. Sol Hart and Lauren Feldman, "Threat Without Efficacy? Climate Change on U.S. Network News," *Science Communication* 36, no. 3 (2014): 341.
107. Wilson and Rucker, "The Strategy."
108. "2012 Presidential Election," 270 to Win, https://www.270towin.com/2012_Election/.

Chapter 6

Hillary Clinton versus Donald Trump in the 2016 Election[1]

The 2016 U.S. presidential election pit Republican Donald Trump against Democrat Hillary Clinton. This election was viewed by the public as one of the most negative elections in history. Lydia Saad, Senior Editor at Gallup, claims that Clinton and Trump both possessed "the worst election-eve images of any major-party presidential candidates Gallup has measured back to 1956."[2] Given the unprecedented negative views many held toward both candidates, it is unsurprising that the 2016 election had the lowest voter turnout in twenty years.[3]

As the general election heated up, the issues that mattered to voters centered heavily on economic and defense issues. According to the Pew Research Center, "84% of registered voters say that the issue of the economy will be very important to them in making their decision about who to vote for in the 2016 presidential election."[4] Following closely behind the economy was the issue of terrorism, which 80 percent said would be very important. This 4 percent differential between the economy and terrorism is a major shift from 2008, where the economy was very important to 87 percent of voters and terrorism was only very important to 68 percent of voters.[5] Thus, there was fertile ground among voters for fear appeals to be made. As the Pew made clear, "Other issues that rank highly on voters' 2016 importance list include foreign policy (75% very important), health care (74%), gun policy (72%) and immigration (70%)."[6] Major social issues were of far less importance. "Fewer than half of voters see abortion (45%) or the treatment of gay, lesbian and transgender people (40%) as very important to their vote."[7]

The remainder of this chapter examines the campaign ads of both candidates through the previously established method of horror framing (see table 6.1). Hillary Clinton and Donald Trump deployed elements of the horror genre in their campaign ads, but each did so in very different ways. Clinton relied

Table 6.1 Hillary Clinton and Donald Trump Campaign Advertisements' Airdates

Hillary Clinton		Donald Trump	
Airdate	Title	Airdate	Title
June 16, 2016	Who We Are	August 19, 2016	Two Americas Immigration
July 7, 2016	Role Models	August 29, 2016	Two Americas: Economy
August 5, 2016	Unfit (D)	September 12, 2016	Deplorables
August 22, 2016	Just One	September 20, 2016	Movement
September 6, 2016	Sacrifice	September 30, 2016	Motherhood
September 13, 2016	Low Opinion	October 19, 2016	Laura
September 23, 2016	Mirrors	October 19, 2016	Predators
October 10, 2016	Respected	November 1, 2016	Choice
October 21, 2016	Captain Kahn	November 2, 2016	United
October 24, 2016	Barbershop	November 3, 2016	Unfit (R)
October 31, 2016	Daisy	November 4, 2016	Donald Trump's Argument for America
November 2, 2016	27 Million Strong		
November 3, 2016	We Are America		
November 7, 2016	Tomorrow		

on both the classic and conflicted horror frames but favored the conflicted frame over the classic when attacking Trump. Clinton did very little in the way of attempting to promote audience efficacy through epideictic self-praise throughout her campaign. On the other hand, Trump consistently evoked the classic horror frame to fashion distinct, otherized monsters out of immigrants, the economy, and Clinton herself. Trump further provided a plan for slaying such constructed ghouls through mob action, thus repeatedly attempting to instill audience efficacy through epideictic self-praise and mass voter response.

HILLARY CLINTON'S TELEVISED HORROR NARRATIVE

First, I make the case that Hillary Clinton's campaign ads did not consistently frame Trump as a dangerous monster, letting his foolishness narratively overwhelm his ghoulishness. Further, the following demonstrates that Clinton did little in her ads to resolve the Trump problem, and those few ads that did suggest her efficacy in addressing Trump's negative vision were late in the campaign and not unifying, being broken up among individual demographic groups. Clinton clearly used both horror frames—the classic and the conflicted—but privileged the conflicted over the classic both in quantity and narrative significance.

It is also briefly worth noting that Clinton spent significantly more on televised advertisements than Trump. While the Trump campaign spent less than $40 million on ads, the Clinton campaign nearly doubled that amount, spending $72 million on TV ads.[8] Indeed, "Through September, Clinton spent an average of $9.1 million dollars a week on televised advertisements in comparison with Trump's $3 million dollar average each week."[9]

Clinton's Portrayal of Trump through a Conflicted Frame

Hillary Clinton's first general election ad, which debuted on June 16, 2016, was titled "Who We Are" and poses a series of questions before answering them for the audience.[10] The questions asked are, "Do we help each other?" "Do we respect each other?" "Do we stand together?"[11] Clinton answers these questions by saying, "I know what I believe. It's wrong to pit people against each other. We've had enough partisan division and gridlock already."[12] She then argues, "It's time to unite behind some simple, common goals."[13] These are as follows: "to build a strong economy that works for everyone, not just those at the top, an economy that creates jobs families can really live on, to work with our allies around the world and keep our families safe at home, to give every man, woman, and child the chance to live up to their god-given potential."[14] Finally, she ends with one more question: "What kind of America do we want to be? Dangerously divided or strong and united."[15] To which she answers, "I believe we are always stronger together."[16]

This first election advertisement works to create the narrative of Trump as unfit for the presidency through his boorishness and foolishness. While Clinton is asking her first series of questions, clips of Donald Trump saying he would like to "punch him in the face," "Knock the crap out of him," and mocking a disabled individual are spliced in between each question.[17] Each of these clips where Donald Trump is speaking is distorted with black lines and darker shading,[18] evoking the ideas of distortion found in the Expressionism of films like *The Cabinet of Dr. Caligari* (1920).[19] This ad, like in *Caligari*, seems to be casting judgment on the psychological state of Trump. In *Caligari*, these distortions are characterized by "unexpected curves and sudden ups and downs."[20] However, in this ad, the distortions are straight lines. Thus, the distortions, while still clearly meant to be disturbing, do not suggest a sporadic nature. They suggest instead the norms for Trump and the larger Republican Party, as Clinton discusses the status quo of the "partisan division" as "Dangerously divided."[21] Here the horror of Trump is not something exceptionally monstrous. Rather, it is a continuation of the hyper-partisanship that has become mundane. Accordingly, Clinton's first general election ad frames Trump through a conflicted horror lens: more misguided, buffoonish, and mundane than outright other. Further, there is no spatial or temporal separation. Trump is undoubtedly American and representative of the politics of the present. However, Clinton clearly argues that he represents the worst aspects of human nature, not the best principles she attempts to embody that epitomize the nation. While there is some positive efficacy given through certain vague economic and international goals, these positive attributes largely disappear until the final, election eve ad of the campaign.

"Sacrifice," which was initially broadcast on September 6, 2016, continues the theme of Trump as unfit—specifically with regard to wielding the powers of commander in chief—by showing veteran responses to Trump's comments.[22] Again demonstrating the conflicted horror frame, Trump is portrayed as ignorant of warfare, highlighted by quotes like "I know more about ISIS than the generals do."[23] Notably, the veterans' responses seem more disappointed and disgusted rather than horrified or fearful. This theme, like "Who We Are," isolates Trump as a fool, but extends the narrative from interactions with ordinary people to a buffoonery in interactions with perhaps the last institution with whom Americans retain high confidence—the military.[24]

The "Sacrifice" ad uses some traditional horror imagery in how it intentionally depicts multiple veterans' disfigurements.[25] Disfigurement of the face and body have long been used "as abject spectacle"[26] within horror. Indeed, disfigurements in the movie *Tarantula* (1955), according to Steffen Hantke, "evoke graphic memories of severe burns, the most common physical disfigurement, together with amputated limbs, of returning WWII veterans."[27] The horrific imagery in this advertisement accordingly is not focused on Trump but on the veterans, drawing sympathy through an obvious focus on their disfigurement. Clearly, one is not meant to cast these veterans as monstrous. This imagery instead moves back to a conflicted frame, where the horror of the ad is sympathetic, oriented spatially and temporally in the here and now.

An example of a pure attack ad against Trump is Clinton's "Low Opinion" ad,[28] which again epitomizes Trump as a fool. Released on September 13, 2016, the ad features more of a "gotcha" message than "Who We Are." "Low Opinion" opens with Trump saying, "You can't lead this nation if you have such a low opinion for its citizens."[29] The ad continues with numerous quotes of Trump disparaging and making fun of different groups and citizens.[30] This commercial ends by repeating the first Trump quote and text that simply says, "Exactly."[31] "Low Opinion" does not use any horrific imagery. Thus, in and of itself, it does not fit within either of the horror frames discussed here. But, when the ads are evaluated as an "extended message,"[32] we still see a continuation on the conflicted horror frame of Trump as misguided rather than evil.

"Mirrors" directed the narrative of Trump's boorish behavior toward his disrespect for women.[33] This ad was released on September 23, 2016, and takes a less comedic approach than that of "Low Opinion." The main horror imagery comes from minor distortions of Trump when he is shown on screen. However, such imagery is far more subtle when compared to the noticeable distortions in "Who We Are"[34] and "Just One."[35] Further, the victimization of women in particular is reminiscent of how sexual violence is depicted in horror. Mark Jancovich argues that horror films often employ violence against women, "violence that is itself highly sexualized."[36] This is fitting with the highly sexual nature of Trump's comments selected for this advertisement, commenting on women's weight and chests. However, the ad utilizes conflicted horror frames because "[o]utright horror distracts from the misogyny."[37] Clinton's ads portray, through a conflicted horror frame, how the sphere of the horrific (sexual victimization of women) has crossed into the sphere of the sadly mundane (institutionalized patriarchy). Trump is thus cast as this crossing of spheres par excellence.

"Respected," which was initially aired on October 10, 2016, continues this theme of Trump's misogyny, using a Republican war veteran in an ad stylized as a personal testimony.[38] Jamieson argues that "personal testimony ads consist of actual individuals reporting their opinions of the opposing candidate's performance"[39] and are deemed fair game because "we are taught that everyone is entitled to express his or her opinion."[40] This ad continues the conflicted frame of "Low Opinion" and "Mirrors" by again emphasizing Trump's attacks on women. The ad accentuates this message of disgust when the Republican veteran concludes: "Donald Trump's America is not the country I fought for so I'm voting for Hillary Clinton."[41] It's notable that this ad focuses on voting for Clinton not because of anything she has done or will do, but because of Donald Trump's character flaws. The veteran in this ad is voting for Clinton out of protest against Trump. Up to this point, there has been little engagement by the Clinton campaign on any positive actions.

"Captain Kahn" is another personal testimony-style ad deployed by the Clinton campaign, which focuses on the father of Captain Kahn, a Muslim American soldier killed in Iraq.[42] The ad, first televised on October 21, 2016, shows Captain Kahn's father, clearly holding back tears, asking Trump, "[W]ould my son have a place in your America?"[43] While he is asking this, a video of a soldier's casket being lowered into a grave is shown with both a wavering distortion and straight black lines.[44] As discussed previously, this type of distortion evokes horror.[45] The horror here is ostensibly that of war, though the ad muddles this with the implication of Trump's racism and anti-Muslim bias. Thus, a conflicted frame is once again used, where there is not one monstrous other on which to blame the horrors of war. In the grander narrative, an argument could be made that Trump's instability and inclination toward war would cause more of these stories of heartbreak. However, this ad is clearly not focused on Trump as a warmonger, but rather Trump as a racist.

"We Are America," which was originally aired on November 3, 2016, takes all the narrative threads of the attacks on Trump throughout the campaign and ties them together.[46] It opens with a classically horrific shot of a decayed, dirty black-and-white house with a colored, disheveled American flag in the center.⁴⁷ At that point, the use of visual horror imagery is largely dropped. Instead, still images of the victims of different controversial Trump comments are shown with desolate music playing. The opening half of the advertisement highlights Trump's comments against women, veterans, disabled individuals, and Latinxs.⁴⁸ The second half of the advertisement moves to all images of children and Trump's comments on war and the use of nuclear weapons, with no change in mood.⁴⁹ In this way, the ad highlights the American youth as victims of these potential wars. The ad ends with a moving image of an American flag flapping in front of the sun, with the text "We are not him."⁵⁰

This ad makes an interesting move. Chronologically prior to this TV spot, any mention of Trump's stance on war and nuclear weapons had been portrayed through a classic horror frame. Additionally, attacks on Trump's explicit and derogatory comments were framed more through a conflicted lens. Here, however, the conflicted frame overtakes the classic frame, with both Trump's derogatory comments *and* his war comments lumped together within the conflicted frame. This highlights the general portrayal of Trump as a misguided, hurtful fool rather than a monstrous other. This also displays how the threats facing the country are largely not external, nor are they spatially or temporally separated. Instead, the threat is Trump and the possibility of his election. This threat is largely focused on his foolishness.

Clinton's Ads that Portray Trump through a Classic Frame

Any ads that the Clinton campaign used to depict Trump as classically monstrous focused almost exclusively on how he would exercise the powers of commander in chief. "Unfit (D)," the third TV spot by Clinton, aired on August 5, 2016.⁵¹ While the ad's title might suggest the continuation of the unfit foolishness narrative, this is the first ad that portrays Trump as beyond unfit, as outright dangerous. The ad focuses entirely on Trump and political pundits' views on his viability for controlling the U.S. nuclear arsenal.⁵² Darkly shadowed images of Trump are intercut with pundits explaining how Trump cannot be trusted with these weapons. One pundit claims Trump would use nuclear weapons "against our Western European allies."⁵³ The ad ends with Charles Krauthammer, a conservative pundit, claiming that he does not want "a person of that temperament" controlling the nuclear codes.⁵⁴ Here, two videos of Trump are shown side by side: one of him erratically mocking a disabled individual and the other of a shadowed Trump looking disappointed.⁵⁵ Bill O'Reilly sighs in disappointment at this comment by Krauthammer and the ad fades out with the text, "Donald Trump Too Dangerous."⁵⁶

This ad suggests the instillation of pure fear for the audience—fear of an irrational Trump controlling the most powerful weapons in the world. The ad plays on perceived threats with little effort to portray positive efficacy. The advertisement moves beyond the crudeness of Trump that had, up to this point, dominated Clinton's TV spots. Instead, Trump is framed as uniquely horrific, warranted by the sense he would contemplate nuclear warfare against his country's own allies. The horror of this ad is also spatially separated, as the fear is not necessarily that war would happen on the home front (although, with a nuclear war, this could be a quite real possibility); rather, the horror is projected to the countries he would attack, including those in Western Europe. The fear is pronounced nonetheless with the ad utilizing the fears of global interconnectedness and nuclear warfare found in 1950s sci-fi horrors such as *War of the Worlds* (1953) and *Them!* (1954).[57] The only perplexing aspect of the ad, in terms of horror framing, is the use of the clip of Trump mocking a disabled person. Out of context, it makes him look more foolish and misguided than monstrous as the other shots of him had conveyed. Thus, there remains a touch of the conflicted frame of a misguided, semi-human monster that is balanced with images of Trump as a deep threat to the future stability of global peace.

"Just One" further demonizes Trump as a warmonger through a classic horror lens, again making the case that his instability could cause war.[58] The ad, which was initially broadcast on August 22, 2016, opens with ominous music and a dark, shadowy White House.[59] The camera then cuts to Trump saying, "Knock the crap out of him" as the narrating voice says, "America depends on steady leadership."[60] The distortion transition effect is continually used for cutting between the White House and examples of Trump's rhetoric. Finally, the narrator states, "Because all it takes is one wrong move" before the image of the White House fades to black.[61] While the image fades to black, Trump is heard exclaiming, "I would bomb the s<beep> out of them" as the sound of a bomb is heard in the background. Simultaneously, the text "JUST ONE WRONG MOVE" is displayed with slight image distortions.[62]

The "Just One" ad moves the Clinton campaign fully into the realm of the classic horror frame, taking the argument of "Unfit (D)" and ramping it up with even more classic horror imagery meant to instill fear. The distortions in this ad, unlike those found in "Who We Are," are wavy and curved. This ad is more directly relatable to the German Expressionism of *The Cabinet of Dr. Caligari* and argues Trump is wildly unpredictable and warlike unlike the predictable partisanship "Who We Are" implies with straight-line distortions.[63] The ominous soundtrack adds to the uneasy affective response elicited by this advertisement. Notably, any imagery of Trump looking foolish is absent from this ad, setting it apart as purely classically horrific. Further, given the way the White House is dimly lit, it is quite evocative of gothic manor settings, reminiscent of the castle setting in the genre-defining novel, *The Castle of Otranto*.[64] This symbolic setting not only brackets the horror spatially, but also temporally in a "What if Trump is elected?" potential timeline. Typically, the White House is a pristine sign of pride for the American public, but the decrepit look created by the shadow effect shows that Trump's mistakes as president, if elected, would allow the White House to fall into corruption, like the decayed building in which Victor Frankenstein creates his monster in Franken*stein* (1931).[65] Once again, this ad intensifies the perception of threat with little in the way of positive efficacy.

"Daisy," which was first aired on October 31, 2016, is a fascinating advertisement within Clinton's campaign from a horror frame perspective.[66] This ad continues the theme of "Unfit (D)" and "Just One" all of which argue that Trump is unfit for the presidency because of his proclivity toward nuclear warfare. The driving force of this ad is the personal testimony from Monique Corzilius Luiz, the young girl in the infamous "Peace Little Girl (Daisy)" advertisement (see figure 6.1).[67] The original "Peace Little Girl (Daisy)" advertisement, the pinnacle of horror imagery in campaign advertising, depicts a young girl counting up as she picks petals off of a daisy.[68] This image of horror is then juxtaposed with a launch countdown that climaxes in a massive nuclear blast with a narrator explaining nuclear war is at stake in the election.[69] This ad, which "engaged viewers as political ads had never done before," has all the elements of fear-mongering horror.[70] Now, the modern rendition of "Daisy" plays on public memory of the ad from 1964, arguing that the same Cold War fear of nuclear war is back with the possibility of a Trump election.[71] The back end of the ad contains clips of Trump expressing his desire to bomb people, news pundits mentioning Trump wanting to

Figure 6.1 Democratic National Committee, "Peace Little Girl (Daisy)." Screenshot captured by author.

use nuclear weapons, and a reminder that there is no check on the commander in chief.[72]

The modern "Daisy" advertisement is interesting primarily because of its classical meta-horror connotations. The horror is being remade through a discussion of an original horrific advertisement. This calls to mind postmodern horror remakes such as Hammer Films' *The Curse of Frankenstein* (1957)[73] or *Bram Stoker's Dracula* (1992),[74] which draw upon audience familiarity of an original horror film and recreate it for contemporary viewers. Thus, "Daisy" tries to evoke the same fear of 1964 in the 2016 election, especially for the political elite. This memory highlights the bracketing of time in classic horror framing since this ad attempts to portray a temporal breakdown where the past bleeds into the present and separates "fear of nuclear war" time from the normal flow of time. Thus, once again, the classic horror frame was used in the context of Trump's comments on war, but ads covering all other aspects seemed to rely far more heavily on the conflicted horror frame. Additionally, the final reminder that there is no check on the commander in chief forces a highly negative message of efficacy onto the audience. The threat is constructed in these classically horrific ads, but little resolve is offered concerning how to defeat this monstrosity. Further, "We Are America," which aired chronologically after "Unfit (D)," "Just One," and "Daisy," took the narrative of Trump as a warmonger and reframed it within the conflicted horror frame. This took the proverbial wind out of the sails of any outright fear appeal narratives that were built up by the previous ads.

Clinton's Portrayal of Trump through a Mixed Frame

There is one ad that warrants its own section because it relies so equally on conflicted and classic horror frames. "Role Models," which was initially televised on July 7, 2016, expands upon clips of Trump acting boorish by focusing attention largely on the derogatory comments from his past.[75] These clips of Trump are interwoven with images of young children seemingly watching Trump utter these statements on television. Their look is somber, and they appear mesmerized by his words, never diverting their eyes from the television screen. The ad then displays the text, "Our children are watching. What example will we set for them?"[76] The TV spot concludes with children watching Clinton speak, where she argues that we need to make a choice of which our children and grandchildren would be proud.[77]

This ad contains two separate but related elements of the horror genre: censorship and possession. Horror films have a long history of battling censorship. Julian Petley argues, "there can be little doubt that horror, after pornography, has been cinema's second most censored genre."[78] Thus, this ad makes the implicit argument that Trump, like pornography and horror, is something *explicit* and horrific that should not be seen or heard by our nation's children. Possession is clearly articulated as well, as the ad implies that the children watching will imitate Trump. This evokes films like *The Exorcist* (1973), which, as Daniel Humphrey notes, "involves a cute, pubescent girl possessed by a demon who then, horrifyingly enough, swears like a foul-mouthed truck driver."[79] It is no wonder, then, that one of the pivotal Trump quotes used in Clinton's case is, "And you can tell them to go f<beep> themselves."[80]

Here, Trump is portrayed as both explicit and demonic. Explicitness, a characteristic of both classic and conflicted horror frames, does not privilege one frame over the other. Possession, additionally, is a tricky mode of horror to frame. The possessing demon obviously signifies a completely otherized, absolute evil in a Manichean sense. But, oftentimes within the horror genre, the demon is left unseen, or its existence questioned. Thus, there are also elements of the conflicted horror frame as these possessions tend to occur in mundane environments as the horrific acts are physically perpetrated by the body of the victim—a "cute" girl in the case of *The Exorcist*.[81] Accordingly, this ad seems to use "multiple and blended frames"instead of solely a classic or conflicted frame.[82] Thus, while there is a case that the classic horror frame is used here to describe an element of Trump that exists outside of his potential warmonger status, it is muddied by an equal dosage of the conflicted frame. Further, since Trump's boorishness is framed through a conflicted frame in every other advertisement, any residual classically framed fear appeal is washed out. As this analysis demonstrates, classic horror framing is almost exclusively used in relation to Trump as a dangerous warmonger.

Clinton's Use of Minimally Horrific Efficacy Ads

To this point, positive efficacy, or the means to defeat the monster/misguided villain, has been surprisingly absent save the very first ad, "Who We Are," that was aired on June 16, 2016.[83] As Bruce E. Gronbeck argues, campaign narratives utilize forensic attacks on the opponent and epideictic praise of the favored candidate.[84] Besides "Who We Are," there are only three ads the Clinton campaign deployed in an effort to mobilize any sort of positive efficacy toward voting late in the game: "Barbershop," "27 Million," and "Tomorrow." Of these ads, only "Tomorrow" used specific policy goals to epideictically praise Clinton.

"Barbershop" utilizes the personal testimony style, which we have seen in "Respected," "Captain Kahn," "Daisy," and "Sacrifice." However, this time there are few horrific elements and the personal testimony focuses on a community of Black folks in a barbershop.[85] Clearly, this ad, which was originally aired on October 24, 2016, is aimed directly at Black Americans, as demonstrated by the interviewees. The tone of the ad is rather upbeat with fun background music. Positive traits of Clinton are given, such as "Her resume," "experience in office," "respect she gives every individual," and her support from Obama.[86] These are contrasted against Trump as purely a businessman.[87] This ad lacks any readily apparent horror tropes, but it is important in that it is one of the few advertisements that features positive qualities of Clinton, giving the audience a possible glimpse of positive efficacy. However, once again, there is no articulation of a future vision of Clinton's America. The positive qualities are entirely based on her past deeds. Further, because this advertisement is exclusively aimed at Black Americans, other demographic groups may have overlooked these brief, positive portrayals of Clinton. Even though this ad is one of Clinton's few *attempts* at positive efficacy messaging, it narratively undercuts itself by falling short of the positive efficacy P. Sol Hart and Lauren Feldman envision. Finally, even though positive efficacy is displayed, there is almost as much negative talk about Trump.[88]

The ad, "27 Million Strong," again emphasizes a get-out-the-vote message for a particular marginalized group.[89] This ad, which the Clinton camp broadcast on November 2, 2016, acts in a similar way to "Barbershop" in its focused nature and its pulling away from horror framing. The ad uses a poem and images of empowered, resilient Latinx people to argue for strong electoral support for Clinton.[90] However, this ad differs from "Barbershop" in that it fails to offer any strengths of Clinton and only obliquely mentions Trump as a "president of United hate."[91] Thus, this advertisement did little to alter the larger narrative of the Clinton television campaign and also, like "Barbershop," was targeted primarily at only one voting demographic. While it attempts to argue for positive efficacy among Latinxs, the absence of epideictic praise of Clinton herself again leaves the ad in a potentially precarious position.

"Tomorrow," aired on November 7, 2016, was the final, election-eve television ad released by the Clinton campaign.[92] This ad consists simply of Hillary Clinton talking into the camera for two minutes, making her case for the presidency. There are no visual horror elements present, though some of her arguments recall the horror framing of past advertisements. She initially argues, "it's not just my name and my opponent's name on the ballot. It's the kind of country we want for our children and grandchildren. Is America dark and divisive or hopeful and inclusive?"[93] Thus, even without the visual horror imagery, the language of horror tinctures Clinton's prolonged monologue, such as when she implies Trump's America would be "dark and divisive."[94] Clinton then praises herself, explaining she will "work my heart out as president to make life better for you and your family."[95] Finally, Clinton vaguely articulates her goals as president for the first time since "Who We Are."

They are "to keep America safe and strong," "make our economy work for everyone," and "to give our kids and every American the chance to live up to their god-given potential."[96] While positive efficacy was offered, it seems vague and disconnected from the rest of her advertising campaign. Thus, when viewed in a larger narrative, this is an ending that could have left the audience scratching their heads, with the positive efficacy conveniently materializing out of thin air. Consistency in efficacy appeals was clearly lacking in the Clinton campaign.

With these final pieces of Clinton's television campaign in place, what was the narrative flow of the ads as a whole? As demonstrated through the ads under review here, the campaign argued that Trump is a misguided, foolish, and ill-tempered candidate, not fit for the presidency. Clinton's appeal was centered more in opposition to Trump, than in favor of herself. The threat to America was, in and of itself, a Trump presidency. This threat ranged from offensive remarks to starting a nuclear war. Only Trump's warmongering was ever fully framed through a classic horror frame, and even that was eventually subsumed into the frame of conflicted horror in the "We Are America" advertisement. Thus, Clinton's campaign mostly avoided narratively constructing Trump as either inhuman or monstrous. Instead, the campaign's ads depicted Trump as an overly flawed human and woefully insufficient presidential candidate. Additionally, a remedy for both Trump and the other fears Americans faced—those outlined explicitly in the Trump campaign—were never fully articulated.

DONALD TRUMP'S TELEVISED HORROR NARRATIVE

Donald Trump, in contrast to Hillary Clinton, almost exclusively framed his television ads through the lens of classic horror. His slogan, "Make America Great Again," by its nature, temporally brackets the present horrors facing America. The slogan at once implies America's previous greatness, announces this absence in the present, and foretells of national revival through the election of Trump. Borrowing language from Ronald Reagan's "Let's make America great again" slogan, Trump argued the horrors facing the nation were a temporal aberration in the history of America.[97] But Trump also attempted to offer positive efficacy to his audience, since America would be great again once he is elected and with "the monster vanquished, normal time returns."[98] Trump kept a consistent narrative frame of classic horror throughout his televised campaign advertisements, creating monstrous threats and consistent attempts at positive audience efficacy. Understanding these advertisements through a primarily classic horror lens helps deepen understanding of the fear appeals and corresponding efficacy appeals deployed heavily throughout the Trump campaign's televised narrative.

Classic Horror Framing of Immigrants

Trump's first general election campaign advertisement, "Two Americas Immigration," which first aired on August 19, 2016, sets up one of Trump's perceived threats to America: illegal immigration.[99] The ad equates Clinton with a system that "stays rigged against Americans" where masses of immigrants and refugees are shown, darkly shaded.[100] The narrator uses disaster language when describing how "Syrian refugees flood in."[101] Jumping from refugees to immigrants, the narrator says, "illegal immigrants convicted of committing crimes get to stay" as blurred-faced immigrants are being incarcerated by police officers.[102] The narrator continues, predicting, "Our border open, it's more of the same but worse" as footage plays of people riding on liquid-container train cars.[103] As an image of Clinton fades out, Trump's alternative solution is shown in the second half of the commercial. The ad argues that "Donald Trump's America is secure" as images are shown of helicopters patrolling the border.[104] Then, a Black American family is shown looking at an American flag as the narrator says, "Our families safe" before an image of a large U.S. Navy vessel is depicted with the text "MAKE AMERICA SAFE AGAIN!" on the screen.[105] Notably, the narrator uses a stern, ominous tone during the first half of the ad, before lightening up when describing Trump's America.[106] This contrast works well to elicit the audio cues of horror that Glenn W. Richardson Jr. argues as evoked through a "deep and serious" narrating tone.[107]

The first half of this advertisement establishes immigration as an existential threat to America, with refugees and illegal immigrants as a monstrous other invading from a spatially separated land. All of this bluntly uses the classic horror frame as a tool of fear creation. The framing of immigrants, as masses ride what could be identified as hazardous waste train cars, suggests impurities threatening "true" America. This view aligns with J. David Cisneros's critical understanding that "immigrants are framed visually and metaphorically, using similar representational strategies, as dangerous and destructive pollutants."[108] Cisneros ultimately observes, "Very few images of immigrants being apprehended by border officials show the immigrants' faces."[109] This is certainly the case for Trump's ad, as immigrants are framed from behind or their faces are blurred when being brought into custody.[110] This visual metaphor of immigrants as pollutants, absent a humanizing visage, allows a rendering of otherized monstrosity evocative of the classic horror frame. Understood from this perspective, Clinton and the presently corrupted America are the villains letting the monstrous in, much like Victor Frankenstein and the creation of his monster.[111]

The second half of the advertisement shows how Trump will defeat this supposedly monstrous other: strengthened border security and military operations. This is in line with the "strategies of deterrence," defined by

Anne Demo as "an infusion of 'enforcement resources' such as Border Patrol agents, fencing, lighting, and surveillance technology" in the hope that such efforts "will make illegal entry appear 'futile' to would-be migrants."[112] The upbeat soundtrack and lighting make an attempt at a strong efficacy appeal. The clear delineation between threat and resolution, without intermixing throughout the ad, helps to narratively create the high threat and high efficacy that Kim Witte argues can lead to "adaptive responses."[113] Thus, Trump gives his visual argument for how to defeat the "horror" of illegal immigration.

"Laura," which was originally broadcast on October 19, 2016, again isolates immigrants as monstrous, but moves them from the category of pollutant as in "Two Americas Immigration" to posit them as gruesomely violent.[114] This ad features Laura Wilkerson, in a personal testimony style advertisement,[115] retelling the horrific account of "an illegal alien" who murdered her son, Joshua.[116] She retells the gruesome details of his murder, saying, "The killer hit him on the head with a closet rod so hard that it broke in four pieces, and then he took him to a field and he doused him with gasoline and set him on fire."[117] While none of these viscerally affective details are visually shown, the verbal description given by the distressed, crying mother is sufficient to form a mental image.[118] Leaving the visual details to the mind's imagination can create an even more horrific effect, as Ivan Butler illustrates through analysis of Val Lewton's *Cat People* (1942),[119] where Lewton prefers to merely suggest the monstrous rather than make it visually explicit.[120] However, there remains an explicit visual cue of horror used through a prolonged, black-and-white shot of a picture of Joshua and his family. This black-and-white shot is one of the key signifiers of horror that Richardson identifies.[121]

The truly horrifying mental imagery of Joshua's murder, solidified through black-and-white filtering, is then linked to Clinton when Laura says, "Hillary Clinton's border policy is going to allow people into the country just like the one that murdered my son."[122] Once again, a relationship similar to *Frankenstein* is created in this classic horror frame. In the 1931 film adaptation, Dr. Frankenstein creates his evil monster in a decrepit manor that is spatially separated from normalcy. The monster then escapes, wreaking havoc on the purity of the mundane townspeople by killing a young girl and threatening others.[123] The Trump campaign makes an analogous claim arguing that the truly monstrous are illegal immigrants, and the one creating and releasing this monstrous problem into "innocent" America is Hillary Clinton through her border policies.

"Choice," which was first televised on November 1, 2016, returns to the story of two Americas once again—a dominant theme throughout Trump's television narrative.[124] The advertisement contrasts Clinton's America, which employs some of the same imagery from earlier ads, with Trump's America, which features large crowds and the same shot of a Navy vessel from

"Two Americas Immigration."[125] However, the visually horrific imagery is enhanced in the first half of the advertisement. First, horizontal straight-line distortions are used,[126] mirroring Clinton's "Who We Are" advertisement.[127] This, once again, is evocative of the German Expressionism of *The Cabinet of Dr. Caligari*.[128] Another shot of a border officer arresting a faceless immigrant is featured, followed by a U.S. flag burning and surrounded by signs with Arabic writing on them.[129] These classically framed horror images are meant to stoke the fires of fear in the voters and to make the explicit link between Hillary Clinton and the existential threats of immigrants and terrorists. The visual depictions conflate immigrants and terrorists. As before, a clear vision of Trump's America is laid out as the avenue toward slaying the monstrous and ending the bracketed time of American downturn, again attempting to instill a sense of audience efficacy.

Trump's final televised campaign ad, "Donald Trump's Argument for America," which was first aired on November 4, 2016, again poignantly highlights immigration as a monstrous threat. The ad mentions "massive illegal immigration" with another faceless immigrant being arrested by border control.[130] This, and the other threats the ad ties together, are blamed as a creation of the Obama administration, directly implicating Clinton as his secretary of state. Trump then calls for mob action against this monstrous corruption, saying, "The only thing that can stop this corrupt machine is you. The only force strong enough to save our country is us. The only people brave enough to vote out this corrupt establishment is you, the American people. I'm doing this for the people and for the movement and we will take back this country for you and we will make America great again."[131] These words are shown over large crowds of Trump supporters. The crowds are reminiscent of mob justice, often an expedient for killing the monster in classic horror films such as *Frankenstein* and *The Wolf Man* (1941).[132] This type of imagery attempts to invoke efficacy through an invitation to the country to join with Trump as he leads his crusade against the monstrous threats to America. Thus, a horror narrative is formed, combining fear, with a specific policy to combat the fear, with an appeal to the audience to join in the fight.

Classic Horror Framing of Economic Decline

The next main threat that Trump's ads construct is that of a decaying economy. He creates this fear appeal again with the theme of two Americas, this time focusing on the economy in these temporally separated Americas. "Two Americas: Economy" initially aired on August 29, 2016, opens with a shadowy shot of Clinton overlooking a dark Capitol Building.[133] This imagery already mentally elicits a decayed manor, like that used in classic gothic horror.[134] The horror framing suggests that audiences recall the hidden, Frankensteinian deeds of a corrupt national government, spearheaded by Hillary Clinton. The narrator argues, "In Hillary Clinton's America, the middle class gets crushed" as an image of a concerned father is shown consoling his son.[135] The narrator continues by claiming, "Hundreds of thousands of jobs disappear" while a decaying factory is seen fenced off with a chain and lock.[136] This locked fence performs the role of synecdoche, representing decline that extends beyond this single, "fireless" factory to the broader decay of American manufacturing and the economy.[137]

The second half of this ad then immediately lightens up the imagery as Trump is shown shaking hands with workers, while happy families and small business owners appear.[138] Once again, the monstrous decay of a corrupt, bracketed America is juxtaposed with the campaign promise of "Make America Great Again!" that is shown prominently at the end of the advertisement.[139] These jovial images utilize the other end of synecdoche, associating the preferred candidate with "happy families."[140] This clear division between the two Americas aims to create audience efficacy, showing who/what is monstrous and who the savior should be.

"Choice," analyzed in the previous section, also includes horrific imagery that bolsters Clinton's connection to the decaying economy. The vertical line distortion this ad deploys is layered onto a darkly shaded picture of Clinton in front of a chain-link fence of a closed factory.[141] Such imagery again reifies economic decay through synecdoche. This horrific image of Clinton is then followed with another darkly shaded shot focused on an apparently distressed woman. She waits in a long line with many other similarly crestfallen people, overwhelmed by their present predicament.[142] The text and narration of "FEWER JOBS" make the connection between unemployment and personalized horror.[143] This ad once again contrasts the positive America of Trump with the negative, horrifying America of Clinton. This divide is meant to make the electoral choice easy for Americans, especially when combined with positive efficacy appeals. There is a monstrous evil on one side and a savior on the other.

Trump's final televised campaign ad, "Donald Trump's Argument for America," returns to the issue of economic decline. The ad argues that the economy has been "bled . . . dry" by "disastrous trade deals" and economic policy brokered by the Establishment.[144] This wording clearly posits the Establishment, headed by Clinton, as vampiric entities like Dracula, draining the blood of the once healthy American economy through corrupt trade deals.[145] The horror wording of "bled our country dry" is accompanied with a very darkly shaded outline of America, with dollar bills draining out the bottom of the country, as if the economic jugular of the country had been slit and left to bleed out.[146]

The ad once again makes the move toward associating decaying factories with Clinton. A shot of Hillary and Bill Clinton is quickly followed by shaded shots of a locked chain-link fence, an abandoned factory floor, and a crumbling brick factory with birds roosting and flying, all evocative of gothic horror manors (see figure 6.2).[147] The inclusion of birds in the shot helps amplify the classically horrific framing of the economy, through an association of birds with horror made famous by Alfred Hitchcock's *The Birds* (1963).[148]

Additionally, positioning the arguments for the country's economic decline in the context of foreign trade deals continues the classic horror framing of spatially separated horror articulated by Caroline Joan (Kay) S. Picart and David A. Frank.[149] Numerous dimly lit shots of Clinton shaking hands with foreign dignitaries are used throughout this ad.[150] Usually, foreign diplomacy would be considered a positive aspect of a potential presidential candidate. Here, however, this notion is inverted as Clinton is portrayed as allowing foreign entities to drain the American economy, paralleling a Dracula-like figure, framed as an explicitly foreign, eastern menace.[151] Further, when Trump blames other nations for stealing America's manufacturing jobs, we see a shot of Asian factory workers wearing disposable sanitization masks, elevating anxieties over foreign diseases.[152]

Many of the ads analyzed throughout this chapter rely on different types of horror framing. Yet, this ad might be the exemplar of the horror genre because of its heavy allusions to various classic horror elements (e.g., vampires, decay, birds, etc.). The Trump campaign's efforts to frame the economy through classic horror tropes combine with attempts to elicit mob justice to

Figure 6.2 *Dracula* **(1931).** Screenshot captured by author.

create a narrative call to action: reform the corrupted, foreign, monstrous economy that is hurting everyday Americans.

The Trump Campaign's Horror Framing of Clinton and the Establishment

The preceding analysis has focused on Trump's construction of illegal immigration and a decaying economy as classically framed, external threats to America. Within this analysis, it was clear that these threats were also explicitly connected to Hillary Clinton. However, Trump also deployed ads that made Clinton monstrous in and of herself, transforming her image from that of a demon, to the devil herself—the center of hell/the Establishment.

"Deplorables" is the first ad by Trump that focuses more on Clinton than an external threat.[153] This advertisement, released on September 12, 2016, relies on Clinton's comment that "You could put half of Trump's supporters into what I call the Basket of Deplorables."[154] This type of attack ad is similar to the bulk of Clinton's campaign attack ads, using what on the surface appears to be a conflicted lens of Clinton as misguided. However, the strength of the language used in the last statement, over an image of a shadowy Clinton, attempts to move this ad into the classic horror frame. The narrator asks and answers the following question: "You know what's deplorable? Hillary Clinton *viciously demonizing* hard working people like you."[155] The ad relies on the classic horror genre by describing Clinton in animalistic terms, calling her vicious, and depicting her actions as demonic.

The "Predators" ad mirrors many of the attack ads that Clinton made against Trump, showing the derogatory things Clinton has said against Black Americans, Bernie Sanders supporters, and Trump supporters.[156] The ad, which originally aired on October 19, 2016, shows Clinton saying Black American youth are "super predators," Sanders supporters live "in their parents' basement," and Trump supporters are "deplorables."[157] All of these depictions fit well into a similar conflicted frame, like that used by the Clinton campaign, where Hillary Clinton is portrayed as a misguided, hurtful person. However, the imagery of Clinton, particularly the last shot, makes her look more monstrous than the narrative of the ad suggests. The last shot is colored in black and white and is extremely unflattering, showing Clinton with her mouth open as if she is about to bite someone,[158] again framing her in a classically horrific way similar to that of *Dracula* or *The Wolf Man*.[159] While the commercial uses the conflicted frame more than Trump's other advertisements, the imagery of Clinton is still shaded in a classically horrific manner.

"Unfit (R)," which was first televised on November 3, 2016, ramps the horror imagery up to a new level, targeting Clinton directly.[160] The ad is focused on Clinton once again coming under FBI investigation because of her connections to the "pervert Anthony Weiner's laptop."[161] The news of another FBI investigation and email scandal in the closing days of the campaign were disastrous for Clinton and "many of her supporters say [it] was responsible for her election defeat."[162] "Unfit (R)" uses potentially the heaviest horror framing analyzed in this work to reach maximum fear appeal potential. The background music in the ad is extremely foreboding, every image of Hillary is heavily shaded to the point of being nearly unrecognizable, and she is pictured in front of a pyramid, a shadowy White House, and a dimly lit Capitol Building, all the while blood-red text is displayed over her.[163]

"Unfit (R)" alludes to a plethora of classic horror concepts and films including decaying manors,[164] blood,[165] *The Mummy* (1932)[166] and even the Illuminati[167] through its use of dark shading, blood-red text, and a seemingly random inclusion of a pyramid in the background. However, Egyptian mythology has deep roots in the horror genre. Kendall R. Phillips describes how horror "films utilized Egyptian mythology in crafting weird tales" given the "Orientalist association between Egypt and the supernatural."[168] Thus, mysticism and conspiracy mix with horror to frame Clinton as inhuman monstrosity. This spot, the final one before Trump's two-minute closing pitch, takes all the classic horror framing, which has been largely aimed at existential threats to America like immigration and the economy, and focuses it on the "evil" Clinton.

Trump's final televised campaign ad, "Donald Trump's Argument for America," takes all of the horrors built up throughout his campaign and aims them squarely at the "political establishment."[169] This advertisement is loaded with distortion transitions between different images of Hillary Clinton and other Establishment members such as President Obama, President Bill Clinton, the Federal Reserve, and the United Nations.[170] This horror imagery is explicitly tied together with the construed threats of immigration and the "economic foreign policies that have bled our country dry."[171] These horrific threats are used to cast Clinton and the Establishment as both monstrous in and of themselves and monstrous as the creators of more monsters. With the call for mob justice in this advertisement, attempts at audience efficacy are given in the face of comprehensive fear appeals.

The Trump Campaign's Appeals to Audience Efficacy

"Movement," which initially aired on September 20, 2016, is almost purely a positive TV spot, using epideictic praise of Trump.[172] Much of the same imagery from the positive halves of "Two Americas Immigration" and "Two Americas: Economy" are reused, creating narrative consistency in the plan Trump has for America. The one-line attack on Clinton is telling of the larger classic horror framing. The narrator says, "Leaving the past behind" as an image of Hillary and Bill Clinton (from Bill Clinton's Lewinsky scandal) is shown on an old television.[173] This works to temporally separate the monstrous Clinton family from Trump's vision of a great American future. Additionally, this advertisement, when viewed in the larger narrative of the television campaign as a whole, helps strengthen a narrative of efficacy through the horror message of how Trump will slay the monster.

"Motherhood" focuses on Ivanka Trump offering personal, epideictic testimony to Donald Trump's capacity for improving the economic conditions of mothers and families.[174] The commercial, which was released on September 30, 2016, is entirely positive, with no attacks made. Further, the TV spot utilizes no readily apparent horror elements. This ad is also the most in-depth spot by either campaign on a specific policy. Ivanka Trump argues, "My father will change outdated labor laws so that they support women and American families. He will provide tax credits for childcare, paid maternity leave, and dependent care savings accounts. This will allow women to support their families, and further their careers."[175] This ad attempts a two-fold narrative. First, it positions Trump as the hero who will vanquish the monstrously sexist economy. Second, this commercial is clearly meant to rebut Clinton's arguments that Trump is a misogynist, a charge featured prominently in her own television campaign. This two-fold nature, bolstered by concrete policy promises, makes this ad a vital piece in the overall narrative of the Trump television campaign.

"United," released on November 2, 2016, is another purely positive, epideictic campaign ad that shows Trump's vision for America through specific policy proposals.[176] These proposals all feed into the narrative that Trump will "Make America Great Again."[177] The policies listed include, "Up to $5,000 in Childcare Tax Credits," "Law and Order," "Justice and Fairness," and "America Respected Again."[178] These specific policies work to make the positive efficacy of the audience clearer. While largely devoid of horror elements, the use of images of large crowds, as has been seen in many of Trump's other ads, is again notable in the context of classic horror framing as a method for eliciting mob response, one potential avenue for amassing voters.[179]

Throughout Trump's campaign, there is a very clear inclination toward using the classic horror frame over the conflicted horror frame. Early in the campaign, there are brief moments where Clinton is partially framed through a conflicted lens, more demon than the devil. But this shifts by the time "Deplorables" is aired on September 12, 2016, putting her at the center of the evils facing America. Further, Trump demonizes two existential threats to America: immigrants and the economy. Both, as Trump argues, are dangerous because of the spatially separated, foreign other. Trump, throughout the entirety of his campaign, brackets the time in which America is not great, looking to continue the normal flow of time by making America great once more. Finally, even though Trump relies heavily on the classic horror frame and fear, he includes a number of positive advertisements. Even Trump's negative ads typically contain a positive, policy-focused conclusion. These themes effectively demonstrate the classic horror frame, which requires positive efficacy to slay the monster and return everything to normalcy. Thus, Trump maintained a highly consistent and focused narrative frame of classic horror throughout his televised campaign advertisements, utilizing threat construction and attempts at positive audience efficacy.

CONCLUSION

As we now know, Donald Trump defeated Hillary Clinton for the presidency in a tightly contested race. Whether either candidate's horror narratives were effective with the American voter audience is still to be determined. However, as this analysis demonstrates, Clinton and Trump took quite different approaches to their respective ads. As I have argued, analysis by horror frame allows us to better understand foundational differences between the campaigns' approaches to electoral persuasion. It suggests important distinctions between the campaign ads, and how their messages were constructed via elements of horror. Horror analysis is invited by the ads themselves, as many of them clearly utilize distinct elements of the genre, such as audio cues, visual cues, and thematic allusions. This analysis revealed that the Trump campaign attempted to horrifically articulate a reason to vote for Trump, whereas Clinton's campaign only seemed to articulate a reason to vote against Trump. Nevertheless, the sheer magnitude of horror framing in this campaign—both quantitatively and qualitatively—exemplify the normative and omnipresent dynamics of horror framing in contemporary campaign advertising.

The Trump campaign consistently used classic horror framing, combined with consistent appeals to audience efficacy. The Clinton campaign, conversely, deployed conflicted and classic frames with minimal appeals to audience efficacy. This analysis is important because it has revealed just how prevalent horror genre elements were in this campaign. Richardson argues that such a generic understanding is crucial in understanding what "glues the components of compelling narratives together."[180] Thus, the examination here has worked to understand how the horror genre was used in differing ways to maintain each campaign's narrative coherence. Trump's glue consisted of monsters and himself as savior. Clinton's glue was primarily Trump's deep flaws.

Clinton was very attack-heavy throughout her campaign ads, wavering between conflicted horror framing and classic horror framing, but tending to favor the conflicted frame. Her conflicted horror frames typically surfaced when she discussed uncivil statements issued by Trump, whereas her classic horror framing was present when discussing Trump as a warmonger. However, as her campaign progressed, Clinton's ads were better characterized as employing the conflicted horror framing rather than the classic frame. She also very rarely ran positive ads and presented few concrete policy positions as remedies to the conflicted monster she rhetorically created. Additionally, her calls to action against the monster were often fractured along demographic lines, steering clear from attempting a mob response to horror.

Conversely, Trump generously employed heavy-handed classic horror framing to instill a fear of both existential threats—namely immigration and the economy—and Hillary Clinton and the Establishment. Even with this strong dose of threat construction through classically horrific frames, Trump's campaign was noticeably more self-praising than Clinton's, with entire ads devoted to epideictic exaltation of Trump and a more explicit explanation of his specific policy proposals. Trump further attempted to evoke positive audience efficacy in response to his fear appeals through a call for mob response, reminiscent of classic horror films such as *Frankenstein* and *The Wolf Man*.[181] Thus, "[w]ith the monster vanquished, normal time returns."[182] In Trump's vision, this normal time is where America is great once again.

This analysis illustrates not only that these horror framing elements were deployed in the 2016 presidential campaign advertising, but also offers an opportunity to better apprehend *how* these elements were deployed. Jamieson argues that narrative consistency is essential.[183] Trump's television campaign was highly consistent in its narrative messaging, while Clinton's was far less so. Another important aspect, examined by Witte, is the use of fear appeals,[184] with classic horror framing creating a completely monstrous other and conflicted horror framing creating something to fear, but also something that is mundane.[185] Trump's campaign almost exclusively used classic horror framing, whereas Clinton's relied far more on the conflicted frame, with some deviances. However, as Hart and Feldman have claimed, simply scaring the audience often isn't the only goal of a persuader. Attempting to instill a high level of perceived efficacy is one important way fear appeal ads try to make the audience act.[186] Trump's campaign prominently featured messages of audience efficacy, of joining the mob. Clinton's campaign, on the other hand, showed few positive messages and calls for efficacy. Those rare Clinton ads that did aim for audience action were demographically segmented, intermixed with negativity, and ran relatively late in the campaign. These characteristics and methods of horrific campaign advertising can and should be applied when analyzing other televised campaign ads from all levels of the political arena, since horror and fear appeals are so central to political efforts. However, the presidential ads of the 2016 election could very well be the exemplar of campaigns that diverge significantly in their usage of differing horror frames. While it is unclear what role advertising played in the historically negative views of both candidates on election night,[187] the overwhelmingly polarizing and demonic elements of this election at least attempted to push voters in that direction.

NOTES

1. Copyright © 2019 by Michigan State University. Portions of this chapter originally appeared as an article in *Rhetoric & Public Affairs* 22, no. 2 (2019): 281–322.
2. Lydia Saad, "Trump and Clinton Finish with Historically Poor Images," *Gallup*. November 8, 2016, http://news.gallup.com/poll/197231/trump-clinton-finish-historically-poor-images.aspx.
3. Gregory Wallace, "Voter Turnout at 20-year Low in 2016," *CNN*, November 30, 2016, https://www.cnn.com/2016/11/11/politics/popular-vote-turnout-2016/index.html.
4. Pew Research Center, "4. Top Voting Issues in 2016 Election," *Pew Research Center*, July 7, 2016, http://www.people-press.org/2016/07/07/4-top-voting-issues-in-2016-election/.
5. Pew Research Center, "4. Top Voting Issues."
6. Pew Research Center, "4. Top Voting Issues."
7. Pew Research Center, "4. Top Voting Issues."
8. "Donald Trump and Hillary Clinton's Final Campaign Spending Revealed," *The Guardian*, December 9, 2016, https://www.theguardian.com/us-news/2016/dec/09/trump-and-clintons-final-campaign-spending-revealed.
9. Prashanth Bhat, Alyson Farzad-Phillips, Morgan Hess, Lauren Hunter, Nora Murphy, Claudia Serrano Rico, Kyle Stephan, Gareth Williams, and Shawn Parry-Giles, "Campaign Advertising 2016: Referendum on Character," *Center for Political Communication and Civic Leadership*, 5.
10. Hillary for America, "Who We Are," *The Living Room Candidate: Presidential Campaign Commercials 1952–2020*, June 6, 2016, http://www.livingroomcandidate.org/commercials/2016/who-we-are.
11. Hillary, "Who We Are."
12. Hillary, "Who We Are."
13. Hillary, "Who We Are."
14. Hillary, "Who We Are."
15. Hillary, "Who We Are."
16. Hillary, "Who We Are."

17. Hillary, "Who We Are."
18. Hillary, "Who We Are."
19. Harry M. Benshoff, "Horror Before 'The Horror Film,'" in *A Companion to the Horror Film*, ed. Harry M. Benshoff (New York: Wiley Blackwell, 2014), 216.
20. Lotte H. Eisner, *The Haunted Screen: Expressionism in the German Cinema and the Influence of Max Reinhardt* (Berkeley: University of California Press, 1965), 21.
21. Hillary, "Who We Are."
22. Hillary for America, "Sacrifice," *The Living Room Candidate: Presidential Campaign Commercials 1952–2020*, September 9, 2016, http://www.livingroomcandidate.org/commercials/2016/sacrifice.
23. Hillary, "Sacrifice."
24. "Confidence in Institutions," *Gallup*, n.d., https://news.gallup.com/poll/1597/confidence-institutions.aspx.
25. Hillary, "Sacrifice."
26. Steffen Hantke, "Science Fiction and Horror in the 1950s," in *A Companion to the Horror Film*, ed. Harry M. Benshoff (New York: Wiley Blackwell, 2014), 259; *Tarantula*, directed by Jack Arnold (1955; Universal Studios Home Entertainment, 2013), DVD.
27. Hantke, "Science Fiction and Horror," 262.
28. Hillary for America, "Low Opinion," *The Living Room Candidate: Presidential Campaign Commercials 1952–2020*, September 13, 2016, http://www.livingroomcandidate.org/commercials/2016/low-opinion.
29. Hillary, "Low Opinion."
30. Hillary, "Low Opinion."
31. Hillary, "Low Opinion."
32. Kathleen Hall Jamieson, *Packaging the Presidency: A History and Criticism of Presidential Campaign Advertising* (New York: Oxford University Press, 1984), 448.
33. Hillary for America, "Mirrors," *The Living Room Candidate: Presidential Campaign Commercials 1952–2020*, September 23, 2016, http://www.livingroomcandidate.org/commercials/2016/mirrors.
34. Hillary, "Who We Are."
35. Hillary for America, "Just One," *The Living Room Candidate: Presidential Campaign Commercials 1952–2020*, August 22, 2016, http://www.livingroomcandidate.org/commercials/2016/just-one.
36. Mark Jancovich, "Gender, Sexuality, and the Horror Film," in *Horror, the Film Reader*, ed. Mark Jancovich (London: Routledge, 2002), 57.
37. Daniel Humphrey, "Gender and Sexuality Haunt the Horror Film," in *A Companion to the Horror Film*, ed. Harry M. Benshoff (New York: Wiley Blackwell, 2014), 91.
38. Hillary For America, "Respected," *The Living Room Candidate: Presidential Campaign Commercials 1952–2020*, October 10, 2016, http://www.livingroomcandidate.org/commercials/2016/respected.
39. Jamieson, *Packaging the Presidency*, 450.
40. Jamieson, *Packaging the Presidency*, 450.

41. Hillary, "Respected."
42. Hillary for America, "Captain Kahn," *The Living Room Candidate: Presidential Campaign Commercials 1952–2020*, October 21, 2016, http://www.livingroomcandidate.org/commercials/2016/captain-kahn.
43. Hillary, "Captain Kahn."
44. Hillary, "Captain Kahn."
45. Benshoff, "Horror Before 'The Horror Film,'" 216.
46. Hillary for America, "We Are America," *The Living Room Candidate: Presidential Campaign Commercials 1952–2020*, November 3, 2020, http://www.livingroomcandidate.org/commercials/2016/we-are-america.
47. Hillary, "We Are America."
48. Hillary, "We Are America."
49. Hillary, "We Are America."
50. Hillary, "We Are America."
51. Hillary for America, "Unfit (D)," *The Living Room Candidate: Presidential Campaign Commercials 1952–2020*, August 5, 2016, http://www.livingroomcandidate.org/commercials/2016/unfit-d.
52. Hillary, "Unfit (D)."
53. Hillary, "Unfit (D)."
54. Hillary, "Unfit (D)."
55. Hillary, "Unfit (D)."
56. Hillary, "Unfit (D)."
57. See Vivian Sobchack, "American Science Fiction Film: An Overview," in *A Companion to Science Fiction*, ed. David Seed (Malden, MA: Blackwell Publishing, 2005), 262; *War of the Worlds*, directed by Byron Haskin (1953; Paramount Pictures, 1999), DVD; and *Them!*, directed by Gordon Douglas (1954; Warner Brothers Pictures, 2020), DVD.
58. Hillary, "Just One."
59. Hillary, "Just One."
60. Hillary, "Just One."
61. Hillary, "Just One."
62. Hillary, "Just One."
63. Eisner, *The Haunted Screen*, 21.
64. See Rosemary Jackson, *Fantasy: The Literature of Subversion* (London: Methuen, 1981), 179; and Horace Walpole, *The Castle of Otranto* (Edinburgh: James Ballantyne & Co., 1811). Walpole's *The Castle of Otranto* is widely considered the literary foundation of the gothic horror genre, using a gothic castle as its primary setting. This setting, a decrepit castle or manor, became a foundational setting element of classic horror. See David Punter and Glennis Byron, *The Gothic* (Malden, MA: Blackwell, 2004) and "The Castle of Otranto: The Creepy Tale that Launched Gothic Fiction," *BBC News*, December 13, 2014, https://www.bbc.com/news/magazine-30313775.
65. *Frankenstein*, directed by James Whale (1931; Universal Studios Home Entertainment, 2016), DVD.

66. Hillary for America, "Daisy," *The Living Room Candidate: Presidential Campaign Commercials 1952–2020*, October 31, 2016, http://www.livingroomcandidate.org/commercials/2016/daisy.

67. Hillary, "Daisy."

68. Democratic National Committee, "Peace Little Girl (Daisy)," September 7, 1964, http://www.livingroomcandidate.org/commercials/1964/peace-little-girl-daisy.

69. Democratic National Committee, "Peace Little Girl."

70. Ashley Killough, "The 'Daisy' Spot and Five Other Compelling Political Ads," *CNN*, September 7, 2014, https://www.cnn.com/2014/09/07/politics/political-ads/index.html.

71. Hillary, "Daisy."

72. Hillary, "Daisy."

73. *The Curse of Frankenstein*, directed by Terence Fisher (1957; Horrortheque, 2010), Digital.

74. *Bram Stoker's Dracula*, directed by Francis Ford Coppola (1992; Sony Pictures, 2017), DVD.

75. Hillary for America, "Role Models," *The Living Room Candidate: Presidential Campaign Commercials 1952–2020*, July 7, 2016, http://www.livingroomcandidate.org/commercials/2016/role-models.

76. Hillary, "Role Models."

77. Hillary, "Role Models."

78. Julian Petley, "Horror and the Censors," in *A Companion to the Horror Film*, ed. Harry M. Benshoff (New York: Wiley Blackwell, 2014), 130.

79. Humphrey, "Gender and Sexuality," 48; *The Exorcist*, directed by William Friedkin (1973; Warner Bros., 2011), DVD.

80. Hillary, "Role Models."

81. Humphrey, "Gender and Sexuality," 48.

82. Caroline Joan (Kay) S. Picart and David A. Frank, *Frames of Evil: The Holocaust as Horror in American Film* (Carbondale: Southern Illinois University Press, 2006): 141.

83. Hillary, "Who We Are."

84. Bruce E. Gronbeck, "Negative Narratives in 1988 Presidential Campaign Ads," *Quarterly Journal of Speech* 78, no. 3 (1992): 337.

85. Hillary for America, "Barbershop," *The Living Room Candidate: Presidential Campaign Commercials 1952–2020*, October 24, 2016, http://www.livingroomcandidate.org/commercials/2016/barbershop.

86. Hillary, "Barbershop."

87. Hillary, "Barbershop."

88. P. Sol Hart and Lauren Feldman, "Threat Without Efficacy? Climate Change on U.S. Network News," *Science Communication* 36, no. 3 (2014): 341.

89. Hillary for America, "27 Million Strong," *The Living Room Candidate: Presidential Campaign Commercials 1952–2020*, November 2, 2016, http://www.livingroomcandidate.org/commercials/2016/27-million-strong.

90. Hillary, "27 Million Strong."

91. Hillary, "27 Million Strong."
92. Hillary for America, "Tomorrow," *The Living Room Candidate: Presidential Campaign Commercials 1952–2020*, November 7, 2016, http://www.livingroomcandidate.org/commercials/2016/tomorrow.
93. Hillary, "Tomorrow."
94. Hillary, "Tomorrow."
95. Hillary, "Tomorrow."
96. Hillary, "Tomorrow."
97. Pamela Engel, "How Trump Came Up with His Slogan 'Make America Great Again,'" *Business Insider*, January 18, 2017, http://www.businessinsider.com/trump-makeamerica-great-again-slogan-history-2017-1.
98. Picart and Frank, *Frames of Evil*, 7.
99. Donald J. Trump for President, "Two Americas Immigration," *The Living Room Candidate: Presidential Campaign Commercials 1952–2020*, August 19, 2016, http://www.livingroomcandidate.org/commercials/2016/two-americas-immigration.
100. Trump, "Two Americas Immigration."
101. Trump, "Two Americas Immigration."
102. Trump, "Two Americas Immigration."
103. Trump, "Two Americas Immigration."
104. Trump, "Two Americas Immigration."
105. Trump, "Two Americas Immigration."
106. Trump, "Two Americas Immigration."
107. Glenn W. Richardson Jr., *Pulp Politics: How Political Advertising Tells the Stories of American Politics* (Lanham, MD: Rowman & Littlefield, 2008), 39.
108. J. David Cisneros, "Contaminated Communities: The Metaphor of 'Immigrant as Pollutant' in Media Representations of Immigration," *Rhetoric & Public Affairs* 11, no. 4 (2008): 570.
109. Cisneros, "Contaminated Communities," 588.
110. Trump, "Two Americas Immigration."
111. *Frankenstein*, Whale.
112. Anne Demo, "Sovereignty Discourse and Contemporary Immigration Politics," *Quarterly Journal of Speech* 91, no. 3 (2005): 296.
113. Kim Witte, "Putting the Fear Back into Fear Appeals: The Extended Parallel Process Model," *Communication Monographs* 59, no. 4 (1992): 345.
114. Donald J. Trump for President, "Laura," *The Living Room Candidate: Presidential Campaign Commercials 1952–2020*, October 19, 2016, http://www.livingroomcandidate.org/commercials/2016/laura.
115. Jamieson, *Packaging the Presidency*, 450.
116. Trump, "Laura."
117. Trump, "Laura."
118. Trump, "Laura."
119. *Cat People*, directed by Jacques Tourneur (1942; Turner Home Entertainment, 2005), DVD.
120. Ivan Butler, *Horror in the Cinema* (Cranbury, NJ: A. S. Barnes and Company, 1979), 76.

121. Richardson, *Pulp Politics*, 39.
122. Trump, "Laura."
123. *Frankenstein*, Whale.
124. Donald J. Trump for President, "Choice," *The Living Room Candidate: Presidential Campaign Commercials 1952–2020*, November 1, 2016, http://www.livingroomcandidate.org/commercials/2016/choice.
125. Trump, "Choice."
126. Trump, "Choice."
127. Hillary, "Who We Are."
128. Benshoff, "Horror Before 'The Horror Film,'" 216.
129. Trump, "Choice."
130. Trump, "Donald Trump's Argument for America," *The Living Room Candidate: Presidential Campaign Commercials 1952–2020*, November 4, 2016, http://www.livingroomcandidate.org/commercials/2016/donald-trumps-argument-for-america.
131. Trump, "Donald Trump's Argument for America."
132. *Frankenstein*, Whale; *The Wolf Man*, directed by George Waggner (1941; Universal Studios Home Entertainment, 2016), DVD.
133. Donald J. Trump for America, "Two Americas: Economy," *The Living Room Candidate: Presidential Campaign Commercials 1952–2020*, August 29, 2016, http://www.livingroomcandidate.org/commercials/2016/two-americas-economy.
134. Jackson, *Fantasy*, 179.
135. Trump, "Two Americas: Economy."
136. Trump, "Two Americas: Economy."
137. Jamieson, *Packaging the Presidency*, 449.
138. Trump, "Two Americas: Economy."
139. Trump, "Two Americas: Economy."
140. Jamieson, *Packaging the Presidency*, 449.
141. Trump, "Choice."
142. Trump, "Choice."
143. Trump, "Choice."
144. Trump, "Donald Trump's Argument for America."
145. *Dracula*, directed by Tod Browning (1931; Peacock TV), Digital.
146. Trump, "Donald Trump's Argument for America."
147. Trump, "Donald Trump's Argument for America."
148. *The Birds*, directed by Alfred Hitchcock (1963; Universal Studios Home Entertainment, 2014), DVD.
149. Picart and Frank, *Frames of Evil*, 7.
150. Trump, "Donald Trump's Argument for America."
151. *Dracula*, Tod Browning.
152. Trump, "Donald Trump's Argument for America."
153. Donald J. Trump for President, "Deplorables," *The Living Room Candidate: Presidential Campaign Commercials 1952–2020*, September 12, 2016, http://www.livingroomcandidate.org/commercials/2016/deplorables.
154. Trump, "Deplorables."

155. Trump, "Deplorables" (emphasis added).

156. Donald J. Trump for President, "Predators," *The Living Room Candidate: Presidential Campaign Commercials 1952–2020*, October 19, 2016, http://www.livingroomcandidate.org/commercials/2016/predators.

157. Donald J. Trump for President, "Predators."

158. Trump, "Predators."

159. See *Dracula*, Browning and *The Wolf Man*, Waggner.

160. Donald J. Trump for President, "Unfit (R)," *The Living Room Candidate: Presidential Campaign Commercials 1952–2020*, November 3, 2016, http://www.livingroomcandidate.org/commercials/2016/unfit-r.

161. Trump, "Unfit (R)."

162. "Hillary Clinton Email Probe—What Was It About?" *BBC News*, May 10, 2017, https://www.bbc.com/news/election-us-2016-37811529.

163. Trump, "Unfit (R)."

164. Jackson, *Fantasy*, 179.

165. See *Dracula*, Browning.

166. *The Mummy*, directed by Karl Freund (1932; Universal Studios Home Entertainment, 2016), DVD.

167. See L.L. Wynn, "Shape Shifting Lizard People, Israelite Slaves, and Other Theories of Pyramid Building," *Journal of Social Archaeology* 8, no. 2 (2008): 272–95.

168. Kendall R. Phillips, *A Place of Darkness: The Rhetoric of Horror in Early American Cinema* (Austin: University of Texas Press, 2018), 77.

169. Trump, "Donald Trump's Argument for America."

170. Trump, "Donald Trump's Argument for America."

171. Trump, "Donald Trump's Argument for America."

172. Donald J. Trump for President, "Movement," *The Living Room Candidate: Presidential Campaign Commercials 1952–2020*, September 20, 2016, http://www.livingroomcandidate.org/commercials/2016/movement.

173. Trump, "Movement."

174. Donald J. Trump for President, "Motherhood," *The Living Room Candidate: Presidential Campaign Commercials 1952–2020*, September 30, 2016, http://www.livingroomcandidate.org/commercials/2016/motherhood.

175. Trump, "Motherhood."

176. Donald J. Trump for President, "United," *The Living Room Candidate: Presidential Campaign Commercials 1952–2020*, November 2, 2016, http://www.livingroomcandidate.org/commercials/2016/united.

177. Trump, "United."

178. Trump, "United."

179. Trump, "United."

180. Glenn W. Richardson Jr., "Pulp Politics: Popular Culture and Political Advertising," *Rhetoric & Public Affairs* 3, no. 4 (2000): 617.

181. *Frankenstein*, Whale; *The Wolf Man*, Waggner.

182. Picart and Frank, *Frames of Evil*, 7.

183. Jamieson, *Packaging the Presidency*, 447.

184. Witte, "Putting the Fear Back," 331.

185. Steffen Hantke, "The Kingdom of the Unimaginable: The Construction of Social Space and the Fantasy of Privacy in Serial Killers Narratives," *Literature/Film Quarterly* 26, no. 3 (1998): 181.

186. Hart and Feldman, "Threat Without Efficacy," 341.

187. Saad, "Trump and Clinton Finish with Historically Poor Images."

Chapter 7

Donald Trump versus Joe Biden in the 2020 Election

The 2020 U.S. presidential election came at a time of great countrywide strife across a variety of issues. Incumbent Republican President Donald Trump faced off against Democratic challenger and former Vice President Joe Biden. While the 2016 election had been one of negativity from and toward both candidates, the 2020 election was a highly partisan contest where both candidates rallied their base and broke popular vote records.[1] Biden centered his campaign on the ongoing COVID-19 pandemic, which was spiking again at the time of the election and had killed 232,000 Americans by election day.[2] Interestingly, while Biden's primary issue of focus was the pandemic that was not the number one issue for Biden voters. As election exit polls bear out, the coronavirus pandemic was the second most important issue for Biden voters. The most important issue was racial inequality, with 92 percent of Biden voters saying it mattered most in deciding their vote compared to 81 percent for the pandemic.[3] These numbers highlight one of the other key contexts of the 2020 election: ongoing protests over police brutality toward Black people. In the wake of the killing of Black man George Floyd by police officers on May 25, 2020, large-scale protests, particularly from Black Lives Matter, were seen throughout the country. Counter-protests from white nationalist groups like the Proud Boys heightened racial tension within the country. It is against this backdrop of racial injustice and an ongoing, out-of-control pandemic that voters made their decision.

Issue positions for Republicans and Trump voters highlight the partisan nature of the election. Trump focused heavily on the economy, jobs, taxes, lawlessness, and the threat of Radical Left policies. This is borne out in exit polls among Republican voters, where the top issue was the economy at 83 percent. Crime and safety, a potential foil to racial inequality in the minds of conservative voters, garnered the next highest total at 71 percent. The

Table 7.1 Donald Trump and Joe Biden Campaign Advertisements' Airdates

Donald Trump		Joe Biden	
Airdate	Title	Airdate	Title
August 3, 2020	Progresista	July 21, 2020	Truth :60
August 3, 2020	Takeover	July 23, 2020	Crossroads
August 7, 2020	The Joe Biden They Are Hiding From You	July 30, 2020	Backbone
August 11, 2020	Meet Phony Kamala Harris!	August 5, 2020	It Is What It Is
August 13, 2020	Record Smashing	August 6, 2020	Better America
August 17, 2020	Don't Let Them Ruin America	August 8, 2020	Donald Trump Failed to Protect Us From COVID-19
August 17, 2020	Watch: Past vs Present	August 8, 2020	How to Build Back Better
August 17, 2020	47 Years of Failure	August 12, 2020	Kamala Harris: Vice President Announcement
August 20, 2020	America First! #MAGA	August 23, 2020	Trump's Boycott
September 24, 2020	Teleprompter Joe	August 28, 2020	Pero Ya No
October 5, 2020	Second Chance	September 8, 2020	Sacred
October 10, 2020	Carefully	October 9, 2020	Same Old
October 16, 2020	Biden Lied	October 20, 2020	Go from There
October 18, 2020	The Real Biden Plan	October 24, 2020	Make Life Better

lowest issue of importance for Trump voters was racial inequality at only seven percent, while the coronavirus was second lowest at 15 percent. This mirroring effect was nearly perfect for Biden voters as well, with the economy as the lowest ranked issue (17%) and crime and safety as the second lowest ranked issue (27%).[4] Accordingly, while both candidates had higher favorability ratings than the 2016 election, citizens were highly polarized along ideological lines, with Trump and Biden voters viewing issues from nearly opposite perspectives.

Given this contextual webbing of voter issues, this chapter analyzes the 2020 campaign ads (see table 7.1)[5] via horror framing. Trump returned to his 2016 strategy of using classic horror framing, usually to target terrorists, immigrants, women, and the Radical Left. However, unlike 2016 when the Trump campaign unleashed this classic frame on Clinton, Biden was largely targeted through a conflicted frame. According to this strategy, the horror of a Biden presidency centered on his mental aptitude and manipulability, both being deeply human flaws. Biden, on the other hand, used relatively tame elements of horror in his campaign. What horror elements he did use were usually conflicted. Many of the fear appeals of his ads were implicit and enthymematic. The Biden campaign seemed to be banking on voters being able to easily fill in the fears surrounding them with subtle reminders of the pandemic and national strife, allowing the Biden campaign to focus on self-positivity. The Biden campaign's televised advertisements were the least horrific since John Kerry's 2004 campaign.

TRUMP'S DUAL FRAMES: A CONFLICTED, MANIPULATED JOE BIDEN AND THE CLASSIC MONSTROSITIES OF TERRORISTS, IMMIGRANTS, WOMEN, AND THE RADICAL LEFT

I begin with a thorough analysis of Trump's general election presidential campaign advertisements. These ads bear out a clear strategy of questioning the mental aptitude and decision-making ability of Biden, while highlighting some of the same horrors from the 2016 campaign against Hillary Clinton. Many of the ads are structured in a similar way to 2016 as well, with the first half of many ads starting horrific before the second half makes appeals to audience efficacy through self-praise of Trump. There are some almost entirely self-positive ads as well, but the brunt of Trump's campaign and its narrative was framed through horror.

Trump's Classic and Conflicted Horrors

Originally aired on August 17, 2020, "47 Years of Failure" is an exemplar of how the Trump campaign mixed the frames of classic and conflicted horror within their 2020 advertisements.[6] The ad begins with a deep-voiced narrator saying, "Joe Biden, 47 years in Washington; 47 years of failure" as a shaded, depressed-looking Biden is presented.[7] The ad then quickly runs through some of Biden's purported failures, such as increased health care and drug prices, higher taxes, terrible trade deals, and the exportation of jobs. Each of these different failures is framed by a montage of dark images with the word "FAILURE" bolded over the image in an ominous shade of blue. Health care and drug prices are visually portrayed as a group of pill bottles, with one pill bottle knocked over. Taxes are linked with a man looking at a piece of paper in frustration, allowing the audience to enthymematically assume he is looking at his taxes in disgust. Disastrous trade deals are framed by Biden toasting China's President Xi Jinping.

With the issue of exportation of jobs, we begin to visually see the connection to classic horror. This Biden failure is visually established with a shot of a run-down, decrepit building that may have been an office or a factory. Windows are broken, and the building is just tall enough that it does not fit entirely in the frame. This run-down building strongly evokes gothic horror, which places a premium on abandoned, decrepit buildings. Gothic horror has always been influential to the horror genre in general, with a recent resurgence in films such as *Crimson Peak* (2015) and the Netflix series *The Haunting of Hill House* (2018) and its sequel, *The Haunting of Bly Manor* (2020).[8] This decrepitness is directly linked, verbally and textually, to China and Mexico, making such devastation foreign and other. As such, economic downturn and a loss of jobs are framed through a classic horror lens, with Biden as the failure who has allowed for such a haunting of America.

From here, "47 Years of Failure" frames Biden as susceptible to influence, a common theme throughout the Trump ads. Biden is shown in front of Radical Left leaders such as Bernie Sanders, Alexandria Ocasio-Cortez, and Ilhan Omar.[9] This positioning visually establishes these more left-leaning politicians as the evil masterminds behind Biden's turn toward "failed policies of the radical left."[10] As such, Sanders, Ocasio-Cortez, and Omar are portrayed through a more classic, monstrous fashion as brainwashers of Biden. It is worth noting that two of these politicians are women of color, as Trump and his campaign have established a theme of typically targeting opposition women with harsher horror framing than opposition men. This is an easy strategy since, as Bernadette Marie Calafell argues, "Women of color already embody monstrosity" in popular culture.[11] As such, this tropological framing is already primed for the primarily white audience Trump is targeting.

Once Biden is established as a pawn of the Radical Left, attacks on more leftist policies are again montaged with images that feature once more the bold, ominous blue text reading "FAILURE."[12] This new set of policy attacks are tax increases, "job-killing regulations," and "amnesty for illegal immigrants."[13] As such, Trump relies on a familiar toolset of threats, framing those horrors in similar ways to the 2016 campaign. "Job killing regulations" once again show a broken, abandoned building that is very evocative of dark horror settings. "Amnesty" is connected with two men, whose faces are obscured, climbing over a pile of dirt in the dark. This relies on nearly an identical visual argument as Trump's 2016 advertisement, "Two Americas Immigration," where immigrants are left faceless to dehumanize them into a monstrous, polluting threat.[14] The ad finishes with Biden looking clueless, as the narrator angrily states, "After 47 years of failure, we've had more than enough."[15] As such, "47 Years of Failure" deploys both the classic and conflicted horror frames. The classic horror frame is reserved for economic decline, immigration, and the Far Left while the conflicted horror frame is used to attack Biden as a foolish, failed, and manipulated puppet. While this is less outright horrific than the classic framings used in the ad, there is an implicit horror to such depictions of manipulability.

While "47 Years of Failure" was a clear exemplar of the Trump campaign's mixing of classic and conflicted horror, many of the ads released just before this advertisement were forming these argumentative threads. "Takeover," first aired on August 3, 2020, quickly establishes the connection between Biden and the Left, using a theme of a horrific lab.[16] The ad opens with a narrator saying, "Joe Biden has embraced the policies of the radical left" as images of Sanders, Ocasio-Cortez, and Omar are displayed. Ominous music plays as these four are visually shaded. The word "RADICAL" flickers electronically, much like a piece of horrific machinery one might find in Frankenstein's laboratory.[17]

Policies similar to those later expressed in "47 Years of Failure" are montaged, with electronic flashes acting as transitions between each visual. Taxes are the first to be attacked, as the ad shows a disembodied hand filling in a tax return form before transitioning to the same man that is used in "47 Years of Failure," looking over tax documents in despair.[18] A video shows Biden saying, "If you elect me . . . your taxes are gonna be raised, not cut."[19] Immigrants are again attacked next, as the same video that is reused in "47 Years of Failure" is displayed of faceless immigrants climbing over a dirt pile.[20] However, a unique clip is tagged on, showing what are presumably migrants climbing out of an inflatable raft. While their faces would be more visible, the combination of black-and-white distortion and a ghostly rendered text, "AMNESTY," distort the subjects' faces beyond recognition. Biden is then shown saying he would provide citizenship for "11 million undocumented folks" as text that reads "11 MILLION" electrically rattles like an old light bulb.[21] Police reform is the next policy that is attacked as the narrator notes that Biden wants to reduce police funding as a heavily shaded video is shown of someone throwing something at a glass wall separating the individual from riot police. Such scenes of civil unrest evoke mob-based horrors such as the recent *The Purge* (2013) film and subsequent sequels.[22]

Once these failed policies are established—many through classic horror framing—the meaning behind the title of the ad, "Takeover," is clarified. The same images as before of Biden, Sanders, Ocasio-Cortez, and Omar are shown. This time the words "RADICAL LEFT" are flickering at the top, as the narrator notes, "[T]he radical left has taken over Joe Biden and the Democratic Party."[23] A bright red flicker effect then transitions the background of the image to a distorted, ghost blue map of the United States, with the narrator continuing, "Don't let them take over America."[24]

"Takeover" deploys a few clear generic allusions to classic horror: body horror, possession, and invasion. While Biden's policies are framed through a classic horror lens, Biden himself is ultimately relieved of some culpability by the end of the advertisement as the narrator depicts an active takeover of his psyche by the Left. In some ways, this can be read like a body horror, where Radical Left policies are grafted onto Biden like a Frankensteinian or Cronenbergian monster.[25] This is audiovisually established through the flickering visual and audio effects reminiscent of a laboratory. Possession is another clear horror element at play, which is made visually apparent through the ghostly blue lettering and distortions. Classic horrors steeped in possession and supernatural meddling, such as *The Exorcist* (1973) and *Poltergeist* (1982), come readily to mind.[26] Finally, the last visual and narration allude to an invasion and takeover of the United States. This is frequently a component of classic horrors and science fiction that deal with aliens. One particularly good example for this generic allusion is *Invasion of the Body Snatchers* (1956), where aliens begin a takeover of an American town by possessing and duplicating the residents' bodies.[27] "Takeover" clearly establishes itself as a primarily classic horror advertisement, dealing heavily in the tropes of a number of horror subgenres. However, there is some conflicted horror in the sense that Biden is being unwittingly manipulated into committing supposedly heinous atrocities like granting amnesty to migrants.

Another ad that further develops this parasitic connection between Biden and the Left is "Meet Phony Kamala Harris!" This ad, which aired just over a week after "Takeover" on August 11, 2020, establishes a clearer connection between Biden and the Radical Left based on his association with vice presidential candidate Kamala Harris.[28] The ad opens with Harris waving as the narrator notes, "Kamala Harris ran for president by rushing to the radical left."[29] Her name is displayed in the middle of the shot as blue arrows pointing to the left reveal two separate texts saying, "radical left."[30] From this point, Harris's policies are attached to the Left. The ad places her next to Sanders and claims she embraced his "socialized medicine."[31] This tactic of connecting Biden and Harris with those who are viewed as having more extreme positions establishes guilt by association and apposition both visually and textually.[32] Harris's tax policy is criticized next, before the advertisement points out that Harris attacked Biden for "racist policies."[33] After establishing these criticisms, the narrator says, "Voters rejected Harris."[34] Up until this point in the ad, there hasn't been a significant amount of horror framing other than fear appeals to negative ideographs like the Radical Left.[35]

The ad starts to move into more subtle horror framing as the relationship between Harris and Biden is explored in more depth in the second half of the advertisement. Harris is described as a "phony" as that word appears over a shaded and distorted image of her. The narrator insinuates that voters recognized her as a phony, "but not Joe Biden. He's not that smart."[36] It is here that we once again get evocations of both the classic and conflicted horror frame. The classic is used against Harris as phony, once again evoking ideas of imposter takeovers like *Invasion of the Body Snatchers*. And much like how authorities and police officers are unable to recognize such an invasion is going on in the movie, Biden fulfills the role of a conflicted, unaware, institutionalized authority figure who unwittingly allows the invasion up until eventually succumbing to it.[37] This passive acquiescence is made clear when the narrator says, "Biden calls himself a transition candidate. He is handing over the reins to Kamala while they jointly embrace the radical left."[38] Here, the exact same images of Sanders, Ocasio-Cortez, and Omar are placed on the sides of Biden and Harris shaking hands, making clear that Harris is the leftist link between unwitting Biden and the monstrous Radical Left.

The ad ends by taking a jab at Biden's mental health, a problematic trope that has deep roots in the horror genre. Harris and Biden are pictured next to each other with vertical television distortions, as the narrator says, "Slow Joe and Phony Kamala. Perfect together, wrong for America."[39] Michael Pementel notes, "So much of horror's history in handling mental health has always been playing into it as a trope; usually it's depicted as a plot device that provides context for a crazed or villainous character . . . [which] continues to perpetuate stigma surrounding mental health."[40] It is the uniquely human nature of mental health that classifies such depictions in the realm of conflicted horror, as classic horror monsters have no humanity from which a mental health issue would be portrayed as different. The connections between mental health and horror can be traced all the way back to the genre's cinematic birth with *The Cabinet of Dr. Caligari* (1920), where the twist reveals that the protagonist has actually been in a mental institution for the entirety of the film.[41] As such, this ad extends the classic horror framing from those representing the Radical Left to Harris, while explicitly applying the conflicted horror frame to Biden through problematic notions of mental health. Argumentatively, Harris acts as a more explicit link between Biden and the Left.

While "Meet Phony Kamala Harris!" attacked Biden's mental health a few times in the second half of the advertisement, "Watch: Past vs Present" makes such attacks the explicit focus of the ad. Originally aired August 17, 2020, this political spot opens with a black-and-white image of Biden slowly fading in as text emerges, reading, "DID SOMETHING HAPPEN TO JOE BIDEN?"[42] The ad then jumps back and forth between clips labeled "PAST" and "PRESENT."[43] The clips labeled as past are brightly colored with no distortions. In the first instance, Biden quips about being vice president to audience laughter. Television interference distortions then hit the screen, morphing "PAST" into "PRESENT," where a now shaded and slightly distorted clip of Biden speaking in 2020 is presented.[44] Biden is seen stumbling over his lines and the camera focuses on his hand seeming to gesture for a teleprompter to move on. The ad continues this pattern, of jumping between colorful moments of charisma from his vice presidency to present moments, tagged with the year 2020 in the top right and always shaded and distorted, where he is stuttering and stumbling over what he is trying to say. These attacks last for a lengthy minute and nineteen seconds, culminating in a black-and-white, shaded picture of Biden looking confused with text, "WHAT HAPPENED TO JOE BIDEN?"[45] Sad music plays as the image lingers. As such, this ad makes Biden's mental health its explicit target, evoking that same conflicted horror trope: attempting to make the audience both remorseful and fearful. Using clips of Biden stuttering seems particularly callous given his well-documented struggle with stuttering.[46]

The final thirty seconds of "Watch: Past vs Present" draws a sharp contrast between the conflicted horror of Biden and the positive self-assessment of Trump. A full-color American flag waves in the wind as the words, "COMMANDER IN CHIEF" are displayed prominently.[47] A deep-voiced narrator speaks for the first time, saying, "Commander in Chief, it's more than just a job."[48] Trump is shown speaking and then saluting, and then images of a U.S. Naval fleet and fighter jets are shown. The narrator says that Trump "rebuilt our military, repaired a broken VA, and eliminated Solemani [sic], Al Baghdadi, ISIS, the world's deadliest terrorists brought to justice."[49] As these military achievements are mentioned, black-and-white images of these figures are displayed with bright red Xs over their faces. When ISIS is mentioned, a black-and-white clip of a masked man wielding a rocket-propelled grenade launcher is shown. These images of foreign, monstrous others clearly evoke classic horror in line with past representations of terrorist threats. This is an attempt to scare the viewer into thinking Trump is their only option for safety, given the portrayed lack of wherewithal from Biden in the earlier portion of the ad. "Watch: Past vs Present" ends with a montage of Trump greeting soldiers, saluting flags, and memorializing dead troops, while the narrator heavily emphasizes safety, saying, "Today America is safer and stronger than ever, because to President Trump, it's more than just a job; it's a sworn duty to Keep America Safe."[50] Essentially, this ad uses the conflicted frame to attack Biden before abruptly switching to self-positive appeals to audience efficacy in the latter portion, which is laced with hints of the classic horror frame as well. This abrupt switch is reminiscent of Trump's 2016 ads like "Two Americas Immigration" and "Two Americas: Economy," although such a switch made a bit more narrative sense in those advertisements.[51]

Another ad that follows the two-part approach, as well as echoing other themes from the 2016 election is "America First! #MAGA." This ad, initially aired on August 20, 2020, draws upon the gendered attacks of 2016, trying to weave Biden into this web.[52] The ad opens with white text reading, "AMERICA STRONG" over a black background. Slowly building music plays as a distorted image of the U.S. Capitol is shown. A montage of older clips of Bill Clinton and Biden are presented, with heavy, horizontal distortions. Text fades in and out saying, "WASHINGTON FLOURISHED" and "POLITICIANS PROSPERED."[53] Trump is heard narrating, saying, "For too long, Washington flourished, politicians prospered, the establishment protected itself. But not the citizens of our country. Their victories have not been your victories. Their triumphs have not been your triumphs."[54] As this narration goes on, the montage moves to clips of Hillary Clinton and Speaker of the House Nancy Pelosi, with some clips of Biden with them interspersed. Some of the clips are older, drawing upon the narrative that these are long-standing politicians. There is an infamous clip of Pelosi, laughing somewhat menacingly while holding an ice cream bar. All of these clips are distorted to highlight them as unsettling. Such distortions are a common visual editing trope within the horror genre.[55] Obama is shown laughing in another clip, before the focus reverts to Hillary Clinton. Finally, Biden is shown toasting China's Jinping. All of these clips deal heavily in guilt by apposition, trying to visually connect Biden to less likeable, already demonized political figures, many of whom are women or people of color, a common attack thread for Trump and his campaign.[56]

Outside of the distortions and somewhat menacing faces being made by the figures in this montage, there is little that overtly casts these individuals as classic horror figures. However, this is where Trump allows collective memory to enthymematically fill in such an understanding. In 2016, the Trump campaign heavily framed Hillary Clinton through a classic horror lens. As Shawn J. Parry-Giles and Trevor Parry-Giles note, "Museums and monuments, history classes, and Hollywood films are just a few of the means by which members of a community come to understand and share collective memory . . . collective memory reveals how history and politics are fundamentally connected."[57] In essence, the way Trump's 2016 horror framing of Clinton both relied upon and influenced horror and our shared understanding of Clinton has stuck with the public. Trump doesn't need to explicitly retread those gendered horror frames. Rather, he simply needs to show Clinton and visually connect her with Biden and the rest of the more moderate members of the Democratic Party. Through this strategy, the Trump campaign has not only connected Biden with the monstrous Radical Left but also the monstrous corrupt Left. Notably, Trump typically connects Biden to the corrupt Left through white women such as Clinton and Pelosi, while he connects Biden to the Radical Left through women of color such as Ocasio-Cortez and Omar. The way these connections work—without an overt need to re-demonize Clinton, Pelosi, Ocasio-Cortez, or Omar—reveals the invasive and insidious qualities of horror framing in presidential campaigning.

The latter half of "America First! #MAGA" is almost entirely self-positive of Trump, providing voters with efficacy in combatting evil, monstrous politicians by voting for Trump. The ad immediately brightens up and we are hit with a flurry of images that heavily feature American flags in different contexts. Trump is interspersed throughout. This portion also relies on apposition, but in an attempt to establish a positive connection. Trump is shown greeting Queen Elizabeth II in one shot, standing next to British Prime Minister Boris Johnson in another, shaking hands with Jinping, and posing next to Canada's Justin Trudeau, among a handful of other images of his diplomacy. While this montage is happening, Trump narrates, "We will rebuild old alliances and form new ones."[58] Of particular note is the use of positive apposition with Jinping in the same ad that used Jinping for negative apposition with Biden. This shows how important subtle audiovisual cues are for audiences in understanding how to read and react to the images and arguments with which they are presented.

While maintaining its self-positivity, "America First! #MAGA" delves briefly into classic horror again when discussing terrorism. Trump says he will unite "the civilized world against radical Islamic terrorism, which we will eradicate completely from the face of the earth."[59] This language establishes such terrorist threats as inhuman, worthy of total annihilation, which the audience can supposedly only achieve by reelecting Trump. Images of massive bombing hits and airstrikes are shown through thermal vision displays as Trump makes this argument. Such visuals distance the viewer from thinking about the depiction of death on their television screen.[60] The ad continues depicting military forces before Trump pivots to his promise that "we will bring back" the economy and protect the border.[61] He then mentions the challenges that we will face, as images show Trump wearing a mask. The pandemic is never verbally or textually mentioned, only alluded to through visuals of Trump and others wearing masks. The ad ends with a flood of images of Trump, crowds, flags, workers, soldiers, fighter jets, and other such visuals as Trump narrates, "This moment is your moment, it belongs to you."[62] The "we" phrasing throughout the ad along with this final appeal is clearly targeted at rousing viewer efficacy and enthusiasm, culminating in a vote for Trump.

First aired on August 17, 2020, "Don't Let Them Ruin America" is another ad that, similar to many of the other ads in Trump's campaign, criticizes Biden through apposition to other individuals and through criticism of his mental aptitude.[63] The ad uses a heavy, classic horror framing of Black Lives Matter protestors in order to establish fear in the audience. Notably, Black Lives Matter or the point of the protests is never explicitly mentioned, with the ad relying on enthymeme. Trump supporters can easily complete that enthymeme, as the identity of the "them" that is ruining America is made clear through dog-whistle politics, which Ian Haney López describes as "coded talk centered on race," a strategy the GOP has long used in their rhetorical appeals.[64] Eerie piano music plays as text appears over violent protests that reads, "JOE & KAMALA LIE TO PROTECT THE RADICAL LEFTIST MOB."[65] A clip of Harris is edited over fireworks and gas in the streets, with a font that looks straight out of a 1930s horror film poster reading, "PHONY KAMALA HARRIS."[66] Harris is quoted calling the demonstrators "peaceful protestors."[67] Horrific screams are heard as the image transitions to a large, blazing inferno. Biden then appears over this inferno, with text reading "SLEEPY JOE BIDEN," once again a dig at his mental aptitude.[68] Biden also emphasizes, "The vast majority of the protestors have been peaceful" as screams and fires continue.[69] The ad then extends this pattern to a wide array of Democrats echoing similar sentiments of peaceful protest, with cameos from people such as Oregon's Attorney General Ellen Rosenblum, *New York Times* reporter Peter Baker, the Governor of Oregon Kate Brown, and Obama's Secretary of Homeland Security Jeh Johnson, among others. Each of these people is tagged with the horror text explaining who they are, emphasizing "DEMOCRAT" for the majority of them.[70] Their claims that the protests are peaceful are juxtaposed with continued background screaming, raging fires, explosions, and building music. The ad then transitions to a broken-down building and a flaming building as the text reads, "DEMOCRATS HAVE RUINED THEIR CITIES. DON'T LET THEM DESTROY AMERICA."[71]

"Don't Let Them Ruin America" clearly frames protestors through a classic horror lens, as demonic entities looking to destroy America, like a pack of monsters raiding a village. The civil unrest narrative is again at play, harkening to dystopian horror films of that genre.[72] The Democrats and members of the media that are attacked in this advertisement are framed through a conflicted lens as humans trying to protect and help this inhuman monstrosity. Similar to how Trump frames migrants without clear shots of their faces, these protestors are largely left faceless to take away a key element of their humanity. Given that these protests were largely in support of Black Lives Matter, this ad easily falls into the category of racist appeal. As described by Charlton D. McIlwain and Stephen Maynard Caliendo, a racist appeal is "one that advantages Whites as a result of systemic racist predispositions about people of color."[73] This strategy of racist appeal is frequently used by Trump in the context of Black Lives Matter and immigration. This is then fused with horror to create a fear response in white viewers. The almost constant flames in the background of those edited into "Don't Let Them Ruin America" is highly evocative of Hell, a possible allusion to where Christians who support Trump might imagine humans framed through a conflicted, evil lens—like Biden—would end up.

Another ad that attempts to criticize Biden through his connections with other individuals is "Biden Lied," which was first released on October 16, 2020.[74] This ad, however, goes a bit beyond the more casual connections of some ads, directly tying Biden in with his son, Hunter Biden, and his Ukrainian business venture. The ad opens with an ominous guitar twang, as an image of Joe and Hunter Biden is presented. The camera zooms in on Hunter Biden as the narrator says, "A Ukrainian company hands Hunter Biden a lucrative deal," as white text is typed across the screen, reading, "2014: Corrupt Burisma gives Hunter Biden an $83,000-a-month job."[75] That text appears over a foggy red background. An interview with Hunter Biden is then presented on a television with horizontal distortions. Hunter Biden is asked if he would have been on the board of Burisma if he wasn't a Biden, to which he replies, "Probably not."[76] The ad then goes on to say that Joe Biden claimed to know nothing about these dealings. An image of Joe and Hunter Biden smiling together is negatively exposed and then zoomed in on with heavier distortion as the ad reveals the cover of the *New York Post* issue claiming to have Biden's secret emails connecting him to Hunter's business. This report was highly contested from its release up through the election, with many claiming that the emails were doctored or even foreign election tampering.[77] Nevertheless, Trump and his campaign heavily featured the contested reports.

The second portion of the ad builds upon this narrative that Biden lied. The narrator says, "Turns out he lied. Biden met personally with a Ukrainian executive after they hired his son."[78] A very unflattering image of Biden is pasted over a faded, blood-red background as the email supposedly connecting Joe Biden to his son's business venture is highlighted. A ghostly image of Hunter Biden fades in on the left side of the screen. The ad ends with two images of Joe Biden, one with him looking disappointed and another extreme close-up of him looking slack-jawed. Both of these images carry the text "BIDEN LIED to the American People."[79] The narrator then wonders aloud, "What else is he lying about?"[80] Therein lies the crux of this attack. Biden is supposedly hiding the connections he has with other people, a deliberately deceptive tactic. The Trump campaign worked relentlessly to connect Biden with other, more monstrous individuals. This ad shows that even if Biden claims he is not deeply connected with those people, he is an evil, conflicted liar who is corrupt and hiding connections with more monstrous, corrupt foreign entities. While this attack is pretty subtle in its conflicted horror, the narrative in combination with the audiovisuals of distortions, close-ups, and blood-red backgrounds make such generic allusions apparent.

Prior to "Biden Lied," "Teleprompter Joe," which was released on September 24, 2020, firmly connected attacks on Biden's mental aptitude with depictions of him as a pawn, grounding this attack in conflicted horror.[81] The ad opens with ominous music as *Fox News* anchor Bret Baier grills Biden's press secretary, TJ Ducklo, about whether or not Biden has ever used a teleprompter during interviews. The ad uses heavy horizontal distortions as a close-up is presented of Ducklo, licking his upper lip during this questioning. Such close-ups establish discomfort for audience members.[82] Before Ducklo can respond, the ad cuts to a clip from a Biden town hall where a portion of a question asked by a Black woman is provided out of context. Biden is then shown saying, "Move it up here," insinuating he is talking about a teleprompter.[83] The text then appears on the screen much like a teleprompter and begins highlighting words as Biden gives his response. Next, a clip of Biden from another address flipping his hand upwards is zoomed in on to insinuate his reading off a teleprompter. Another clip shows Biden repeating a line as distorted teleprompter text moves up the screen, again trying to substantiate a teleprompter conspiracy. Next, Biden is shown holding up a picture of his sons that supposedly shows a teleprompter in the reflection. That reflection is circled and highlighted with the text, "TELEPROMPTER."[84] The ad then goes back to the Ducklo interview by Baier, where Baier claims Ducklo cannot give a yes or no answer on if Biden uses teleprompters. From here, the ad cuts back to Biden waving his hand up as teleprompter text reads, "[ANSWER] YES. IS THIS SOMEONE YOU CAN COUNT ON?"[85] The spot then shifts to more distorted shots of Biden as teleprompter text highlighted in blue reads, "JOE CAN'T SPEAK FOR HIMSELF."[86] That text then moves up and is replaced by new text highlighted in red for the first time, asking, "WHO IS REALLY IN CHARGE?"[87] The screen fades to black as the text flickers.

The audiovisuals of "Teleprompter Joe" combine with the underlying message of the ad to cast Biden once again as a conflicted horror figure. He is not himself targeted as an inhuman monster, but rather as one being brainwashed, manipulated, and controlled by unnamed, nefarious forces. However, with some of these other ads as context, we can enthymematically fill in who these forces might be as either the Radical Left or the corrupt, Establishment Left, or both. Accordingly, attacks on Biden's mental aptitude are combined with continued conspiracy messaging to establish a conflicted horror frame where the presidential candidate you might vote for is not really the one making the decisions. Instead, that is left up to ominous and nefarious actors.

"The Real Biden Plan," first aired on October 18, 2020, is one of the few Trump ads that attempts to use classic and conflicted horror to attack Biden for his own policies without establishing him as a pawn. The ad opens with a somewhat upbeat narrator asking, "What would Joe Biden's plan do for you?"[88] The ad then abruptly shifts tones as a record scratch is heard and a visual distortion moves over an image of Biden. A colorized, happy image of Biden is now replaced with a black-and-white, menacing image of the former vice president. White text reads, "THE REAL BIDEN PLAN:" with the space after the colon being filled in with blood-red text throughout multiple shots. These texts that fill in the statement include, "14% TAX HIKE," "82% OF AMERICANS WOULD PAY MORE," and "GIVE ILLEGAL IMMIGRANTS AMNESTY AND HEALTHCARE."[89]

As these various attacks are levied, a montage plays of highly distorted, faded shots of Biden looking evil. He laughs in slow-motion in one shot, establishing a somewhat monstrous appearance. A shot of money being forced down a wet drain is also presented, before a heavily distorted image of Biden and Sanders both raising their hands is shown. When immigration is discussed, two individuals climbing what appears to be a border wall are shown, once again making out illegal immigrants as inhuman, monstrous threats. The final portion of the ad claims that Biden is "a career politician who spent decades raising taxes."[90] The text echoes this sentiment with "RAISING TAXES" highlighted in blood red as Biden smirks. A quick, distorted clip of Biden saying, "Come on man," is intercut as the narrator concludes, "So what would the Biden plan do for you? Raise your taxes."[91] This final sentence is visually emphasized in red text placed over an empty wallet. As such, "The Real Biden Plan" toes the line between conflicted and classic horror. While it does not delve much into temporal or spatial horrors, other than the crossing of the border by migrants, it does frame Biden fairly monstrously through highly unflattering, distorted shots. This is further emphasized by the repeated use of blood-red text and subtle, anxiety-inducing music.

A Few Isolated Instances of Trump Framing Biden through Classic Horror

Interestingly, while many of the Trump campaign's advertisements frame Biden through the conflicted frame, there is a grouping of ads that definitively break that mold in a way that moves beyond "The Real Biden Plan." First aired on August 7, 2020, "The Joe Biden They Are Hiding From You" firmly frames Biden as monstrous for racist comments he made in the past. This ad tries to counter the narrative of Trump as racist by establishing Biden as racist in the midst of nationwide Black Lives Matter protests. The ad opens with a deep, booming, ominous noise as white words on a black background read, "JOE BIDEN, IN HIS OWN WORDS."[92] You then hear Biden start talking as one's speakers almost rattle from the ominous bass. The text reads, "AUG 5, 2020."[93] Biden's voice is distorted as he says, "Unlike the African American community with notable exceptions, the Latino community is an incredibly diverse community."[94] A camera flashes after this comment and a highly zoomed in, incredibly unflattering shot of Biden flares across the screen. The ominous noises continue as a new Biden quote from May 22, 2020, plays where he says, "If you have a problem figuring out whether you are for me or Trump, then you ain't black."[95] Another camera flash effect and this time a close-up of Biden, looking menacing and grabbing a person's shoulder is presented. This pattern of date, racist quote, camera flash, and shaded, menacing picture continues throughout the advertisement until about forty seconds in. Then, after an audience is heard laughing at Biden for recounting how Black people call him "Boy," a series of camera flashes erupt that bring an extremely unflattering, monstrous image of Biden closer and closer with each flash.[96] The next quote plays where Biden says, "They're going to put you all back in chains," followed by an extremely angry, demonic Biden close-up and then an image of just his mouth with teeth bared.[97] Then, Biden is quoted talking about Obama as the "first . . . African-American, who is articulate and bright and clean, nice-looking guy."[98] Here, each adjective from articulate through guy gets highlighted with horrific sound effects as if viewing old, haunted documents. An image of Biden smiling menacingly fades in just enough to be recognizable before fading back out. Harris is then heard criticizing Biden for supporting politicians who "built their reputation and career on the segregation of race" as Biden is pictured in a shadowed, black-and-white collage with the two men.[99] Harris asks Biden if he's going to apologize and he says, "Apologize for what?"[100] The "for what?" echoes as the same unflattering photo that was zoomed in on multiple times is zoomed in on again. There is again an audio bass boom and this time the image flashes as a photo negative on one of the zooms. The image fades with a screeching, horrific noise as the text reads, "THE JOE BIDEN THEY ARE HIDING FROM YOU."[101]

"The Joe Biden They Are Hiding From You" is interesting both in how heavily it frames Biden through the classic horror frame and in its substantial use of close-ups to visually convey horror. Shot distance is a critical component of how visual mediation shapes audience reactions to candidates. As Diana C. Mutz and Byron Reeves argue, "the distance deemed appropriate for face-to-face interactions with public figures in American culture is beyond 12 feet, yet most citizens' exposure to politicians via television has the appearance of being far closer."[102] That is in the context of typical television, where this ad even extends beyond that for extreme close-ups. This invasion of typical spatial norms almost certainly intensifies the already negative affect being instilled through the ad's horrific audio effects and quotes. As such, "The Joe Biden They Are Hiding From You" frames Biden through a monstrous, classic horror frame using a plethora of audiovisual tricks in combination with Biden's well-documented gaffes on race.

Another ad that targeted Biden through a more classic horror frame is "Progresista," an ad that is almost entirely in Spanish and clearly aimed at Latinx voters. Notably, this ad was put out by the Latinos for Trump PAC. This would typically disqualify it from my analysis, however, given the importance of Latinx voters in Florida in the 2020 election—specifically Cubans in Miami who many argue swung Florida in Trump's favor—and the extreme horror framing it uses, a brief analysis of the ad felt fitting.[103] Further, I do not give it much weight in my overall analysis. "Progresista" first aired on August 3, 2020.[104] The ad opens with Biden saying, "I'm gonna go down as one of the most progressive presidents in American history."[105] This statement is translated to Spanish and displayed across a distorted video of Biden. The ad then cuts to a highly distorted, unflattering image of Biden with big red text reading, "¿Progresista?"[106] Ominous, pounding music plays as Biden is put in visual apposition with a number of Latin American dictators. Distorted clips of Hugo Chávez, Fidel Castro, Gustavo Petro, and Nicolás Maduro are all played in which they are advocating for progressive and socialist policies. Biden is then pictured with Sanders with bold text over a red background that reads, "CUANDO DICEN PROGRESISTA" which transitions to "QUIEREN DECIR . . ." over a wavy, color faded image of Biden.[107] Then a heavily distorted image of Castro ranting at a podium appears with the finishing phrase in white and blood-red text, "UNA REVOLUCIÓN SOCIALISTA EN . . . LOS ESTADOS UNIDOS."[108] Roughly translated, this series of texts read, "When they say progressive, they mean a socialist revolution in the United States."[109] The ad ends with a faded image of Biden greeting Maduro with yellow text over red background that reads, "PROGRESISTA = SOCIALISTA."[110]

"Progresista" works on a number of levels when it comes to horror framing. First, it frames Biden classically through his connection to foreign dictators. This foreignness is invocative of the classic frame, which often positions monstrosity as something foreign, existing outside of normal spatiality and temporality. The reference to older clips of dictators also works to violate this temporality. The threat of this connection between Biden and socialism is then made explicit with the Castro clip as the ad argues that Biden wants a socialist revolution in the United States. This again works through generic reference to invasion horrors that were especially popular during the Cold War and McCarthyism.[111] The apposition between Biden and these corrupt, foreign leaders makes his classic framing clear. The visual distortions and frequent use of deep, blood red in the texts makes this frame even stronger.

Trump's Self-Positive Advertising

Released on August 13, 2020, "Record Smashing" is one of Trump's primarily self-positive advertisements that instills a sense of audience efficacy through reference to his purported achievements as president.[112] The ad opens with grandiose music as Trump walks out of the shadows in front of a well-lit American flag, perhaps symbolizing Trump emerging from his fight with supposed dark forces. An upbeat narrator says, "President Trump built a great economy, and amidst a global pandemic he's doing it again."[113] Trump is seen speaking in front of a rally of workers, shaking hands with a woman in a business suit, and pumping his fist at some sort of manufacturing plant.

The visuals then cut to a sunny, full-color American flag with the text, "THE GREAT AMERICAN COMEBACK."[114] The narrator echoes this wording, before rattling off his economic achievements during the pandemic, mostly touting adding jobs. At one point the narrator notes that under Trump "women and minorities [are] going back to work in record numbers," while two Black men on an assembly line and then a woman of color on an assembly line are shown.[115] Trump's campaign is clearly trying to hit back against notions that he is bigoted here. However, it is certainly worth noting that this is the only point in the ad that individuals of color are prominently displayed. Other than that, every person focused on is white.

Another facet worth noting is the ad clearly downplays the threat of the COVID-19 pandemic. While the ad mentions the word "pandemic," it frames that threat as something Trump has already defeated. Visually, there are only two instances in the entire ad where individuals are seen with masks. One is a "blink and you miss it" background individual and another is someone working on intricate machinery, making it ambiguous whether the mask is pandemic, or job related. Trump is never shown with a mask and none of those directly interacting with him are wearing one either. As such, Trump does not want to scare his voters with this self-positive ad. Rather, Trump and his campaign are trying to instill a sense of hope and overcoming in the audience. The narrator ends by saying, "and the best is yet to come" as Trump gives the audience a thumbs up in front of an American flag.[116] In the midst of a pandemic that has caused fear and economic turmoil, "Record Smashing" is an effort to convince viewers that their best form of protection—especially for their wallets—is voting for Trump.

"Carefully," which first aired on October 10, 2020, is another relentlessly self-positive ad that attempts to downplay the fears surrounding COVID-19 by providing Trump as an example of efficacy.[117] The ad uses soft, upbeat music and an optimistic sounding narrator. The narrator says, "President Trump is recovering from the coronavirus. And so is America."[118] A clip of Trump waving with a mask on transitions to a video of a woman switching a closed sign on a business door to "OPEN."[119] The narrator then espouses a message of togetherness, touting the things Trump has done to fight the pandemic as images of families, scientists, doctors, and patients montage. Dr. Anthony Fauci is then brought into the ad, where he says, "I can't imagine that . . . anybody could be doing more."[120] This works to counter some of Biden's attacks that cast Trump as an enemy of the scientific community. The ad ends with a montage of scientists, two Black teenagers greeting each other, and a mother and daughter touching noses through their masks. The narrator makes a push for unified efficacy as she says, "We'll get through this together. We'll live carefully, but not afraid."[121] As such, this self-positive ad directly attempts to counter the Biden ad narrative, which either explicitly or implicitly tries to remind Americans of their lingering fear of COVID-19. The ad positions Trump, someone who got the virus and recovered, as a person voters can put their trust in to overcome this monstrous, viral threat.

First broadcast on October 5, 2020, "Second Chance" is a highly self-positive ad that tries to provide evidence of how Trump has supposedly helped Black communities.[122] The ad centers on Tony Rankin, a Black man who is prominently identified as a "US Army Veteran."[123] Rankin narrates about how he was homeless and sleeping in his car as black-and-white shots of a very beat-up car are shown. He says, "I didn't have hope for a very long time" before a woman narrator says, "Then, Tony Rankin was offered a second chance."[124] The music becomes more upbeat as the narrator highlights how Trump's "opportunity zones gave new investments to neglected communities."[125] Persons of color are then predominantly shown doing construction tasks as Rankin comes back on the screen, saying, "Life is good now. Life is worth living. The President does want to help people like myself to be lifted back up in these low-income communities."[126] As Rankin makes these positive assessments of Trump, a montage of Trump meeting with Black folks is intercut with construction workers, implying that Trump is listening to people of color and helping them with jobs production.

"Second Chance" is an attempt by the Trump campaign to make a targeted call to efficacy for low-income communities, which the ad conflates with BIPOC communities. In essence, a vote for Trump can make your life meaningful again by providing construction jobs, as these are the only jobs visualized in the ad. This plays into the white savior trope, common to both political campaigns and cinema alike. As Matthew W. Hughey describes it, white savior narratives "rely on an implicit message of white paternalism and antiblack stereotypes of contented servitude, obedience, and acquiescence."[127] "Second Chance" does just that, presenting a case where Trump has "graciously" given Black folks construction jobs and that they are content in their servitude of Trump and the capitalist system.

Ultimately, the Trump campaign relied heavily on horror framing in order to attack Biden and the Left. Typically, Trump unleashed the classic horror frame on the Radical Left (especially women who fit that grouping), the Establishment, immigrants, terrorists, and other such groups of people. Biden was typically framed through the conflicted lens given his supposed manipulability. There were a couple of ads that framed Biden through the classic lens, but ultimately Trump's narrative was one of brainwashing and invasion. Biden was connected either directly or through Kamala Harris to more radical policies than he ever endorsed as a fairly moderate candidate. Trump, then, as a continuation of his 2016 campaign, is framed as a leader who will fight the good fight against the monstrous Left and the pawn, Biden. This falls in line with how James West describes Trump and his followers, "Trump acolytes placed him into epic action films such as *300*, *Gladiator*, and *Troy*, depicting him as a fearless warrior fighting back against a variety of enemies which included the Democratic political machine."[128] As such, horror framing does the heavy lifting for Trump's argument against Biden that is constructed throughout his campaign narrative, allowing him to continue his own narrative as epic savior even when his concrete policy actions as president do not meet that threshold.

BIDEN'S IMPLICITLY HORRIFIC ADVERTISING CAMPAIGN

Many things were near opposites in the 2020 campaign and presidential election, and strategy surrounding the use of horror in campaign advertising was no exception. While Trump clearly leaned heavily on the genre, Biden focused much more on self-positive messages that instill hope and audience efficacy. The horror was still there, sometimes rearing its head or, more often, existing in the realm of implication and enthymeme given the real-life horrors surrounding American voters during this campaign. As such, Biden's campaign was vastly less horrific than the Trump campaign.

Biden's Subtly Horrific Advertisements

Originally aired on July 23, 2020, "Crossroads" uses some light conflicted horror framing at its beginning in order to bolster the self-positive assessment of Biden.[129] The spot opens with a montage of masked medical workers, a masked priest reading the Bible over a hospital bed, and masked protestors with a sign reading, "LISTEN TO BLACK VOICES."[130] The narrator says over a somber musical piece, "Right now we're at a crossroads."[131] The ad then cuts to a slightly shaded image of Trump looking smug and then videos of protestors getting tear gassed. The narrator notes, "We've seen what can happen when we elect a leader determined to divide us."[132] All of this happens within the first ten seconds of the ad, and the rest of the advertisement becomes exclusively positive. Trump is carefully framed through a conflicted horror lens, implying that all of the ills facing America were created or exacerbated by him and his human failure. The actual horrors are left somewhat ambiguous. COVID-19 is never verbalized and only seen as part of text later in the ad for a hyperlink on Biden's plan. A priest reading over a hospital bed is readily understandable as a sign of impending death, with some possible connections to exorcist horrors at play.[133] Police brutality, something that is very much monstrous to Black communities, is shown but again never verbalized as such. This seems indicative of a broader trend the Biden campaign capitalized on: they didn't need to be overly horrific or rely on fear appeals, Americans were already fearful. As such, they could let audiences carry that fear with them and focus much more strongly on self-positive appeals to efficacy, explaining how Biden could rid them of their fears.

The latter two-thirds of "Crossroads" is relentlessly positive. Biden is seen trotting down steps to a large crowd of supporters as the narrator pivots, "As President Joe Biden will forge a new path by growing an economy that works for working families."[134] Workers on an assembly line are shown, followed by two men lifting heavy bags, a medical worker walking down a hall, a woman and child on a video call, and finally kids riding down a hill on bikes. Triumphant music plays as the narrator speaks over these images, claiming Biden will restore small business, improve health care access, and "lead us on the path forward paved with opportunity for us all."[135] That final line, "OPPORTUNITY FOR US ALL," is emblazoned in the sky over a home as the sun is either setting or rising.[136] Such imagery could indicate the end of America's ills or the rising of a better America (the ambiguous nature of the shot may imply both). As such, "Crossroads" is a mostly self-positive ad with some light horror framing at the beginning. This brief negativity is likely meant to stir audience's already held fears, not exacerbate them anymore.

A Biden ad that was less subtle in its use of horror is "'It Is What It Is,'" which was first released on August 5, 2020.[137] This ad opens with an interview with Trump where he says, "I think it's under control. I'll tell you what—."[138] Trump is then interrupted by the interviewer who asks, "How? A thousand Americans are dying a day."[139] Trump then retorts, "They're dying. It's true. And you . . . it is what it is."[140] A siren and a slow, disconcerting beat begin with this line as black-and-white images of body bags and medical workers appear. A montage of masked medical workers and patients is then presented throughout the ad as the text, "'It is what it is' President Donald J. Trump" remains over the screen. The audio clip of that line repeats multiple times as the sirens and ominous, booming soundtrack continues. The final two images are of makeshift caskets lined up and an older woman pressing her hand against a window as a toddler does the same on the other side.

"'It Is What It Is'" once again frames Trump through a conflicted lens, while turning up the classic horror frame on COVID-19. The Biden campaign's conflicted framing of Trump is achieved primarily through his human callousness, seeming indifferent to those dying from the disease. Interestingly, COVID-19 is once again never mentioned by name. The Biden campaign has again assumed that viewers are well-aware of the pandemic and that visual cues are all they need to remember the fear they hold. As such, they don't need to go overboard. However, the images they select strike a deep chord with pandemic or zombie horror films such as *Outbreak* (1995),

Contagion (2011), and *28 Days Later* (2002).[141] In fact, with movie productions largely shut down or delayed during the pandemic, these political ads are on the cutting edge of what the horror genre might look like in the wake of the pandemic. Some predict that the number of contagion and zombie films will grow significantly, as horror is a genre that is deeply connected with the fears of the contemporary era.[142] "'It Is What It Is'" is one of the more horrific ads the Biden campaign released, framing Trump through the conflicted lens and the pandemic through the classic lens. Nevertheless, the horror elements of this ad are still relatively subdued, relying highly on audiovisual connections the audience would likely make.

Another attack ad against Trump was "Donald Trump Failed to Protect Us From COVID-19," which first hit television screens on August 8, 2020.[143] The ad works by fluctuating back and forth between what Trump did in response to the pandemic and what Obama and Biden did to prepare for a pandemic. The ad opens with a slightly distorted video of Trump saying, "Nobody knew there'd be a pandemic or an epidemic of this proportion."[144] The ad then cuts to a black screen with white text using a slight, shrill sound effect. The text reads "The Obama-Biden Administration knew."[145] Somewhat motivating music plays as Obama and Biden are pictured in blue with text reading, "Created 69-page PANDEMIC PLAYBOOK."[146] A dashed line moves downward from a simplified image of a book to an X on a red-shaded image of Trump with his back turned. An electronic rejection sound effect is heard as the text "IGNORED" appears.[147] The ad continues this pattern of showing Obama and Biden in blue with a policy they created to fight pandemics, a dashed line moving down to a red-shaded image of Trump with his back turned, and an X with text describing how Trump failed to extend those policies. The ad ends with an unfiltered version of the Obama and Biden picture with text that reads, "They PREPARED US," followed by an unfiltered, zoomed-in version of the picture of Trump with his back turned. Text is placed next to Trump which reads, "He tore it apart."[148]

Once again, this ad is subtly horrific, framing Trump in a conflicted manner as someone who eliminated America's defenses against a pandemic. The verticality of the ad plays a number of roles in visualizing the argument the Biden team is making. First, as Kristen Whissel notes, "verticality automatically implies the intersection of two opposed forces—gravity and the force required to overcome it—it is an ideal technique for visualizing power."[149] As such, the Biden campaign is displaying their supremacy in tactics for handling a pandemic, instilling audience efficacy with a vote for Biden. However, there is a further slight horror twist to this that is visually implied. The red filtering of Trump in combination with his downward placement should make immediate connections with Western, Christian notions of Hell. Descending into Hell has been a trope in horrific Christian fictions for centuries, with

Dante's *Inferno* as a notable literary foundation of such a vertical-visual connection.[150] As such, Trump is subtly implied as both inferior to Biden in his pandemic response and worthy of damnation for how he metaphorically turned his back on the American people. Such visual arguments of damnation highlight Trump's intense, flawed humanness, connecting him with the conflicted horror frame, unless of course the connection implies Trump as the devil himself, in which case classic monstrosity would be invoked. This ambiguity is left for the viewer to determine.

"Truth :60," originally aired on July 21, 2020, is the ad that frames the pandemic most strongly through a classic horror lens.[151] The ad opens with a masked Biden, who begins narrating, "Today we're facing a serious threat. We have to beat it as one country."[152] Already, in those first two lines, Biden has established a horrific threat—the pandemic—and a call for audience efficacy to defeat that threat established using "we."[153] During the threat portion of Biden's statement, distorted images of health workers and crowds of people are shown, visually linking the threat with the ongoing pandemic with visuals similar to "It Is What It Is."[154] During the call for action, Biden is pictured speaking in front of a large American flag. The ad pivots back to framing the pandemic through classic horror as Biden says, "Numbers don't lie. Infection rates are now going up in more states than they're going down."[155] As Biden makes this argument, a distorted map with states being filled in with red is presented, intercut with health care workers suiting up in heavy pandemic gear. Such visuals again connect with pandemic horror films, as well as with invasion narratives.[156] The choice of red to represent states where COVID-19 cases are increasing further exacerbates the horror elements of this ad. Biden's statement that "Numbers don't lie" further aligns this advertisement with centrist sci-fi horrors, where experts such as scientists and health officials are cast in a heroic light.[157]

After another horror framing, "Truth :60" bounces back to calls for unity and audience efficacy. Biden says, "We gotta fight this together. Wear a mask. Keep your distance. Look at the size of the crowds. It may be inconvenient. It may be uncomfortable. But it's the right thing to do as an American."[158] As Biden lists these actions, a montage of socially distanced, mask-wearing individuals plays. A shot of an empty baseball stadium is also briefly shown. Biden comes back onto the screen as he delivers his line about it being "the right thing to do."[159] The second half of the ad consists almost entirely of a montage of images of a masked Biden speaking with other people. Biden argues, "We need a president who will level with the American people . . . tell us the unvarnished truth . . . take responsibility, instead of always blaming others . . . listen to the experts, follow the science, allow them to speak."[160] These statements which especially highlight the centrality of experts and scientists to fighting COVID-19 again connect with centrist invasion films that place a premium on such expertise. "Truth :60" ultimately relies on classic horror framing to establish the fear of the COVID-19 pandemic. However, it does very little to target Trump other than through indirect mentions. Ultimately, while this ad does establish itself using horror it ultimately relies most heavily on audience efficacy by giving concrete actions for Americans to take on top of voting for Biden. And even though the horror elements are washed out by the steps for moving forward, this ad still sticks out because it is more horrific than many of Biden's later ads. The Biden campaign largely stepped away from even this relatively weak horrific framing as the campaign progressed.

One ad that did not relinquish this horror framing was "Pero Ya No," originally aired on August 28, 2020.[161] Targeted primarily at Latinx voters, "Pero Ya No" interwove horror and slight comedic elements through the Puerto Rican pop song of the same name as the ad, "Pero Ya No" by Bad Bunny.[162] The ad "Pero Ya No" plays the song throughout as images of Trump and his supporters celebrating at large rallies are juxtaposed with scenes of families crying and being separated at the border and police marching toward protestors. A slow-motion effect is used on some dancing and clapping Trump supporters, that gives both a light comedic impact as well as a horrific one when the things they are cheering for, like stronger restrictions on immigration, are put in stark contrast. Horror and comedy have a deep connection, as films such as *Evil Dead II* (1987), *Shaun of the Dead* (2004), and *The Cabin in the Woods* (2011) demonstrate.[163] The lyrics of the song "Pero Ya No" would have further meaning for Spanish-speaking viewers which, when translated into English, mean things like, "I used to love you, but not anymore" and "I was down for you, but not anymore."[164] As such, these lyrics can have two meanings in the context of this ad: voters used to like Trump, but not anymore or Trump used to like voters—specifically Latinx voters—but not anymore. The ad continues to criticize Trump as horrifically foolish, as he is seen hugging a flag and tossing paper towels into a crowd in Puerto Rico after Hurricane Maria. These images are juxtaposed with someone being loaded into an ambulance, again highlighting the pandemic. The ad ends with Trump turning away before showing a brief montage of Biden smiling while interacting with Latinx folks. As such, "Pero Ya No" uses a mixture of comedy and horror to lightly frame Trump and his supporters through a flawed, conflicted lens to Latinx voters.

Originally broadcast on August 6, 2020, "Better America" relies on a similar strategy as "Pero Ya No" by targeting a specific voting demographic, this time Black Americans.[165] The ad relies on a soul soundtrack as the narrator says, "The story of Black America is the story of America."[166] Images of Black protestors from the civil rights era are visually compared with images of contemporary Black Lives Matter protestors. The narrator continues, "Black people have always believed in the promise of a better America," as clips play of a Black man serving barbeque, a Black woman in a mask, a laughing, smiling Black woman, and another laughing Black woman playfully boxing with a Black man.[167] The ad cuts some from these upbeat images as a Black woman in hazmat gear is shown with text that reads, "CORONAVIRUS DEVASTATING BLACK COMMUNITIES."[168] A bar graph shows that while Black people make up 13 percent of the population, they account for 22 percent of pandemic deaths.[169] The narrator notes, "So, at this moment we're in now, we must choose to fight for that better America."[170] An image of protestors holding signs demanding the right to vote from the civil rights movement is placed next to a contemporary Black person holding a sign that says "REGISTER TO VOTE."[171] From here, the atrocities of police brutality in the 1950s and 1960s are pictured with a dog attacking a Black man, police dragging a Black man by his feet, and Black people having bayonetted rifles pointed at them. The narrator says, "And just like our ancestors, who stood up to the violent racists of a generation ago, we will stand up to this president, and say NO MORE."[172] An image of Trump appears with heavy, horizontal distortion lines. That image is then replaced with Trump supporters carrying torches and wearing MAGA hats from the white supremacist monument protests. The words "NO MORE" flash on the screen as a contemporary Black Lives Matter protest is presented. These images of the past, which are then connected with Trump and the modern presidency, establish a deep synergy with the classic horror frame's breach of time. Caroline Joan (Kay) S. Picart and David A. Frank argue, "The classic horror film also breaches the ontology of normal time. The time sequence of horror is bracketed, as the transgressive monster emerges at a definitive moment and, in classic American Gothic, is eventually conquered. With the monster vanquished, normal time returns."[173] As such, the way this ad frames a resurgence of past horror establishes Trump and his supporters through classic horror, especially through the violent visuals connected from the past to the present.

The latter portion of "Better America" relies heavily on establishing audience efficacy through Biden. The narrator argues, "America is better than him, so we choose to be bigger. We choose to be bolder. We choose to bring back justice, respect, and dignity to the country."[174] A montage of Black folks is presented, some smiling, some going to church, some just looking into the camera. The words "JUSTICE," "RESPECT," and "DIGNITY" are presented in text over different clips of Black people in unison with the narrator. Here, the ad pivots to the self-positive assessment of Biden as the narrator says, "We choose Joe Biden to lead us all to that American promise together."[175] Here a flurry of clips is shown of Biden interacting with Black supporters, concluding the advertisement. As such, the horror of Trump and his supporters is presented to Black viewers. While this horror breaches the normal flow of time, Biden is presented as a remedy to this horrific breach, setting the country back on a course for righting systemic racial injustices. Thus, Black viewers are presented efficacy in this ad both through protest and by voting for Biden. This makes this ad a clear exemplar of racial appeal. According to McIlwain and Caliendo, racial appeals are "racial in nature but do not target anti-minority sentiment for their efficacy."[176] Accordingly, while Biden combines elements of race and horror, this ad emphasizes the horror of Trump and his continuation of anti-Black policies, establishing it as an ad using racial appeals and steering it away from Trump's ads that rely on racist appeals.

"Kamala Harris: Vice President Announcement," which was first televised on August 12, 2020, is one of the most Harris-centric ads the campaign ran.[177] It presented parallels to the story of Black folks shown in "Better America" as mediated through vice presidential candidate Harris. The ad opens with text reading "August 11, 2020" as a clip fades in on Biden calling Harris via laptop to confirm that she is ready to run as his vice presidential candidate. Biden asks, "You ready to go to work?" to which Harris responds, "Oh God, I'm so ready to go to work."[178] Harris then narrates her own story as images of her as a child montage on the screen. Harris says, "My mother knew that she was raising two black daughters who would be treated differently for how they looked. Growing up whenever I got upset about something, my mother would look me in the eye and ask, 'So what are you going to do about it?'"[179] Harris then walks through her political career, starting as a lawyer, then California attorney general, then U.S. senator.

After this self-positive, inspiring story, "Kamala Harris: Vice President Announcement" transitions into some horror framing similar to some of the ads before it. Harris narrates, "Right now, America needs action. In the middle of a pandemic, the president is trying to rip away health care. While small businesses close, he's given breaks to his wealthy donors."[180] Trump is shown using a filter that fades the colors of the shots he is in. This is juxtaposed with images of health care workers, someone locking a business, and Black Lives Matter protesters. The use of the verb phrase "rip away" to describe Trump's approach to health care is evocative of violent horror.[181] Harris continues, saying, "when the people cried out for support, he tear gassed them."[182] A video of police tear gassing protesters is shown, establishing a visual connection with horror films that rely upon narratives of dystopian futures and civil unrest.[183] Such callousness horrifically frames Trump, however without the explicit temporal framing of "Better America," this framing reverts back toward the conflicted frame as this indifference is a deeply human horror.

Harris acknowledges this horror, saying, "America is in crisis" but provides efficacy, claiming, "I know Joe Biden will lead us out of it. He's a man of faith, decency, and character."[184] Here videos of Harris and Biden smiling together are presented as Harris discusses the quality of Biden's family. Harris briefly returns to a horrific narrative of good vs. evil as she argues, "'We're in a battle for the soul of this nation.' But together it's a battle we can win. We just have to take action."[185] Here, Harris again uses an allusion to the earlier horror elements to establish audience efficacy through action: primarily voting for a Biden-Harris administration. A photo of Biden and Harris holding their hands up together in celebration fades away as the ad returns to the video call from the beginning. Biden asks, "First of all, is the answer yes?" to which Harris replies, "The answer is absolutely yes, Joe."[186] Both Biden and Harris appear very excited as the ad ends. "Kamala Harris: Vice President Announcement," an ad that runs almost two minutes, uses a brief stint of horror in its middle portion to galvanize a call for audience efficacy through voting for Biden-Harris in the latter portion of the ad.

"How to Build Back Better" is another long-form advertisement, which was released on August 8, 2020.[187] The ad works by framing a set of crises America is facing because of Trump's failures and then explaining Biden's policy proposals in response to those issues. Biden opens by explaining, "Over a hundred and fifty thousand Americans are dead from Covid-19."[188] A red line graph with a red shaded background is shown representing these depths, immediately evoking subtle horror through the color red and death. Biden then runs through the crises he addresses in the ad. Each crisis is presented with text at the bottom of the screen, a picture symbolizing the crisis, and a black-and-white, faded, distorted, slightly red-tinted image of Trump looking angry on the side. The crises are a health crisis, economic crisis, racial justice crisis, and climate crisis. Biden briefly explains why each of these crises has been exacerbated by Trump's actions, such as his "words of hate" or "denial of science."[189] An emerging theme from Biden's ads is his characterization of science and scientists as noble truth seekers. This connects his advertisement with centrist science fiction horrors, which cast extremists like Trump as the conflicted, evildoers.[190]

With these crises laid out, Biden uses nostalgia to craft an understanding of the past, present, and future that is similar to, but distinct from, Trump's "Make America Great Again." Biden instead opts for a temporal slogan of "Build Back Better."[191] To establish this position, Biden's campaign presents a series of historic images, such as an early nurse, soldiers in World War II, a Black man at a podium, a man on the moon, and Presidents Franklin D. Roosevelt, John F. Kennedy, and Barack Obama speaking. Biden narrates this past, saying, "Over the last century America has defined itself by rising to meet existential challenges."[192] As Parry-Giles and Parry-Giles note, "Nostalgia is a powerful political/rhetorical appeal because of its emotional resonance with an audience . . . [it] invokes an idealized, mythologized past" which fills in for a lack in the present.¹⁹³ Biden is doing just this when invoking great moments and leaders of the past. However, unlike Trump who fully yearns for this nostalgic return, Biden makes a caveat: "in order to meet the challenges today we can't just build back the way things were before; we have to build back better."¹⁹⁴ Thus, Biden establishes a progressive nostalgia, which seeks to right the horrific wrongs of the present by rebuilding a better version of the past into the future. From here, Biden continues his balancing of the past and future by showing efforts in the past and then explaining his policies for the future in relation to each of the crises he highlighted. The latter portions of this ad are relentlessly upbeat as Biden optimistically proclaims how he will fix the major ills in America. The ad ends with Biden noting, "Times are tough now in America, but we've been here before. We can do this."¹⁹⁵ "How to Build Back Better" uses progressive nostalgia as Biden's weapon for battling against the classic horrors of disease, economic decline, racial injustice, and climate change. Trump is, at worst, positioned as a conflicted enabler of these crises. At best, he is a failure who is unable to fix these major issues. As such, Biden provides a clear path to efficacy for voters to slay the monsters threatening America through his detailed policy proposals.

"Trump's Boycott—Goodyear OH," which was initially aired on August 23, 2020, doesn't rely much on horror framing but does use a similar appeal to nostalgia as was seen in "Build Back Better."¹⁹⁶ The central premise of this ad is that Trump is calling for a boycott of Goodyear, a major auto parts manufacturer in Ohio. A newscast is presented reporting on Trump's push for a boycott. An overhead shot of what is presumably Akron, Ohio is then shown with a quote from the Mayor of Akron, reading, "When you come after Goodyear, you're coming after Akron."¹⁹⁷ A distorted clip of Trump is then presented, where he is supposedly advocating for such a boycott. It is after this quote that the ad applies nostalgia, as black-and-white videos of antique cars are shown driving with a special focus on their tires. The narrator says, "A company with 122-year history in Akron, Ohio. Thousands of American workers and competitors all over the world. And a sitting president who's spinning out of control, who'd risk American jobs to try and save his own."¹⁹⁸ Clips are shown of workers supporting Goodyear, juxtaposed with a graph of international competitors and a slightly distorted shot of Trump. The ad ends with a traditional Biden message of approval, followed by Biden looking into the camera with a smug smile and aviator sunglasses as he revs the engine of a sports car. As such, the Biden campaign does not really rely on horror in this ad but uses nostalgia, which has been linked with horror in other ads, to juxtapose Trump's boycott of Goodyear with Biden's support of the company and industry more broadly.

On the other hand, "Sacred," which was originally aired on September 8, 2020, firmly places Trump in the realm of conflicted horror as it attacks

Trump's potential policies toward Social Security.[199] The ad opens with Biden speaking over a montage of elderly Americans, saying, "For our seniors, social security [sic] is a sacred obligation, a sacred promise made."[200] Such language, referring to a sacred promise elicits Christian theological understandings of covenant and pure good. This is then sharply juxtaposed with Trump, who Biden claims, "The current president is threatening to break that promise. He's proposing to eliminate a tax that pays for almost half the social security [sic] without any way of making up for that lost revenue."[201] Here we see the juxtaposition of a man's fall from grace by breaking a sacred covenant. Trump is visually presented with horizontal distortions and faded coloring. He is signing a law and then out golfing while Biden makes these severe assessments. Such a human flaw, turning away from sacred covenant, puts Trump in the realm of conflicted horror, in line with many stories from the Old Testament of the Bible that depict humans turning from God's covenant and being punished severely for such misdeeds.

From here, the ad shifts to a self-positive assessment of how Biden will protect that covenant. Biden looks directly into the camera, points his finger and firmly says, "I will not let that happen."[202] A montage of Biden speaking with older supporters is then presented, as Biden concludes, "If I am your President we are going to protect social security and Medicare [sic]. You have my word."[203] As such, Biden positions himself as a Social Security fearing man, as it were. He will uphold that sacred covenant. In "Sacred," Biden aligns himself with ultimate good, while Trump is positioned as a fallen man who will deprive senior citizens of their God/government-given inheritance.

First broadcast on October 9, 2020, "Same Old" uses elements of the classic horror frame, particularly temporal bracketing, to paint a picture of voter suppression and encourage Black voter turnout.[204] The main narrator of this ad is Black actor Samuel L. Jackson. He begins by saying, "Voter suppression has taken many forms" as a black-and-white image of the Selma March in 1965 is shown.[205] White police officers are presented in the forefront of this image and the one that follows it, emphasizing who it is that was enforcing voter suppression. A clip of Martin Luther King Jr. speaking to the press is presented next, where he says, "People have been denied the right to vote for well nigh 80 years."[206] A montage of Black folks waiting in lines to vote is shown. Jackson comes back to narrate, explaining the different methods of voter suppression that have been used over the years, including the poll tax, literacy tests, and "racial terrorism and violence."[207] Here black-and-white images of the Ku Klux Klan and police beating Black people are shown to solidify the horrors of racist voting suppression. Finally a clip from Paul Weyrich of the Heritage Foundation is shown, where he says, "I don't want everyone to vote."[208] From here, Jackson is visually presented for the first time where he displays very apparent displeasure, temporally bracketing voter suppression, bemoaning, "New day, same old dirty tricks."[209] As such, the violent horrors of the past are temporally extended into the present, establishing a key characteristic of classic horror.

With past voter suppression horrors established, the second third of the ad links those wrongs to present, ongoing efforts to suppress Black voters. Obama is heard narrating, "There are those in power who are doing their darndest to discourage people from voting."[210] As Obama establishes the present temporality of voter suppression, images of Republican Senate Majority Leader Mitch McConnell and Trump are presented in montage with signs explaining voter ID laws. This establishes the visual argument that Trump and Republican leaders are pushing for the suppression of voters, particularly Black voters. A news anchorwoman narrates next, reporting that there are accusations of voter suppression. Another anchorwoman says, "President Trump [is] sabotaging efforts to vote by mail," as protestors hold signs in favor of voting by mail.[211] Thus, Trump is firmly established as a reincarnation of the classic voter suppression horrors of the past.

Jackson returns for the final portion of the advertisement to make a firm pitch to go out and vote. A montage of voting signs, Black activists, and modern demonstrators in Selma are shown as Jackson argues, "If your vote didn't matter, they wouldn't try so hard to take it from you. Vote early, vote like your life depends on it."[212] Here we see how the anxiety around the need to vote is amplified by establishing it as a life or death action. Jackson begins wrapping up the ad, noting, "I'm exercising my right to vote and you should too, not because I want you to but because he doesn't."[213] Right before Jackson delivers the line of "but because he doesn't," a series of unflattering images of Trump yelling is flashed across the screen, visually establishing who the person is that doesn't want Black people voting.[214] The idea of a white man dictating what he does or does not want Black folks to do is highly evocative of contemporary Black horrors like *Get Out* (2017), where Black people are brainwashed by a white family (see figure 7.1).[215]

The classic Biden Harris approval card is shown, and Harris figures prominently in the foreground of the image and Biden in the background. Jackson comes back on with a final note of urgency, yelling, "Vote dammit, vote!"[216] As such, "Same Old" establishes Trump and the Republican Party as a classic horror through their breach of temporal norms. Even though many might think the horror of racist voter suppression and violence was resolved during the civil rights movement, this ad argues that such monstrosity is alive and well with Trump as its new iteration. One can think of a host of horror franchises where sequel after sequel revives the same monster.[217] Such an element of temporal bracketing and an inability to fully kill the beast is presented here. Accordingly, Jackson's desperate plea to vote is

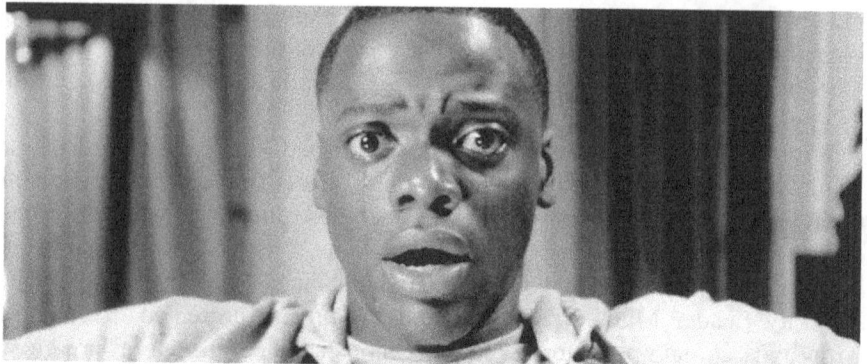

Figure 7.1 *Get Out* (2017). Screenshot captured by author.

a call for a communal resealing of the monster through audience efficacy, a vote for Biden and Harris.

Biden's Almost Exclusively Self-Positive Political Spots

"Backbone," which was originally aired on July 30, 2020, is primarily a self-positive assessment of Biden, which juxtaposes his upbringing with Trump's business background.[218] The ad opens with a fly-over shot of Scranton, Pennsylvania as a narrator says, "Scranton is a long way from Wall Street. You won't find skyscrapers or big-city bankers."[219] Next, Biden's childhood home is shown as the narrator connects his roots to this working-class neighborhood. Family pictures and videos of Biden's father and Biden as a child are presented. The advertisement then transitions to images of Biden when he is slightly older, explaining why he went into public service. Finally, images of Biden with Obama are displayed before the ad cuts into a brief juxtaposition attack on Trump. Distorted images of a younger Trump are shown as the narrator notes that Trump "ran for president for himself and for his friends on Wall Street."[220] An image of Trump's cabinet is presented with text showing how much each member of his cabinet is worth. The ad then shifts again back to Biden, advocating for him as a leader who can help working-class Americans. Trump is shown again briefly with slight distortions as it discusses the pandemic, but ultimately focuses in on Biden and working Americans. The ad ends with an image of Biden smiling with three Black women as the narrator concludes that Biden will "build back better."[221] While "Backbone" does attack Trump, it is not done with much horror other than some slight distortions. Rather, that attack is used to bolster Biden by juxtaposition as a candidate of the people, someone who can lead those people in a fight against the ills and fears that surround them.

Another highly self-positive advertisement for the Biden campaign is "Go from There," which was first released on October 20, 2020.[222] The ad uses a piano rendition of the Star-Spangled Banner as a somewhat rugged-voiced narrator speaks over a visual progression of classic American landscapes. The narrator expresses a deeply nonpartisan position as he says, "There is only one America. No Democratic rivers, no Republican mountains. Just this great land, and all that's possible on it, with a fresh start."[223] Here, Biden visually enters the narrative as he is seen shaking hands and interacting with potential supporters, including a young child. This montage of Biden clips is interspersed with shots of people working, including two football players celebrating with each other. The narrator lists some of the specific things Biden could assist with, such as cures and work. The ad ends with shots of Biden as the narrator notes, "Joe Biden doesn't need everyone in this country to always agree, just to agree we all love this country and go from there."[224] "Go from There" works as a highly self-positive advertisement for Biden that emphasizes both nonpartisan unity and an efficacy for the audience in Biden who will provide resolution for voter fears, such as cures and jobs.

"Make Life Better" is extraordinarily similar to "Go from There" in terms of a self-positive message of non-partisan unity. "Make Life Better" was first released on October 24, 2020.[225] The minute-long political spot is based on a very simple premise, both visually and textually. The ad is essentially a montage of Biden interacting with a wide range of potential voters. Many of the shots show him smiling, shaking hands, and embracing people across race, gender, age, and class lines. Supporters are shown being happy and excited to meet him. The narrator emphasizes that Biden will reach across party lines and be a president for all Americans, those who have served, those who are Democrat, those who are Republican, and those who are "somewhere in between."[226] The narrator also emphasizes that people want someone who will fight to make their lives better. As such, the messaging is a simple one of unity that shows how Biden can provide efficacy for those who are worried about the country, no matter where they fall on the political spectrum.

Biden's campaign strategy was one that relied heavily on self-positive appeals to efficacy, usually holding back on very strong appeals to horror, instead allowing audience members to enthymematically fill in that gap with the fears that were surrounding them from the pandemic to a divided country. Biden did use horror at times, especially when referencing voter suppression of the past or imagery related to the pandemic. Nevertheless, compared to recent campaigns and especially compared to the Trump campaign, the Biden campaign's use of horror framing was exceptionally mild.

CONCLUSION

While there was much hand-wringing over the results of the 2020 election, Joe Biden ultimately defeated Donald Trump, winning a few key states by razor-thin margins. As remains a common refrain in this work, it is unclear what effect, if any, the different campaign strategies of Donald Trump and Joe Biden had on this election. Nevertheless, Trump ultimately maintained his horror framing from 2016, which represents peaks in the genre's demonic implications on presidential elections. Trump relentlessly attacked the Radical Left using a classic frame, especially women of color he placed in that group like Ocasio-Cortez and Omar. He also grouped immigrants and terrorists into this group, using visual apposition to connect these supposedly demonic groups with Biden. Trump's attacks on Biden ultimately relied more heavily on the conflicted horror frame, highlighting his contested mental status and his supposed manipulability. These are deeply human horrors that culminate in an unease about such a supposedly flawed candidate becoming president.

On the other side, Biden marked a stark decline in the prevalence of horror framing when compared with the elections preceding this one. Biden's campaign felt analogous to John Kerry's 2004 campaign, where both candidates' campaign teams seemed hesitant to use strong, horrific attack advertisements. This similarity could potentially be a result of the already heightened fears of the public. In 2004, people were worried about the War on Terror. In 2020, voters feared the COVID-19 pandemic, racial injustice, and a deepening partisan divide in the country. Thus, even though Biden's campaign displayed a restraint that has not been seen by either side for multiple elections, the 2020 campaign still exemplifies the ramifications of the polarizing implication of horror advertising. The political environment of this election was deeply polarized along lines of voting issues.[227] While Biden did not lash out at Trump through his advertisements nearly as much as he could have, there were clearly no courtesies provided. The election was framed by the Biden campaign as us vs. them, good vs. evil, science vs. superstition, racist vs. anti-racist, and so on. That last point, on racial injustice, was often where the Biden campaign struck out against Trump the harshest. Biden's linking of Trump's present actions with past, violent voter suppression and racism, created a classic horror frame, if only in small doses.

Further, while Biden's horror usage was limited, it was still there, however subtly, in many of his advertisements. Coupled with Trump's overtly horrific campaign, we can see the omnipresence of horror framing at play. Further, even though Biden's team was careful not to overplay horror in terms of the ongoing pandemic, this very real threat was one of the key cornerstones of the narrative of the campaign, playing into the normative component of horror in his campaign. This subtly highlights the insidious implication of horror, where such notions seep into campaigns even when they largely avoid such generic allusions. Trump's campaign was much less insidious and much more invasive, once again making stark, polarized monsters out of opposition leaders and various groups of people.

Interestingly, this campaign pushes back some against the political nihilism of horror framing. This election saw all-time high voter turnout. There is a full gambit of reasons this might have happened. While horror was still dominant in the Trump campaign and implied in the Biden campaign, there were also plenty of appeals to efficacy through self-praise. Perhaps these appeals accomplished the sense of efficacy P. Sol Hart and Lauren Feldman find necessary for the public to engage politically.[228] Maybe, as Martha C. Nussbaum points out, fear is "asocial," but only asocial across party lines, not within partisan constructs.[229] Perhaps Biden's decreased horror framing accounts for decreased political fear, as both candidates were seen more favorably than in 2016. Maybe both campaigns simply had better get out the vote strategies. Ultimately, these are all speculations that a future researcher could investigate with more depth. Nevertheless, while there was a one-sided decline in horror framing in the 2020 election, the trend throughout the twenty-first century still seems to indicate that horror will continue to play a significant role in presidential campaign advertising for the foreseeable future. What remains to be seen is the long-term impact such heightened political fearmongering will have on American democracy.

NOTES

1. Sophie Lewis, "Joe Biden Breaks Obama's Record for Most Votes Ever Cast for a U.S. Presidential Candidate," *CBS News*, November 7, 2020, https://www.cbsnews.com/news/joe-biden-popular-vote-record-barack-obama-us-presidential-election-donald-trump/. Biden had a positive favorability at 52 percent in exit polls, while Trump had a 46 percent favorability. In 2016, Trump had a favorability index of 38 percent while Hillary Clinton held a 43 percent favorability. See "Exit Polls," *CNN*, November 23, 2016, https://www.cnn.com/election/2016/results/exit-polls; "National Exit Polls: How Different Groups Voted," *New York Times*, November 3, 2020, https://www.nytimes.com/interactive/2020/11/03/us/elections/exit-polls-president.html.

2. Nigel Chiwaya and Corky Siemaszko, "Covid-19 Cases, Deaths Rising Rapidly Ahead of Election Day," *NBC News*, November 2, 2020, https://www.nbcnews.com/news/us-news/covid-19-cases-deaths-rising-rapid-rate-ahead-election-day-n1245780.

3. "National Exit Polls," *New York Times*.

4. "National Exit Polls," *New York Times*.

5. Worth noting, "Progresista" is a PAC ad, but as I explain in the analysis of that ad, it felt like an important example to include as a standalone. "Personal" from the Biden campaign was not included in this analysis because it was released August 27, 2019, well before Biden won the Democratic nomination. Trump's "Text 'BORDER' to 88022" was not included for a similar reason, as it was released January 5, 2019. Trump's "Vision for America" was also not included because it was less of an ad and more of an intro for the televised Republican National Convention. Further, *The Living Room Candidate* uploaded a handful of ads after final copies of this book manuscript were due and are sadly not included here. These ads do not conflict with this chapter, and in fact further enhance the arguments of this chapter and book. In particular, Trump's ads on defunding the police use exceptionally horrific framing.

6. Trump, "47 Years of Failure," *The Living Room Candidate: Presidential Campaign Commercials 1952–2020*, August 17, 2020, http://www.livingroomcandidate.org/commercials/2020/47-years-of-failure.

7. Trump, "47 Years of Failure."

8. For a more complete understanding of gothic horror, see, David Punter, *The Literature of Terror: A History of Gothic Fictions from 1765 to the Present Day* (London: Longman, 1980). See also, *Crimson Peak*, directed by Guillermo del Toro (2015; Universal Studios, 2015), DVD; *The Haunting of Hill House*, created by Mike Flanagan (2018; Netflix), Digital; *The Haunting of Bly Manor*, created by Mike Flanagan (2020; Netflix), Digital.

9. Trump, "47 Years of Failure."

10. Trump, "47 Years of Failure."

11. Bernadette Marie Calafell, *Monstrosity, Performance, and Race in Contemporary Culture* (New York: Peter Lang, 2015), 12.

12. Trump, "47 Years of Failure."

13. Trump, "47 Years of Failure."

14. Donald J. Trump for President, "Two Americas Immigration," *The Living Room Candidate: Presidential Campaign Commercials 1952–2020*, August 19, 2016, http://www.livingroomcandidate.org/commercials/2016/two-americas-immigration. For discussion on the visual framing of immigrants as faceless pollutants, see J. David Cisneros, "Contaminated Communities: The Metaphor of 'Immigrant as Pollutant' in Media Representations of Immigration," *Rhetoric & Public Affairs* 11, no. 4 (2008): 569–601.

15. Trump, "47 Years of Failure."

16. Trump, "Takeover," *The Living Room Candidate: Presidential Campaign Commercials 1952–2020*, August 17, 2020, http://www.livingroomcandidate.org/commercials/2020/takeover.

17. See *Frankenstein*, directed by James Whale (1931; Universal Studios Home Entertainment, 2016), DVD; *The Curse of Frankenstein*, directed by Terence Fisher (1957; Horrortheque, 2010), Digital.

18. Trump, "Takeover"; Trump, "47 Years of Failure."

19. Trump, "Takeover."

20. Trump, "Takeover"; Trump, "47 Years of Failure."

21. Trump, "Takeover."
22. *The Purge*, directed by James DeMonaco (2013; Universal Studios, 2013), DVD.
23. Trump, "Takeover."
24. Trump, "Takeover."
25. For examples, see films like *Frankenstein*, Whale; *The Curse of Frankenstein*, Fisher; *The Fly*, directed by Kurt Neumann (1958; 20th Century Fox), Digital; *The Fly*, directed by David Cronenberg (1986; 20th Century Fox), Digital.
26. *The Exorcist*, directed by William Friedkin (1973; Warner Bros., 2011), DVD; *Poltergeist*, directed by Tobe Hooper (1982; Warner Home Video, 2010), DVD.
27. *Invasion of the Body Snatchers*, directed by Don Siegel (1956; Republic Pictures, 1998), DVD.
28. Trump, "Meet Phony Kamala Harris!" *The Living Room Candidate: Presidential Campaign Commercials 1952–2020*, August 17, 2020, http://www.livingroomcandidate.org/commercials/2020/meet-phony-kamala-harris.
29. Trump, "Meet Phony Kamala Harris!"
30. Trump, "Meet Phony Kamala Harris!"
31. Trump, "Meet Phony Kamala Harris!"
32. For more on apposition's use in campaign advertising, see Kathleen Hall Jamieson, *Dirty Politics: Deception, Distraction, and Democracy* (New York: Oxford University Press, 1992), 47–60.
33. Trump, "Meet Phony Kamala Harris!"
34. Trump, "Meet Phony Kamala Harris!"
35. For more on ideographs, see Michael Calvin McGee, "The 'Ideograph': A Link Between Rhetoric and Ideology," *Quarterly Journal of Speech* 66, no. 1 (1980): 1–16.
36. Trump, "Meet Phony Kamala Harris!"
37. *Invasion of the Body Snatchers*, Siegel.
38. Trump, "Meet Phony Kamala Harris!"
39. Trump, "Meet Phony Kamala Harris!"
40. Michael Pementel, "Representations of Mental Health in Horror: From Establishing Stigmas to Tearing Them Down," *Bloody Disgusting*, August 2, 2018, https://bloody-disgusting.com/editorials/3513603/representations-mental-health-horror-establishing-stigmas-tearing/. For more on the rhetorical framing of horror and archaic mental health practices, see Jenell Johnson, *American Lobotomy: A Rhetorical History* (Ann Arbor: University of Michigan Press, 2015).
41. See *The Cabinet of Dr. Caligari*, directed by Robert Wiene (1920; Horrortheque, 2010), Digital; Pementel, "Representations of Mental Health in Horror."
42. Trump, "Watch: Past vs Present," *The Living Room Candidate: Presidential Campaign Commercials 1952–2020*, August 17, 2020, http://www.livingroomcandidate.org/commercials/2020/watch-past-vs-present.
43. Trump, "Watch: Past vs Present."
44. Trump, "Watch: Past vs Present."
45. Trump, "Watch: Past vs Present."

46. "Joe Biden," *Stuttering Foundation*, https://www.stutteringhelp.org/content/joe-biden.

47. Trump, "Watch: Past vs Present."

48. Trump, "Watch: Past vs Present."

49. Trump, "Watch: Past vs Present."

50. Trump, "Watch: Past vs Present."

51. Trump, "Two Americas Immigration."; Donald J. Trump for America, "Two Americas: Economy," *The Living Room Candidate: Presidential Campaign Commercials 1952–2020*, August 29, 2016, http://www.livingroomcandidate.org/commercials/2016/two-americas-economy.

52. Trump, "America First! #MAGA," *The Living Room Candidate: Presidential Campaign Commercials 1952–2020*, August 20, 2020, http://www.livingroomcandidate.org/commercials/2020/america-first-maga.

53. Trump, "America First! #MAGA."

54. Trump, "America First! #MAGA."

55. Harry M. Benshoff, "Horror Before 'The Horror Film,'" in *A Companion to the Horror Film*, ed. Harry M. Benshoff (New York: Wiley Blackwell, 2014), 216.

56. See Jamieson, *Dirty Politics*, 47–60.

57. Shawn J. Parry-Giles and Trevor Parry-Giles, "Collective Memory, Political Nostalgia, and the Rhetorical Presidency: Bill Clinton's Commemoration of the March on Washington, August 28, 1998," *Quarterly Journal of Speech* 86, no. 4 (2000): 418–19.

58. Trump, "America First! #MAGA."

59. Trump, "America First! #MAGA."

60. For a discussion of how this tactic applies to drone pilots, see Joshua Olson and Muhammad Rashid, "Modern Drone Warfare: An Ethical Analysis," *2013 ASEE Southeast Section Conference*, 2013, http://se.asee.org/proceedings/ASEE2013/Papers2013/157.PDF.

61. Trump, "America First! #MAGA."

62. Trump, "America First! #MAGA."

63. Trump, "Don't Let Them Ruin America," *The Living Room Candidate: Presidential Campaign Commercials 1952–2020*, August 17, 2020, http://www.livingroomcandidate.org/commercials/2020/dont-let-them-ruin-america.

64. Ian Haney López, *Dog Whistle Politics: How Coded Racial Appeals Have Reinvented Racism & Wrecked the Middle Class* (New York: Oxford University Press, 2014), 4.

65. Trump, "Don't Let Them Ruin America."

66. Trump, "Don't Let Them Ruin America."

67. Trump, "Don't Let Them Ruin America."

68. Trump, "Don't Let Them Ruin America."

69. Trump, "Don't Let Them Ruin America."

70. Trump, "Don't Let Them Ruin America."

71. Trump, "Don't Let Them Ruin America."

72. See films like *The Purge*, DeMonaco; and other films from this series.

73. Charlton D. McIlwain and Stephen M. Caliendo, *Race Appeal: How Candidates Invoke Race in U.S. Political Campaigns* (Philadelphia, PA: Temple University Press, 2011), 16.

74. Trump, "Biden Lied," *The Living Room Candidate: Presidential Campaign Commercials 1952–2020*, October 16, 2020, http://www.livingroomcandidate.org/commercials/2020/biden-lied.

75. Trump, "Biden Lied."

76. Trump, "Biden Lied."

77. For example, see Ben Collins and Brandy Zadrozny, "How a Fake Persona Laid the Groundwork for a Hunter Biden Conspiracy Deluge," *NBC News*, October 29, 2020, https://www.nbcnews.com/tech/security/how-fake-persona-laid-groundwork-hunter-biden-conspiracy-deluge-n1245387.

78. Trump, "Biden Lied."

79. Trump, "Biden Lied."

80. Trump, "Biden Lied."

81. Trump, "Teleprompter Joe," *The Living Room Candidate: Presidential Campaign Commercials 1952–2020*, September 24, 2020, http://www.livingroomcandidate.org/commercials/2020/teleprompter-joe.

82. Diana C. Mutz and Byron Reeves, "The New Videomalaise: Effects of Televised Incivility on Political Trust," *American Political Science Review* 99, no. 1 (2005): 3.

83. Trump, "Teleprompter Joe."

84. Trump, "Teleprompter Joe."

85. Trump, "Teleprompter Joe."

86. Trump, "Teleprompter Joe."

87. Trump, "Teleprompter Joe."

88. Trump, "The Real Biden Plan," *The Living Room Candidate: Presidential Campaign Commercials 1952–2020*, October 18, 2020, http://www.livingroomcandidate.org/commercials/2020/the-real-biden-plan.

89. Trump, "The Real Biden Plan."

90. Trump, "The Real Biden Plan."

91. Trump, "The Real Biden Plan."

92. Trump, "The Joe Biden They Are Hiding from You," *The Living Room Candidate: Presidential Campaign Commercials 1952–2020*, August 7, 2020, http://www.livingroomcandidate.org/commercials/2020/the-joe-biden-they-are-hiding-from-you.

93. Trump, "The Joe Biden They Are Hiding From You."

94. Trump, "The Joe Biden They Are Hiding From You."

95. Trump, "The Joe Biden They Are Hiding From You."

96. Trump, "The Joe Biden They Are Hiding From You."

97. Trump, "The Joe Biden They Are Hiding From You."

98. Trump, "The Joe Biden They Are Hiding From You."

99. Trump, "The Joe Biden They Are Hiding From You."

100. Trump, "The Joe Biden They Are Hiding From You."

101. Trump, "The Joe Biden They Are Hiding From You."

102. Mutz and Reeves, "The New Videomalaise," 3.

103. See Sabrina Rodriguez, "How Miami Cubans Disrupted Biden's Path to a Florida Win," *Politico*, November 4, 2020, https://www.politico.com/news/2020/11/04/biden-miami-cubans-election-2020-433999.

104. Latinos for Trump, "Progresista," *The Living Room Candidate: Presidential Campaign Commercials 1952–2020*, August 3, 2020, http://www.livingroomcandidate.org/commercials/2020/progresista.

105. Latinos for Trump, "Progresista."

106. Latinos for Trump, "Progresista."

107. Latinos for Trump, "Progresista."

108. Latinos for Trump, "Progresista."

109. Latinos for Trump, "Progresista," my translation.

110. Latinos for Trump, "Progresista."

111. See *It Came from Outer Space*, directed by Jack Arnold (1953; Universal Studios, 2017), Blu-ray; *War of the Worlds,* directed by Byron Haskin (1953; Paramount Pictures, 1999), DVD; *The Monolith Monsters*, directed by John Sherwood (1957; Willette Acquisition Corp., 2015), DVD.

112. Trump, "Record Smashing," *The Living Room Candidate: Presidential Campaign Commercials 1952–2020*, August 13, 2020, http://www.livingroomcandidate.org/commercials/2020/record-smashing.

113. Trump, "Record Smashing."

114. Trump, "Record Smashing."

115. Trump, "Record Smashing."

116. Trump, "Record Smashing."

117. Trump, "Carefully," *The Living Room Candidate: Presidential Campaign Commercials 1952–2020*, October 10, 2020, http://www.livingroomcandidate.org/commercials/2020/carefully.

118. Trump, "Carefully."

119. Trump, "Carefully."

120. Trump, "Carefully."

121. Trump, "Carefully."

122. Trump, "Second Chance," *The Living Room Candidate: Presidential Campaign Commercials 1952–2020*, October 5, 2020, http://www.livingroomcandidate.org/commercials/2020/second-chance.

123. Trump, "Second Chance."

124. Trump, "Second Chance."

125. Trump, "Second Chance."

126. Trump, "Second Chance."

127. Matthew W. Hughey, *The White Savior Film: Content, Critics, and Consumption* (Philadelphia, PA: Temple University Press, 2014), 8. See also, Nicole Maurantonio, "'Reason to Hope?': The White Savior Myth and Progress in 'Post-Racial' America," *Journalism & Mass Communication Quarterly* 94, no. 4 (2017): 1130–45.

128. James West, "Get Out (of the White House): The Trump Administration and YouTube Horror Parody as Social Commentary," in *Make America Hate Again:*

Trump-Era Horror and the Politics of Fear, ed. Victoria McCollum (New York: Routledge, 2019), 264.

129. Biden, "Crossroads," *The Living Room Candidate: Presidential Campaign Commercials 1952–2020*, July 23, 2020, http://www.livingroomcandidate.org/commercials/2020/crossroads.

130. Biden, "Crossroads."
131. Biden, "Crossroads."
132. Biden, "Crossroads."
133. See films like *The Exorcist*, Friedkin; *The Vatican Tapes*, directed by Mark Neveldine (2015; Lionsgate Home Entertainment, 2015), DVD; *The Crucifixion*, directed by Xavier Gens (2017; Lionsgate Home Entertainment, 2017), DVD; or any of the other films in the vast subgenre of possession/exorcism horror films.
134. Biden, "Crossroads."
135. Biden, "Crossroads."
136. Biden, "Crossroads."
137. Biden, "'It Is What It Is,'" *The Living Room Candidate: Presidential Campaign Commercials 1952–2020*, August 5, 2020, http://www.livingroomcandidate.org/commercials/2020/it-is-what-it-is.
138. Biden, "'It Is What It Is.'"
139. Biden, "'It Is What It Is.'"
140. Biden, "'It Is What It Is.'"
141. *Outbreak*, directed by Duncan Henderson (1995; Warner Home Video, 2010), DVD; *Contagion*, directed by Steven Soderbergh (2011; Warner Home Video, 2012), DVD; *28 Days Later*, directed by Danny Boyle (2003; 20th Century Fox Home Entertainment, 2008), DVD.
142. Megan McCluskey, "Horror Films Have Always Tapped Into Pop Culture's Most Urgent Fears. COVID-19 Will Be Their Next Inspiration," *Time*, October 7, 2020, https://time.com/5891305/horror-movies-coronavirus-history-genre/.
143. Biden, "Donald Trump Failed to Protect Us From COVID-19," *The Living Room Candidate: Presidential Campaign Commercials 1952–2020*, August 8, 2020, http://www.livingroomcandidate.org/commercials/2020/donald-trump-failed-to-protect-us-from-covid-19.
144. Biden, "Donald Trump Failed to Protect Us."
145. Biden, "Donald Trump Failed to Protect Us."
146. Biden, "Donald Trump Failed to Protect Us."
147. Biden, "Donald Trump Failed to Protect Us."
148. Biden, "Donald Trump Failed to Protect Us."
149. Kristen Whissel, "Tales of Upward Mobility: The New Verticality and Digital Special Effects," *Film Quarterly* 59, no. 4 (2006): 23.
150. See Dante, *The Inferno*, trans. Marvin R. Vincent (New York: Charles Scribner's Sons, 1904).
151. Biden, "Truth :60," *The Living Room Candidate: Presidential Campaign Commercials 1952–2020*, July 21, 2020, http://www.livingroomcandidate.org/commercials/2020/truth-60.
152. Biden, "Truth: 60."

153. Biden, "Truth: 60."
154. Biden, "'It Is What It Is.'"
155. Biden, "Truth: 60."
156. For pandemic horrors, see films like *Outbreak*, Henderson; *Contagion*, Soderbergh; *28 Days Later*, Boyle. For invasion horrors, see films like *Invasion of the Body Snatchers*, Siegel; *It Came from Outer Space*, Arnold; *War of the Worlds*, Haskin; *Independence Day*, directed by Roland Emmerich (1996; 20th Century Fox Home Entertainment, 2016), DVD.
157. Peter Biskind, *Seeing is Believing: How Hollywood Taught Us to Stop Worrying and Love the Fifties* (New York, Henry Holt, 1983), 129.
158. Biden, "Truth: 60."
159. Biden, "Truth: 60."
160. Biden, "Truth: 60."
161. Biden, "Pero Ya No," *The Living Room Candidate: Presidential Campaign Commercials 1952–2020*, August 28, 2020, http://www.livingroomcandidate.org/commercials/2020/pero-ya-no.
162. Bad Bunny, "Pero Ya No," track 3 on *YHLQMDLG*, Rimas Entertainment, 2020, digital.
163. *Evil Dead II*, directed by Sam Raimi (1987; Lionsgate, 2018), DVD; *Shaun of the Dead*, directed by Edgar Wright (2004; Universal Home Video, 2007), DVD; *The Cabin in the Woods*, directed by Drew Goddard (2011; Lionsgate, 2011), DVD.
164. "Bad Bunny—Pero Ya No (English Translation)," *Genius*, https://genius.com/Genius-english-translations-bad-bunny-pero-ya-no-english-translation-lyrics.
165. Biden, "Better America," *The Living Room Candidate: Presidential Campaign Commercials 1952–2020*, August 6, 2020, http://www.livingroomcandidate.org/commercials/2020/better-america.
166. Biden, "Better America."
167. Biden, "Better America."
168. Biden, "Better America."
169. Biden, "Better America."
170. Biden, "Better America."
171. Biden, "Better America."
172. Biden, "Better America."
173. Caroline Joan (Kay) S. Picart and David A. Frank, *Frames of Evil: The Holocaust as Horror in American Film* (Carbondale: Southern Illinois University Press, 2006), 7.
174. Biden, "Better America."
175. Biden, "Better America."
176. McIlwain and Caliendo, *Race Appeal*, 16.
177. Biden, "Kamala Harris: Vice President Announcement," *The Living Room Candidate: Presidential Campaign Commercials 1952–2020*, August 12, 2020, http://www.livingroomcandidate.org/commercials/2020/kamala-harris-vice-president-announcement.
178. Biden, "Kamala Harris."
179. Biden, "Kamala Harris."

180. Biden, "Kamala Harris."
181. Biden, "Kamala Harris."
182. Biden, "Kamala Harris."
183. See films like *The Purge*, DeMonaco.
184. Biden, "Kamala Harris."
185. Biden, "Kamala Harris."
186. Biden, "Kamala Harris."
187. Biden, "How to Build Back Better," *The Living Room Candidate: Presidential Campaign Commercials 1952–2020*, August 8, 2020, http://www.livingroomcandidate.org/commercials/2020/how-to-build-back-better.
188. Biden, "How to Build Back Better."
189. Biden, "How to Build Back Better."
190. Biskind, *Seeing is Believing*, 129.
191. Biden, "How to Build Back Better."
192. Biden, "How to Build Back Better."
193. Parry-Giles and Parry-Giles, "Collective Memory, Political Nostalgia, and the Rhetorical Presidency," 421.
194. Biden, "How to Build Back Better."
195. Biden, "How to Build Back Better."
196. Biden, "Trump's Boycott—Goodyear OH," *The Living Room Candidate: Presidential Campaign Commercials 1952–2020*, August 23, 2020, http://www.livingroomcandidate.org/commercials/2020/trumps-boycott-goodyear-oh; Biden, "How to Build Back Better."
197. Biden, "Trump's Boycott."
198. Biden, "Trump's Boycott."
199. Biden, "Sacred," *The Living Room Candidate: Presidential Campaign Commercials 1952–2020*, September 8, 2020, http://www.livingroomcandidate.org/commercials/2020/sacred.
200. Biden, "Sacred."
201. Biden, "Sacred."
202. Biden, "Sacred."
203. Biden, "Sacred."
204. Biden, "Same Old," *The Living Room Candidate: Presidential Campaign Commercials 1952–2020*, October 9, 2020, http://www.livingroomcandidate.org/commercials/2020/same-old.
205. Biden, "Same Old."
206. Biden, "Same Old."
207. Biden, "Same Old."
208. Biden, "Same Old."
209. Biden, "Same Old."
210. Biden, "Same Old."
211. Biden, "Same Old."
212. Biden, "Same Old."
213. Biden, "Same Old."
214. Biden, "Same Old."

215. *Get Out*, directed by Jordan Peele (2017; Universal Studios, 2017), Blu-ray.

216. Biden, "Same Old."

217. For examples, look at franchises that developed out of the following films: *Halloween*, directed by John Carpenter (1978; Lionsgate Home Entertainment, 2007), DVD; *Friday the 13th*, directed by Sean S. Cunningham (1980; Paramount, 2017), Blu-ray; *A Nightmare on Elm Street*, directed by Wes Craven (1984; New Line Home Video, 2010), Blu-ray.

218. Biden, "Backbone," *The Living Room Candidate: Presidential Campaign Commercials 1952–2020*, July 30, 2020, http://www.livingroomcandidate.org/commercials/2020/backbone.

219. Biden, "Backbone."

220. Biden, "Backbone."

221. Biden, "Backbone."

222. Biden, "Go from There," *The Living Room Candidate: Presidential Campaign Commercials 1952–2020*, October 20, 2020, http://www.livingroomcandidate.org/commercials/2020/go-from-there.

223. Biden, "Go from There."

224. Biden, "Go from There."

225. Biden, "Make Life Better," *The Living Room Candidate: Presidential Campaign Commercials 1952–2020*, October 24, 2020, http://www.livingroomcandidate.org/commercials/2020/make-life-better.

226. Biden, "Make Life Better."

227. "National Exit Polls," *New York Times*.

228. P. Sol Hart and Lauren Feldman, "Threat Without Efficacy? Climate Change on U.S. Network News," *Science Communication* 36, no. 3 (2014): 344.

229. Martha C. Nussbaum, *The Monarchy of Fear: A Philosopher Looks at Our Political Crisis* (New York: Simon & Schuster, 2018), 28.

Chapter 8

Conclusion

This book has sought to construct the historical and methodological basis of horror framing present in presidential election campaign ads in the twenty-first century. Through the textual analysis of the 2000, 2004, 2008, 2012, 2016, and 2020 presidential campaigns, I have shown that televised campaign ads have significantly featured elements of the horror genre in U.S. presidential elections, given the proclivity of both horror and presidential campaigns toward affective fear appeals. Further, I have made apparent that presidential campaigns have used this generic tool in very different ways. There are four remaining goals that this conclusion will accomplish. First, I will briefly review the strategies used by each of the campaigns explored in this work. Second, I will explain some of the implications of this work as it pertains to the use of horror advertising in our political system. Third, I will demonstrate how the constitutive rhetorical forces of this building trend of horrific advertising have potentially rippled into the real-world consequences of the January 6, 2021, Capitol riots. Finally, I will offer a possible corrective for this spiral of political horror: the justified horror frame.

Of all the elections analyzed here, the Gore and Bush campaigns from 2000 were the most similar in their usage of horror framing although there are salient and subtle differences, nonetheless. Both Gore and Bush relied heavily on self-positive campaign advertisements that attempted to set themselves up as the hero capable of realizing audience efficacy. Gore and Bush also relied on both the conflicted and classic horror frames. To an extent that I observed differences, Bush used the conflicted frame a little more heavily than Gore. They also differed in the temporal focus of their praise, with Gore leaning heavily on future policy proposals and Bush relying on both future policy and past accomplishments.

While the 2000 election had a number of evident examples of the classic and conflicted horror frames in use, it would be hard to argue that these frames were the driving narrative of the campaigns as a whole, or as Glenn W. Richardson Jr. calls it, the "crucial connective cement."[1] To be certain, horror framing was a noticeable component of that mixture. However, as later campaigns showed, both the scale and scope of horror themes amplified significantly.

The 2004 election once again featured George W. Bush taking on challenger John Kerry. Whereas Bush had relied heavily on self-positive advertising in the 2000 election, the campaign decided to shift to a much stronger horror offensive, deploying the conflicted frame against Kerry while using the classic horror frame to depict external threats like terrorism. Kerry, on the other hand, tried not to use horror framing early but eventually did in relation to his Vietnam War experiences and the war in Iraq. Generally, a sitting president would seem less willing to scare voters, since they typically want Americans to feel good about the last four years. However, given 2004 was the first election after September 11 and the ensuing wars, Bush amped up the horror themes against a decorated war veteran with more military and foreign policy experience than Bush. Bush used such horror appeals to undermine Kerry's advantage in foreign policy experience to drive voters away from Kerry and to himself.[2]

In the 2008 election, both Barack Obama and John McCain relied heavily on horror framing. McCain was extremely consistent in his usage of the classic and conflicted frames: the classic frames were aimed at existential threats to the United States, while he reserved the conflicted frame for Obama. The Obama campaign seemed to mirror some of the tropes of the McCain campaign early on, but as the campaign progressed and the 2008 financial crisis deepened, Obama moved from using the conflicted frame to the classic frame when attacking his opponent. Obama used the classic horror frame later in the campaign to fully exploit the fear growing amongst voters. Images of economic decline, such as rusted, locked, chain-link fences, are deployed in direct relationship to McCain's economic policies in ads like "This Year."[3] Further, Obama moves McCain from merely being associated with the monstrous Bush, to being his own, evil entity on par with Bush.

However, the long-term shift between the 2000 and 2008 campaigns might not be most apparent in the usage of horror tropes (although it is very apparent there), but rather in the extreme difference in the usage of self-positive appeals to audience efficacy. The Gore and Bush campaigns were both loaded to the brim with policy and self-positive assessments. The Kerry campaign in 2004 also used a similar heavy amount of positive advertising. The Obama and McCain campaigns felt relatively devoid of these features, and when they were used, they were used haphazardly. The Obama campaign started with the self-positive ad, "Country I Love,"[4] but almost completely abandoned appeals to audience efficacy until some of the last ads, such as "Defining Moment"[5] and "Something."[6] McCain appealed to audience efficacy at times in his campaign, but he usually only did this through the notion of his status as a "Maverick." This created a conundrum for audience members. Mavericks typically go it alone, leaving little room for voters to feel a call to join the cause. Shifts in both horror and audience efficacy were apparent in the 2000, 2004, and 2008 elections.

Obama and Romney's 2012 faceoff featured another heavy dosage of horror framing. Romney consistently used the classic horror frame to attack what he viewed as threats to the United States: Obama, China, and the deficit. Romney's advertisements, like some of McCain's, used notions of racistly charged hypnotism, although this time aligned more with a classic horror frame than a conflicted one. On the other hand, the Obama campaign used a significant amount of conflicted horror alongside its positive advertising.[7] Obama deployed the conflicted frame early and often to surgically attack Romney's character as someone uncaring and disconnected from lower- and middle-class issues. Ultimately, the Obama campaign shifted its strategy from 2008 to the 2012 election by using the conflicted frame far more than the classic. This made sure that voters were not led to fear the status quo, an ill-advised campaign strategy for most incumbent presidents. Rather, they were primarily guided to mistrust and fear a Mitt Romney presidency.

The 2016 election followed suit in its dominant usage of horror framing, diverging some in how the frames were deployed and how their intensity differed across ads. The Clinton campaign used both the conflicted and classic horror frames to depict Trump. Her usage of the conflicted frame was aimed heavily at Trump's name-calling and various rhetorical gaffes. She used these clips in combination with a conflicted horror frame to paint the picture that Trump diverges significantly from common, decent American values. While the majority of Clinton's attacks on Trump used the conflicted frame, she also unleashed the classic frame against him when discussing how he would use the powers of commander in chief. For example, "Daisy" uses postmodern horror, relying on public memory of an earlier presidential campaign ad to argue that Trump will plunge the world back into the atomic fears of the Cold War.

Trump took a far different approach from Clinton. Instead of using both the classic and conflicted frames, Trump almost exclusively relied upon the classic horror frame, using it to frame immigrants, economic decline, and Clinton all as monstrous threats.[8] "Unfit (R)" might very well be the most classically horrific campaign advertisement analyzed in this work, and it aims the classic horror frame directly at Clinton.[9] This ad deployed a heavy dosage of dark shading, blood-red typography, and even allusions to the occult in order to connect Clinton with Anthony Weiner.

Clinton and Trump both diverged on their appeals to audience efficacy as well. Clinton had very few appeals to audience efficacy throughout her televised campaign. When she did make those appeals, they were very rarely grounded in her own achievements and policy. Further, they were often aimed at only one voting demographic. Trump, on the other hand, balanced his heavy use of the classic horror frame with plenty of self-positive assessments. Many of his advertisements relied on juxtaposing the decrepit, monstrous state of the United States before contrasting it with his vision of a future where America is great once again. Trump also had some purely self-positive advertisements aimed at much wider voter segments than Clinton.

The 2020 presidential campaign between Donald Trump and Joe Biden split, in that it saw more of the same from Donald Trump while Biden's strategy seemed most analogous to Kerry's 2004 campaign in terms of horror framing. For Trump's campaign, he again relied heavily on the classic horror frame, predominantly targeting terrorists, immigrants, women, and the Radical Left. Worth particular note is how much Trump attacked those last two categories, women and the Radical Left, neither of which describe Biden very well. If anything, the campaign showed how much more comfortable Trump and his team were with attacking women of color that they deemed radical than a moderate, white man. The attacks against Alexandria Ocasio-Cortez, Ilhan Omar, and Kamala Harris were all significantly stronger and more classically framed in terms of horror. When attacking Biden himself, the conflicted horror frame was predominantly used. Attacks on Biden's mental health took the forefront, connecting with a problematic trope that has deep roots in the horror genre. Biden was framed as someone who was losing their mental wherewithal through age and becoming more and more susceptible to manipulation by his running mate, Kamala Harris, and other radical forces. Like many of his 2016 ads, much of Trump's 2020 ads ended on positive notes about his presidency and audience efficacy. However, with multiple crises bearing down on him, these self-positive appeals felt more forced and less authentic than in 2016.

Biden's campaign, on the other hand, marked a significant retreat from the continued amplification of horror framing in presidential campaigns. There were still certain elements of horror at play in Biden's campaign, but many dealt more with allusion and enthymeme than outright horror. The pandemic was primarily discussed in these terms, where quick montages of health care workers, hospitals, patients, and so on, was all that was needed to remind people of the ongoing pandemic in the country. The Biden campaign also used racial advertising, distinct from racist strategies, to encourage specific, targeted audience efficacy for particular demographics. In fact, it was these racial ads' attacks on Trump that carried the heaviest horror framing, not Trump's handling of the pandemic.

While the horror frame was used lightly throughout the Biden campaign, self-positive appeals to audience efficacy were frequently presented. One has to imagine that the Biden campaign was well aware that people were scared given the pandemic and nationwide unrest. Rather than exacerbate those fears even further, the campaign largely angled toward a message centered around the phrase, "Build Back Better." Biden was framed as a hero of the working class, presenting his background narrative as someone who grew up in working-class America.[10]

THE IMPLICATIONS: PRESIDENTIAL HORROR ADVERTISING

Based on this analysis, I offer seven intrinsic implications of contemporary campaign horror framing before discussing the ramifications, ethics, and morality of these trends. Specifically, I argue that horror frames in presidential advertising in the post–9/11 campaigns are *omnipresent, normative, polarizing, demonic, invasive, insidious,* and *nihilistic*. These seven implications have become integral to the use and consumption of horror in political life.

First, horror framing is *omnipresent*. Candidates have consistently turned to horror framing in varying amounts throughout twenty-first-century presidential campaign ads. Winner and loser, Republican and Democrat, incumbent and challenger, all candidate types used both the conflicted and classic horror frames, reflecting the foundational nature of horror frames in most recent presidential campaigns. Horror framing dominates many campaigns in the twenty-first century as candidates seemly assume that voters are motivated most by fear.

Second, candidates have increasingly made horror frames a *normative* component of their campaigns since 9/11. While the horror frame was clearly used in pre–twenty-first-century campaign advertisements, they were not *the* narrative cornerstone of a campaign. Famous ads like Lyndon B. Johnson's "Peace Little Girl (Daisy)" or Ronald Reagan's "Bear" gained notoriety because of how they eschewed the norms of campaigning and utilized exemplary horror framing.[11] A large sum of arguably more horrific ads have been produced in the twenty-first century, and yet they have gained seemingly less notoriety. Why? Because contemporary campaign advertising has become immoderate. Horror is no longer a spice to sprinkle into a campaign, it is often the main ingredient.

Further, while horror frames permeate all campaigns in the twenty-first century, the degree to which they deploy this generic tool has mostly increased throughout the century. This project has shown a sharp increase in the use of horror framing from the 2000 election and the 2008 election, and again between 2008 and 2016, as well as the elections that fall in between. These jumps in horrific fear appeals have consistently built upon themselves in the wake of September 11. Indeed, Mary K. Bloodsworth-Lugo and Carmen R. Lugo-Lugo maintain that "ways of managing fears and anxieties assume a particular relevance to post–9/11 American audiences."[12] Polling data backs this up, showing that U.S. citizens have suffered "a long-term, routinized, mass anxiety . . . about terrorism that has shown little sign of waning," permanently altering "the American mind."[13] This environment of collective, heightened anxiety has provided the perfect breeding ground for increasingly normative political fear mongering. Of course, the 2020 campaign seems to offer somewhat of a counter to this as Biden relied less heavily on horrific appeals than elections prior. However, that is because much of the horror relied on enthymeme where the audience could easily plug in their own overwhelming fears about the pandemic and national unrest. It will be interesting to observe if the Biden campaign remains a blip, like the 2004 Kerry campaign, in comparison to future elections, or if this is a turning point for horror to wane as a generic device in campaign advertising.

Third, horror frames in presidential campaigns are *polarizing*. Clearly, any slight courtesy to opposition candidates has all but eroded through the extreme nature of attack campaign advertising. This creates a fertile political landscape for a demagogic rhetoric that deepens an us versus them mentality that Patricia Roberts-Miller captures: "Demagoguery is about identity. It says that complicated policy issues can be reduced to a binary of us (good) versus them (bad)."[14] This is precisely how modern campaign advertising has used the horror frame, to exacerbate a fear of "them"—the opposition party, "threatening" groups, foreign enemies—and position the candidate and their supporters as reflective of all that is good in "us." Even the Biden campaign dealt heavily with this "us versus them" rhetoric, but this is a theme that is overwhelming in stronger horror appeals.

The fourth theme of political horror framing is *demonic*, an extension of the demagogic us versus them mentality. When a candidate or group is cast as "them," they either become monsters or fools depending on which horror frame is deployed. At best, an opposition candidate's humanity is barely preserved by casting them as deeply flawed, foolish, unprepared, and dangerous. At worst their humanity, as well as the humanity of entire groups of people, is negated and turned into monstrosity.

These campaign monstrosities are clearly connected with big screen horrors. Kendall Phillips suggests that "we may well be in the midst of the Third Golden Age of Horror," owing much to Trump's ascendancy and his reliance on fears and anxieties.[15] The work presented in this book completes Phillips's chain of horror and turns it into a more predictable component of twenty-first-century campaigning. In other words, campaigns instill fear in audiences already primed for the horror aesthetic given its pervasiveness in popular culture, elevating the likelihood that citizens vote for more demagogic candidates and presidents. These more demagogic presidents in turn inspire new and frightening avenues for cinematic horror, ratcheting up the horror themes from the previous election cycle. New cinematic horror developments inspire new and heightened horror usage in their campaign advertising counterparts. This process continues to spiral into greater and greater political horror as shown with each subsequent presidential campaign.[16] The horrors of the 2016 campaign advertisements might very well be the "Golden Age" counterpart to cinematic horror. A lingering question then is if Biden's 2020 campaign has done anything to break that chain.

The fifth theme is the classic horror frame's *invasiveness*. From a practical perspective, the classic horror frame seems the most readily problematic of the advertising techniques discussed here. It is deployed to actively create outright fear, and while sometimes that fear is directed at an inanimate structure such as the economy, it is often directed at individuals or groups of people. Using the classic frame, which by definition dehumanizes its object of horror, can very quickly lead to toxic representations and reactionary ideologies. As Victoria McCollum describes the Trump era, these problematic ideologies include increasing rhetorics of "nationalism, America firstism, and xenophobia."[17] The 2020 campaign also extended these attacks to women of color deemed to be a part of the "Radical Left." We have certainly seen the progression of these exclusionary and hateful fear tactics as the new century has unfolded. Thus, while Trump has elevated the usage of the classic horror frame to a new intensity with a wide array of targets, presidential campaigning has been intensifying these otherizing fears in audiences through the classic frame since the initial kindling of September 11. The classic horror frame—when applied to people and not abstract institutions—is one potential driver of increasingly narcissistic political dread.[18]

The invasiveness of classic horror framing becomes most apparent, however, as it reveals its ability to propagate these ideologies into the day-to-day lives of the U.S. people. The fears they produce slowly seep into the daily lives of those who become consumed by the spectacle of horror. People can begin fearing members of opposition parties, different nationalities, and different backgrounds outside of political rhetoric, in their everyday encounters. An invasion of horror and fear is increasingly apparent in the modern Trump era, but this destructive and pervasive trend has been building throughout the new century before Trump won and lost the presidency.

Sixth, horror framing is an *insidious* component of contemporary political campaigns. That is, while not as bold and brash as the classic horror frame, conflicted frames can creep into conflicted horror framing. For example, racist notions of who can and can't be a hero—like what occurred in a number of McCain's advertisements—illuminate how the conflicted horror frame can be used to maintain status-quo inequities through more insidious means. The antagonist is not as outwardly inhuman: they are just unprepared, unqualified, or unreliable.

Weakly conflicted and purely positive ads can still fall within the grander horror narrative through the insidious nature of campaigns. John S. Nelson and G. R. Boynton hint at this theme when they argue, "Even when popular genres are not overt and controlling in political ads, their conventions often endow the spots with meaning and coherence for viewers."[19] This insidious quality means that positive advertisements are read in a context of horror, inviting the public to put their faith in increasingly demagogic "heroes." Conflicted horror framing might not overtly otherize groups or individuals, but through insidious means they are cast aside as unsuitable for political office. Thus, the horror of campaign ads trickles into everyday life through their insidious nature.

The horror genre is not a genre that simply rests in the realm of the fantastic. Its purpose is not only to scare children with tales of ghosts, ghouls, and other monstrosities. The horror genre also bleeds into everyday life as people go about making decisions. This work has shown one such area of contamination: presidential campaign ads. However, the toxic ooze is not contained there. As campaigns frame immigrants, various minorities, Republicans or Democrats, and opposition candidates within the realm of horror, those notions become accepted by large swaths of the population. Monstrosity is not contained to horror films, but as Bernadette Marie Calafell explains, it is also "the monstrosity of everyday life through acts of violence."[20] Thus, classic horror framing, which relies on spatial distance to create monsters, adds even domestic groups to the list of supposedly foreign horrors.

Finally, horror framing possesses a *nihilistic* quality as fear mongering continues to build in U.S. politics. As both sides of the political spectrum continue to diverge further and further, civic engagement declines as citizens retreat from polarized campaign rhetoric. Indeed, political scientists, including P. Sol Hart and Lauren Feldman, tell us just that "if the public lacks a sense of self- (or internal) and external efficacy, political engagement becomes less likely."[21] Twenty-first-century presidential campaign ads provide only one solution: voting for one of two, increasingly radical parties.

For many potential voters, that option is a no-go, and, without a viable solution, the nihilism erodes voter turnout and political engagement. In fact, in the 2016 election, there were fourteen states where "more people voted in the Senate races than voted for president. The overall results show that nearly 2.4 million people nationwide cast ballots but left the presidential line blank."[22] Large swaths of voters and potential voters were clearly unhappy with their options in the election. Further, in many key swing states which received significant advertising attention, voting rates dropped: "[T]urnout rates dropped by 1.3 percent in Iowa, 3 percent in Wisconsin and nearly 4 percent in Ohio in 2016, a combination that became a death knell for Clinton's presidential hopes."[23] Thus, as the parties become more and more partisan, many voters disengage, creating a radical, nihilistic environment where people fear each other within the same country. Indeed, many scholars point to "declining social trust" as the catalyst of U.S. democratic woes.[24] Martha C. Nussbaum makes clear that "Fear is not just primitive, it is also asocial."[25] What better way to lose trust in people than fearing people themselves? While the connection is certainly inconclusive, the fact that many more people voted in 2020, an election that saw one candidate scale back horror framing significantly, is worth pause and could certainly provide fertile research grounds for future projects.

RIPPLES OF CONSTITUTIVE FORCE: THE JANUARY 6 CAPITOL RIOTS AND A PATH FORWARD

As the implications listed above make clear, there are numerous intrinsic reasons why horror framing—especially classic horror framing of opposition candidates or groups of people—are morally reprehensible. There need not be further explication of why it is wrong to cast your opposition as demonic—or unprepared due to dog-whistle racism—or to establish a demagogic us versus them binary. As such, the intrinsic implications of much classic and conflicted horror framing used in campaigns are already a reason to reject such a practice.

However, beyond the intrinsic harms of unjust horror framing come the constitutive forces these campaigns can impart in a wider trend of growing partisanship and demagoguery. Of course, there is no way to fully quantify how a single ad, ad campaign, or even the trends revealed in this book over decades impact our political systems. However, better understanding the constitutive rhetorical forces at play in these advertisements and trends can give us clues.

When examining rhetorical texts through constitutive forces, one can look at the intentional and extensional influences of the text. As James Jasinski argues, rhetorical texts exhibit intentional "constitutive potential through the invitations inscribed in various discursive forms."[26] These invitations can take the shape of tropes and arguments, and the majority of this work thus far has focused on such intentional constitutive forces. However, we now shift to the extensional constitutive forces these texts establish. Jasinski claims that texts demonstrate extensional constitutive force "through the cultural circulation and discursive articulation of their textual forms in ways that enable and constrain subsequent practice."[27] As such, viewers are initially invited to engage with a text by the text, but the way that text is circulated and transformed is then in the hands of the audience.[28]

Here is where the true moral harm of horrific campaign appeals can be recognized. This book has worked in-depth to reveal the intentional constitutive potential of these campaign advertisements through the tropes of horror and the horror-based arguments they present. The question then is, what constitutive force do these tropes and arguments have extensionally when they are culturally circulated by their intended audiences? The aftermath of the 2020 election gives us some insight on that front.

As has already been established, Joe Biden won the 2020 election by securing extremely thin margins in a number of key states. Donald Trump was unwilling to accept these results on the basis of false, rigged-election charges, with himself and his Republican allies protesting the certification of the election results at each step of the way. Even as some of Trump's allies realized that there was "no substantial evidence of election fraud," others continued to feed the president unfounded conspiracy theories.[29] Thus, Trump ultimately pushed forward with a lie that he "had been grooming for years," "his lie of an election stolen by corrupt and evil forces."[30] This lie was "so convincing to some of his most devoted followers that it made the deadly Jan. 6 assault on the Capitol almost inevitable."[31] While there were certainly a myriad of rhetorical mediums through which Trump groomed and propagated his lies surrounding the election and evil forces in America, the analysis in this book of the 2016 and 2020 elections—elections where Trump relied heavily on the classic horror framing of his enemies—certainly rang true with his conspiracy of evil cultural forces in America. However, January 6, 2021, is truly the day where, by some accounts, Trump lost control of his rhetorical narrative as it circulated among his far-right supporters. Others go even further, arguing Trump achieved his goal of staging an attempted coup.[32] Regardless, on that day Trump-aligned rioters stormed the U.S. Capitol while Congress was trying to certify the election results in favor of Biden, an unprecedented attack on a core democratic institution of the United States.

Of course, many connect Trump's protest of the election results to the Capitol invasion.[33] But the Trump campaign's use of horror frames arguably played a precursory role in constituting what his radicalized supporters conceived as an apocalyptic and constitutional crisis where they insisted an election had been stolen from Donald Trump. Trump used the "MAGA" identity to deputize those supporting his cause as "warriors" in the constitutional fight to "stop the steal."[34] Trump's campaign discourse certainly provided a vocabulary for his supporters: be it his ads establishing two, split Americas, his use of conspiratorial, illuminati imagery in his "Unfit (R)" ad, or his general demonizing of Hillary Clinton, Nancy Pelosi, Alexandria Ocasio-Cortez, Ilhan Omar, and others he grouped in with the evil, "Radical Left."[35]

We can see this type of language and thinking when examining what the insurrectionists said on and about the January 6 coup. One rioter said of those he believed to be rigging the election, "they have morphed into pure evil."[36] And in order to respond to that evil, "We must smite them now and drive them down."[37] Here, we see the vocabulary of the classic horror frame used to full effect, casting Democrats and those opposed to Trump as "pure evil" that must meet a violent end. Another insurrectionist said, "We can't kill nobody. . . . I mean, it may come to that. I hope it don't but it's a democrat house, a crooked democrat house . . . they're anti-Christian and they're in charge now and ain't nothing we can do to stop it."[38] Again, we see the demonic demagoguery of us versus them at play as the opposition is considered "anti-Christian." Violence is once again not eliminated as a potential response to this demonization. This attitude of violence was seen frequently, as another member of the mob wrote, "MURDER THE MEDIA" across one of the Capitol double doors.[39]

One of the most infamous Capitol invaders—Jacob Chansley, known widely as the "QAnon Shaman"—said that he made it into the U.S. Senate "by the grace of God" and called the Vice President "a child-trafficking traitor" for his refusal to stop the certification process.[40] Here, we again see the dichotomy of good versus evil warped around political rhetoric. Another insurrectionist from Texas, said, "We are fighting good versus evil, dark versus light."[41] Again, this shows how horrific political framings often create a do-or-die, ultimate showdown between pure good and pure evil. Once supporters start thinking in these terms, violence is an unsurprising outcome. One member of the attempted coup was prepared for just that, as he allegedly stockpiled ammo and said he wanted to "put a bullet in (Pelosi's) noggin."[42] Pelosi was a common target of Trump's horror framing, making it unsurprising that insurrectionists supporting his cause would choose to target her as well. Other protestors prepared for the violent overthrow of supposed evil by building gallows on the National Mall.[43]

These are but a small collection of many similar thoughts, utterances, and actions by Trump supporters surrounding the January 6 U.S. Capitol invasion. It is immediately apparent that the classic horror messages of Trump's campaign and presidency syngergized with the attitudes of those who stormed the Capitol through the rhetoric with which they justified their actions. As has been revealed, political advertising campaigns often combine horror elements with appeals to audience efficacy: a way for the audience to do something about the things they fear. Generally, that "something" is to get out and vote. Even though Trump lost in 2020, he did not stop seeking to activate his supporters. With the vote no longer an option, Trump used the already established horror frame to move his audience to stand against the certification of the election results and stop the steal, resulting in a governmental insurrection.

Of course, it was not just campaign advertisements that led to this event. Trump's rhetoric in general, QAnon, and even a 150-year trend of apocalyptic evangelicalism all likely played significant roles.[44] But simultaneously, it is difficult to look at the similitudes between Trump's advertising rhetoric and the rhetoric of the crowd and ignore the connection. Accordingly, on January 6, the nation felt the force of the extensional ripples of Trump's rhetoric—campaign or otherwise—which had been building since at least the 2016 campaign.

Yet, solely laying the blame on Trump for the trend of horror framing in campaigning falls into a familiar trap of partisanship and demagoguery. As this work has clearly shown, horror has been used by both Republicans and Democrats in mostly increasing intensities throughout the twenty-first century. So, the question then remains: Is there any room for the horror genre in political campaigning and what is our path out of the contemporary trend of spiraling horror? In response, I propose an ethical frame of justified horror. One thing that is important to establish here is that negative campaigning is not inherently bad and, as Richardson argues, is actually good for democracy.[45] However, there is clearly a difference between negative advertisements that rationally assess an opponent's policy choices, concrete experience (or lack thereof), and character versus ad hominem attacks that go beyond character attacks into the realm of demagogic horror. The former are essential for informed voting, the latter only perpetuate partisan demagoguery.

Justified horror finds itself in the middle of standard negative campaigning and classic and conflicted horror framing. Justified horror exists when elements of the horror genre are used without hyperbole to discuss instances of real-life horror. War is horrific. A pandemic is horrific. Racist violence is horrific. These issues do not need to be sanitized of horror elements when being depicted. We have seen these topics covered by campaigns time and time again throughout the past two decades. Justified horror naturally overlaps with the classic and conflicted frames to a certain degree. However, horror framing leaves the realm of justified horror when it does one or both of two things. First, if it begins to unjustly demonize an opponent or group of people, that horror no longer falls within a just framework. Second, if the horror begins to exaggerate a situation such that the real-world horror is ratcheted up exponentially in the name of unreasonable fear mongering, that horror leaves the realm of justified horror framing.

No campaign analyzed in this book stuck strictly to the realm of justified horror and many relied on little to no justified horror whatsoever. However, the 2020 campaign advertisements certainly seemed to establish a fork in the road for American political campaigning. The Trump campaign relied heavily on classic and conflicted horror that was largely unjust, attacking Biden, Harris, and other "Radical Left" figures through monstrosity. The Biden campaign, on the other hand, came closer to a consistent, justified horror framing. The Biden campaign was typically reserved in their use of horror, frequently relying on more subtle visual cues to remind the audience of the horrors of the pandemic. They were less restrained in their framing of racist violence, but that again is a real-world, justifiable horror. The Biden campaign did start to veer away from justified horror when falling into a familiarly demagogic, us versus them framing. Nevertheless, the Biden campaign certainly marked a notable drop in horror framing in general that hadn't been seen since the 2004 Kerry campaign. As such, future political campaigns will determine which path our election system continues to follow: one of increasingly unjust classic and conflicted horror where such frames become more deeply omnipresent and normative, or one of deescalating horror usage that could give way to a justified horror framing in American politics.

The campaign ads of the twenty-first century are haunted by an overwhelming sense of doom and decay. Whether it be the 2000, 2004, 2008, 2012, 2016, or 2020 presidential election, campaigns horrifically frame supposed threats to the United States, some more real than others. However, with the very real and widely televised videos of the September 11 attacks, the subsequent War on Terror, the economic collapse of 2008, the violence from mass shootings and racist killings, and the COVID-19 pandemic, the far-away monsters of classic horror are coming closer to home, especially in the imagery of presidential campaign ads. Many argue that cinematic horror provides a mirror of sorts for people to productively reflect on society and "our general fears and anxieties."[46] While this is certainly true for the cinematic genre, this reflective aspect becomes weaponized when the genre is used by increasingly partisan political structures. It is impossible to predict what future presidential elections might entail, but if this trend of spiraling horror continues, appeals to voters may be made less by means of thoughtful policy deliberation and more through the horrors that keep us up at night and the candidate who can supposedly protect the American village from those monstrosities.

NOTES

1. Glenn W. Richardson Jr., "Pulp Politics: Popular Culture and Political Advertising," *Rhetoric & Public Affairs* 3, no. 4 (2000): 611.

2. David R. Jones, "Why Bush Won," *CBS News*, November 3, 2004, https://www.cbsnews.com/news/why-bush-won-02-11-2004/.

3. Obama for America, "This Year," *The Living Room Candidate: Presidential Campaign Commercials 1952–2020*, October 5, 2008, http://www.livingroomcandidate.org/commercials/2008/this-year.

4. Obama for America, "Country I Love," *The Living Room Candidate: Presidential Campaign Commercials 1952–2020*, June 20, 2008, http://www.livingroomcandidate.org/commercials/2008/country-i-love.

5. Obama for America, "Defining Moment," *The Living Room Candidate: Presidential Campaign Commercials 1952–2020*, October 25, 2008, http://www.livingroomcandidate.org/commercials/2008/defining-moment.

6. Obama for America, "Something," *The Living Room Candidate: Presidential Campaign Commercials 1952–2020*, October 30, 2008, http://www.livingroomcandidate.org/commercials/2008/something.

7. That is not to say they did not also use the classic frame, as is apparent in "Firms," which bears striking similarities to Romney's "Political Payoffs and Middle Class Layoffs" ad. Obama, "Firms," *The Living Room Candidate: Presidential Campaign Commercials 1952–2020*, July 14, 2012, http://www.livingroomcandidate.org/commercials/2012/firms; Romney, "Political Payoffs and Middle Class Layoffs," *The Living Room Candidate: Presidential Campaign Commercials 1952–2020*, July 16, 2012, http://www.livingroomcandidate.org/commercials/2012/political-payoffs-and-middle-class-layoffs.

8. See Donald J. Trump for President, "Two Americas Immigration," *The Living Room Candidate: Presidential Campaign Commercials 1952–2020*, August 19, 2016, http://www.livingroomcandidate.org/commercials/2016/two-americas-immigration; Donald J. Trump for America, "Two Americas: Economy," *The Living Room Candidate: Presidential Campaign Commercials 1952–2020*, August 29, 2016, http://www.livingroomcandidate.org/commercials/2016/two-americas-economy.

9. Donald J. Trump for President, "Unfit (R)," *The Living Room Candidate: Presidential Campaign Commercials 1952–2020*, November 3, 2016, http://www.livingroomcandidate.org/commercials/2016/unfit-r.

10. Biden, "Backbone," *The Living Room Candidate: Presidential Campaign Commercials 1952–2020*, July 30, 2020, http://www.livingroomcandidate.org/commercials/2020/backbone.

11. Democratic National Committee, "Peace Little Girl (Daisy)," *The Living Room Candidate: Presidential Campaign Commercials 1952–2020*, September 7, 1964, http://www.livingroomcandidate.org/commercials/1964/peace-little-girl-daisy; Reagan-Bush '84, "Bear," *The Living Room Candidate: Presidential Campaign Commercials 1952–2020*, October 2, 1984, http://www.livingroomcandidate.org/commercials/1984/bear.

12. Mary K. Bloodsworth-Lugo and Carmen R. Lugo-Lugo, "The Monster Within: Post-9/11 Narratives of Threat and the U.S. Shifting Terrain of Terror," in *Monster Culture in the 21st Century: A Reader*, ed. Marina Levina and Diem-My T. Bui (New York: Bloomsbury, 2013), 246.

13. John Mueller and Mark Stewart, "Terrorism in the American Psyche: Why Fears of Attacks are So Overblown," *Foreign Affairs*, December 10, 2015, https://www.foreignaffairs.com/articles/united-states/2015-12-10/terrorism-american-psyche.

14. Patricia Roberts-Miller, *Demagoguery and Democracy* (New York: The Experiment, 2017), 8.

15. Kendall Phillips, "Foreword," in *Make America Hate Again, Trump-Era Horror and the Politics of Fear*, ed. Victoria McCollum (New York: Routledge, 2019), ix. For more documentation of Trump-era horror outside of campaign advertising, see Debbie Jay Williams and Kalyn L. Prince, *The Monstrous Discourse in the Donald Trump Campaign: Implications for National Discourse* (Lanham, MD: Lexington Books, 2018).

16. For another example of how Hollywood films and political events cyclically engage one another, see Fielding Montgomery, "*Rogue One*: A U.S. Imperialism Story," *Journal of Popular Film and Television* 48, no. 1 (2020): 27–37.

17. Victoria McCollum, "Introduction," in *Make America Hate Again, Trump-Era Horror and the Politics of Fear*, ed. Victoria McCollum (New York: Routledge, 2019), 22.

18. For more on the narcissistic qualities of political fear, see, Martha C. Nussbaum, *The Monarchy of Fear: A Philosopher Looks at Our Political Crisis* (New York: Simon & Schuster, 2018).

19. John S. Nelson and G. R. Boynton, *Video Rhetorics: Televised Advertising in American Politics* (Urbana: University of Illinois Press, 1997), 86.

20. Bernadette Marie Calafell, *Monstrosity, Performance, and Race in Contemporary Culture* (New York: Peter Lang, 2015), 7.

21. P. Sol Hart and Lauren Feldman, "Threat Without Efficacy? Climate Change on U.S. Network News," *Science Communication* 36, no. 3 (2014): 344. Also see Steven J. Rosenstone and John Mark Hansen, *Mobilization, Participation, and Democracy in America* (New York: Pearson, 2003).

22. Rebecca Harrington and Skye Gould, "Americans Beat One Voter Turnout Record—Here's How 2016 Compares with Past Elections," *Business Insider*, December 21, 2016, https://www.businessinsider.com/trump-voter-turnout-records-history-obama-clinton-2016-11.

23. Michael D. Regan, "What Does Voter Turnout Tell Us about the 2016 Election?" *PBS*, November 20, 2016, https://www.pbs.org/newshour/politics/voter-turnout-2016-elections. For ad targeting, see "2016 Campaign Ad Archive," *The New Republic*, https://newrepublic.com/political-ad-database.

24. Theda Skocpol and Morris P. Fiorina, *Civic Engagement in American Democracy* (Washington, DC: Brookings Institution, 1999), 6. See also, Robert D. Putnam, *Bowling Alone* (New York: Simon & Schuster, 2000).

25. Nussbaum, *The Monarchy of Fear*, 28.

26. James Jasinski, "A Constitutive Framework for Rhetorical Historiography: Toward an Understanding of the Discursive (Re)constitution of 'Constitution' in the Federalist Papers," in *Doing Rhetorical History: Concepts and Cases*, ed. Kathleen J. Turner (Tuscaloosa: University of Alabama Press, 1998), 74.

27. Jasinski, "A Constitutive Framework for Rhetorical Historiography," 74.

28. Jasinski, "A Constitutive Framework for Rhetorical Historiography," 74–75.

29. Jim Rutenberg, Jo Becker, Eric Lipton, Maggie Haberman, Jonathan Martin, Matthew Rosenberg, and Michael S. Schmidt, "77 Days: Trump's Campaign to

Subvert the Election," *New York Times*, February 12, 2021, https://www.nytimes.com/2021/01/31/us/trump-election-lie.html.

30. Rutenberg et al., "77 Days: Trump's Campaign to Subvert the Election."

31. Rutenberg et al., "77 Days: Trump's Campaign to Subvert the Election."

32. Rosalind S. Helderman, Spencer S. Hau, and Rachel Weiner, "'Trump Said to Do So,': Accounts of Rioters Who Say the President Spurred Them to Rush the Capitol Could Be Pivotal Testimony," *Washington Post*, January 16, 2021, https://www.washingtonpost.com/politics/trump-rioters-testimony/2021/01/16/01b3d5c6-575b-11eb-a931-5b162d0d033d_story.html.

33. For examples, see Ben Leonard, "Former Defense Secretary Miller Blames Trump's Speech for Jan. 6 Insurrection," *Politico*, March 11, 2021, https://www.politico.com/news/2021/03/11/chris-miller-trump-capitol-riot-475404; Charlie Savage, "Incitement to Riot? What Trump Told Supporters Before Mob Stormed Capitol," *New York Times*, January 12, 2021, https://www.nytimes.com/2021/01/10/us/trump-speech-riot.html; Sam Cabral, "Capitol Riots: Did Trump's Words at Rally Incite Violence?" *BBC*, February 14, 2021, https://www.bbc.com/news/world-us-canada-55640437.

34. Donald J. Trump in Brian Naylor, "Read Trump's Jan. 6 Speech, A Key Part of Impeachment Trial," *NPR*, February 10, 2021, https://www.npr.org/2021/02/10/966396848/read-trumps-jan-6-speech-a-key-part-of-impeachment-trial.

35. For examples, see Trump, "Two Americas Immigration"; Trump, "Two Americas: Economy"; Trump, "Unfit (R)"; Trump, "America First! #MAGA," *The Living Room Candidate: Presidential Campaign Commercials 1952–2020*, August 20, 2020, http://www.livingroomcandidate.org/commercials/2020/america-first-maga.

36. United States of America v. Jessica Marie Watkins, Donovan Ray Crowl, Thomas Edward Caldwell, Case: 1:21-mj-00119—Amended Criminal Complaint—District Court (United States District Court for the District of Columbia, 2021), 21.

37. United States of America v. Jessica Marie Watkins, 21.

38. United States of America v. Joshua Matthew Black, Case 2:21-mj-00010—Memorandum in Support of Pretrial Detention—District Court (United States District Court for the Northern District of Alabama, 2021), 11.

39. Sabrina Tavernise and Matthew Rosenberg, "These Are the Rioters Who Stormed the Nation's Capitol," *New York Times*, January 7, 2021, https://www.nytimes.com/2021/01/07/us/names-of-rioters-capitol.html.

40. Dan Mangan, "QAnon 'Shaman' Jacob Chansley Held Without Bail after Storming Senate during Capitol Riot by Trump Supporters," *CNBC*, January 15, 2021, https://www.cnbc.com/2021/01/15/trump-rioters-planned-to-kill-congress-members-fed-probe.html.

41. Elizabeth Dias and Ruth Graham, "How White Evangelical Christians Fused with Trump Extremism," *New York Times*, January 19, 2021, https://www.nytimes.com/2021/01/11/us/how-white-evangelical-christians-fused-with-trump-extremism.html.

42. Shelly Bradbury, "Colorado Man Who Threatened to Kill Nancy Pelosi Brought Guns and 2,500 Rounds to D.C., Feds Say," *Denver Post*, January 13, 2021, https://www.denverpost.com/2021/01/13/cleveland-meredith-pelosi-threat-colorado/.

43. David A. Graham, "We're Just Finding Out How Bad the Riot Really Was," *Atlantic*, January 16, 2021, https://www.theatlantic.com/ideas/archive/2021/01/it-was-much-worse-it-looked/617693/.

44. Matthew Avery Sutton, "The Capitol Riot Revealed the Darkest Nightmares of White Evangelical America," *New Republic*, January 14, 2021, https://newrepublic.com/article/160922/capitol-riot-revealed-darkest-nightmares-white-evangelical-america.

45. Glenn W. Richardson Jr., *Pulp Politics: How Political Advertising Tells the Stories of American Politics* (Lanham, MD: Rowman & Littlefield, 2008),

46. See Kendall R. Phillips, *Projected Fears: Horror Films and American Culture* (Westport, CT: Praeger, 2005), 197; Robin Wood, "An Introduction to the American Horror Film," in *The American Nightmare*, eds. Robin Wood and Richard Lippe (Toronto: Festival of Festivals Publications, 1979), 7–33; Harry M. Benshoff, "Preface," in *A Companion to the Horror Film*, ed. Harry M. Benshoff (New York: Wiley Blackwell, 2014), xiv.

Bibliography

28 Days Later. DVD. Directed by Danny Boyle. 20th Century Fox Home Entertainment, 2008.
"2004 Presidential Election." 270 to Win. https://www.270towin.com/2004_Election/.
"2012 Presidential Election." 270 to Win. https://www.270towin.com/2012_Election/.
The Babadook. DVD. Directed by Jennifer Kent. Shout Factory, 2015.
"Bad Bunny—Pero Ya No (English Translation)." Genius. https://genius.com/Genius-english-translations-bad-bunny-pero-ya-no-english-translation-lyrics.
Bad Bunny, "Pero Ya No." Track 3 on *YHLQMDLG*. Rimas Entertainment, 2020, Digital.
Benshoff, Harry M. "Preface." In *A Companion to the Horror Film*, edited by Harry M. Benshoff, xiii–xix. New York: Wiley Blackwell, 2014.
Benshoff, Harry M. "Horror Before 'The Horror Film.'" In *A Companion to the Horror Film*, edited by Harry M. Benshoff, 225–36. New York: Wiley Blackwell, 2014.
Bhat, Prashanth, Alyson Farzad-Phillips, Morgan Hess, Lauren Hunter, Nora Murphy, Claudia Serrano Rico, Kyle Stephan, Gareth Williams, and Shawn Parry-Giles. "Campaign Advertising 2016: Referendum on Character." *Center for Political Communication and Civic Leadership*.
The Birds. DVD. Directed by Alfred Hitchcock. Universal Studios Home Entertainment, 2014.
Biskind, Peter. *Seeing is Believing: How Hollywood Taught Us to Stop Worrying and Love the Fifties*. New York: Henry Holt, 1983.
The Blair Witch Project. Blu-ray. Directed by Daniel Myrick and Eduardo Sanchez. Lionsgate, 2010.
Bloodsworth-Lugo, Mary K. and Carmen R. Lugo-Lugo. "The Monster Within: Post-9/11 Narratives of Threat and the U.S. Shifting Terrain of Terror." In *Monster Culture in the 21st Century: A Reader*, edited by Marina Levina and Diem-My T. Bui, 243–56. New York: Bloomsbury, 2013.
The Body Snatcher. Digital. Directed by Robert Wise. Google Play, 2009.

Bradbury, Shelly. "Colorado Man Who Threatened to Kill Nancy Pelosi Brought Guns and 2,500 Rounds to D.C., Feds Say." *Denver Post*. January 13, 2021. https://www.denverpost.com/2021/01/13/cleveland-meredith-pelosi-threat-colorado/.

Bram Stoker's Dracula. DVD. Directed by Francis Ford Coppola. Sony Pictures, 2017.

Brophy, Philip. "Horrality: The Texture of Contemporary Horror Films." In *The Horror Reader*, edited by Ken Gelder, 276–84. London: Routledge, 2000.

Browning, John Edgar. "Classical Hollywood Horror." In *A Companion to the Horror Film*, edited by Harry M. Benshoff, 207–24. New York: Wiley Blackwell, 2014.

Burke, Kenneth. "Four Master Tropes." *The Kenyon Review* 3, no. 4 (1941): 421–38.

Butler, Ivan. *Horror in the Cinema*. Cranbury, NJ: A. S. Barnes and Company, 1979.

The Cabinet of Dr. Caligari. Digital. Directed by Robert Wiene. Horrortheque, 2010.

The Cabin in the Woods. DVD. Directed by Drew Goddard. Lionsgate, 2011.

Cabral, Sam. "Capitol Riots: Did Trump's Words at Rally Incite Violence?" *BBC*. February 14, 2021. https://www.bbc.com/news/world-us-canada-55640437.

Calafell, Bernadette Marie. *Monstrosity, Performance, and Race in Contemporary Culture*. New York: Peter Lang, 2015.

Campbell, Karlyn Kohrs and Kathleen Hall Jamieson. *Presidents Creating the Presidency: Deeds Done in Words*. Chicago, IL: University of Chicago Press, 2008.

"The Castle of Otranto: The Creepy Tale that Launched Gothic Fiction." *BBC News*, December 13, 2014. https://www.bbc.com/news/magazine-30313775.

Cat People. DVD. Directed by Jacques Tourneur. Turner Home Entertainment, 2005.

Chiwaya, Nigel and Corky Siemaszko. "Covid-19 Cases, Deaths Rising Rapidly Ahead of Election Day." *NBC News*. November 2, 2020. https://www.nbcnews.com/news/us-news/covid-19-cases-deaths-rising-rapid-rate-ahead-election-day-n1245780.

Cisneros, J. David. "Contaminated Communities: The Metaphor of 'Immigrant as Pollutant' in Media Representations of Immigration." *Rhetoric & Public Affairs* 11, no. 4 (2008): 569–601.

Clover, Carol J. *Men, Women, and Chain Saws: Gender in the Modern Horror Film*. Princeton, NJ: Princeton University Press, 1992.

Cloverfield. Blu-ray. Directed by Matt Reeves. Paramount, 2017.

Coleman, Robin R. Means. *Horror Noire: Blacks in American Horror Films from the 1890s to Present*. New York: Routledge, 2011.

Coleman, Robin R. Means. "We're in a Golden Age of Black Horror Films" *The Conversation*. May 29, 2019. http://theconversation.com/were-in-a-golden-age-of-black-horror-films-116648?utm.

Collins, Ben and Brandy Zadrozny. "How a Fake Persona Laid the Groundwork for a Hunter Biden Conspiracy Deluge." *NBC News*. October 29, 2020. https://www.nbcnews.com/tech/security/how-fake-persona-laid-groundwork-hunter-biden-conspiracy-deluge-n1245387.

"Confidence in Institutions." *Gallup*. https://news.gallup.com/poll/1597/confidence-institutions.aspx.

Contagion. DVD. Directed by Steven Soderbergh. Warner Home Video, 2012.
Crimson Peak. DVD. Directed by Guillermo del Toro. Universal Studios, 2015.
The Crucifixion. DVD. Directed by Xavier Gens. Lionsgate Home Entertainment, 2017.
The Curse of Frankenstein. Digital. Directed by Terence Fisher. Horrortheque, 2010.
Dante. *The Inferno*. Translated by Marvin R. Vincent. New York: Charles Scribner's Sons, 1904.
Davis, Blair. "Horror Meets Noir: The Evolution of Cinematic Style, 1931–1958." In *Horror Film: Creating and Marketing Fear*, edited by Steffen Hantke, 191–212. Jackson: University Press of Mississippi, 2004.
Demo, Anne. "Sovereignty Discourse and Contemporary Immigration Politics." *Quarterly Journal of Speech* 91, no. 3 (2005): 291–311.
Demon Seed. DVD. Directed by Donald Cammell. Warner Archive Collection, 2017.
Dias, Elizabeth and Ruth Graham. "How White Evangelical Christians Fused with Trump Extremism." *New York Times*. January 19, 2021. https://www.nytimes.com/2021/01/11/us/how-white-evangelical-christians-fused-with-trump-extremism.html.
"Donald Trump and Hillary Clinton's Final Campaign Spending Revealed." *The Guardian*. December 9, 2016. https://www.theguardian.com/us-news/2016/dec/09/trump-and-clintons-final-campaign-spending-revealed.
Dracula. Digital. Directed by Tod Browning. 1931, Peacock TV.
Eddy, Cheryl. "The Biggest Horror Trends of the Last Decade." *Gizmodo*. November 21, 2019. https://io9.gizmodo.com/the-5-biggest-horror-trends-of-the-last-decade-1838973130.
Eisner, Lotte H. *The Haunted Screen: Expressionism in the German Cinema and the Influence of Max Reinhardt*. Berkeley: University of California Press, 1965.
"Election Results 2008." *New York Times*. 2008. https://www.nytimes.com/elections/2008/results/president/map.html.
Engel, Pamela. "How Trump Came Up with His Slogan 'Make America Great Again.'" *Business Insider*. January 18, 2017. http://www.businessinsider.com/trump-make-america-great-again-slogan-history-2017-1.
Evil Dead II. DVD. Directed by Sam Raimi. Lionsgate, 2018.
"Exit Polls." *CNN*. November 23, 2016. https://www.cnn.com/election/2016/results/exit-polls.
The Exorcist. DVD. Directed by William Friedkin. Warner Bros., 2011.
Finnegan, Cara A. "Studying Visual Modes of Public Address: Lewis Hine's Progressive Era Child Labor Rhetoric." In *The Handbook of Rhetoric & Public Address*, edited by Shawn J. Parry-Giles and J. Michael Hogan, 250–70. West Sussex, United Kingdom: Wiley-Blackwell, 2010.
The Fly. Digital. Directed by David Cronenberg. 20th Century Fox, 1986.
The Fly. Digital. Directed by Kurt Neumann. 20th Century Fox, 1958.
Frankenstein. DVD. Directed by James Whale. Universal Pictures Home Entertainment, 2016.

Friday the 13th. Blu-ray. Directed by Sean S. Cunningham. Paramount, 2017.

Get Out. Blu-ray. Directed by Jordan Peele. Universal Studios, 2017.

Graham, David A. "We're Just Finding Out How Bad the Riot Really Was." *Atlantic.* January 16, 2021. https://www.theatlantic.com/ideas/archive/2021/01/it-was-much-worse-it-looked/617693/.

Gronbeck, Bruce E. "Negative Narratives in 1988 Presidential Campaign Ads." *Quarterly Journal of Speech* 78, no. 3 (1992): 333–46.

The Grudge. DVD. Directed by Takashi Shimizu. Sony Pictures, 2009.

Hall, Melissa Mia. "The Siren." In *Icons of Horror and the Supernatural: An Encyclopedia of Our Worst Nightmares*, edited by S. T. Joshi, 507–36. Westport, CT: Greenwood Press, 2007.

Halloween. DVD. Directed by John Carpenter. Lionsgate Home Entertainment, 2007.

Hantke, Steffen. "Science Fiction and Horror in the 1950s." In *A Companion to the Horror Film*, edited by Harry M. Benshoff, 255–72. New York: Wiley Blackwell, 2014.

Hantke, Steffen. "The Kingdom of the Unimaginable: The Construction of Social Space and the Fantasy of Privacy in Serial Killers Narratives." *Literature/Film Quarterly* 26, no. 3 (1998): 178–95.

Hantke, Steffen. "They Don't Make 'Em Like They Used To: On the Rhetoric of Crisis and the Current State of American Horror Cinema." In *American Horror Film: The Genre at the Turn of the Millennium*, edited by Steffen Hantke, 7–32. Jackson: University Press of Mississippi, 2010.

Harrington, Rebecca and Skye Gould. "Americans Beat One Voter Turnout Record—Here's How 2016 Compares with Past Elections." *Business Insider.* December 21, 2016. https://www.businessinsider.com/trump-voter-turnout-records-history-obama-clinton-2016-11.

Hart, Adam Charles. "Millennial Fears: Abject Horror in a Transnational Context." In *A Companion to the Horror Film*, edited by Harry M. Benshoff, 329–44. New York: Wiley Blackwell, 2014.

Hart, P. Sol and Lauren Feldman. "Threat Without Efficacy? Climate Change on U.S. Network News." *Science Communication* 36, no. 3 (2014): 325–51.

The Haunting of Bly Manor. Digital. Created by Mike Flanagan. Netflix, 2020.

The Haunting of Hill House. Digital. Created by Mike Flanagan. Netflix, 2018.

Helderman, Rosalind S., Spencer S. Hau, and Rachel Weiner. "'Trump Said to Do So,': Accounts of Rioters Who Say the President Spurred Them to Rush the Capitol Could Be Pivotal Testimony." *Washington Post.* January 16, 2021. https://www.washingtonpost.com/politics/trump-rioters-testimony/2021/01/16/01b3d5c6-575b-11eb-a931-5b162d0d033d_story.html.

Helmers, Marguerite and Charles A. Hill. "Introduction." In *Defining Visual Rhetorics*, edited by Charles A. Hill and Marguerite Helmers, 1–24. New York: Routledge, 2009.

Hereditary. DVD. Directed by Ari Aster. Lionsgate, 2018.

"Hillary Clinton Email Probe—What Was It About?" *BBC News.* May 10, 2017. https://www.bbc.com/news/election-us-2016-37811529.

The Horror of Dracula. Blu-ray. Directed by Terence Fisher. Warner Bros. Digital Distribution, 2018.
Hostel. Blu-ray. Directed by Eli Roth. Mill Creek, 2019.
Hughey, Matthew W. *The White Savior Film: Content, Critics, and Consumption*. Philadelphia, PA: Temple University Press, 2014.
Humphrey, Daniel. "Gender and Sexuality Haunt the Horror Film." In *A Companion to the Horror Film*, edited by Harry M. Benshoff, 38–55. New York: Wiley Blackwell, 2014.
Independence Day. DVD. Directed by Roland Emmerich. 20th Century Fox Home Entertainment, 2016.
Invasion of the Body Snatchers. DVD. Directed by Don Siegel. Republic Pictures, 1998.
It Came from Outer Space. Blu-ray. Directed by Jack Arnold. Universal Studios, 2017.
Ivie, Robert L. and Oscar Giner. *Hunt the Devil: A Demonology of U.S. War Culture*. Tuscaloosa: University of Alabama Press, 2015.
Jackson, David. "Obama Ad Stresses 'Challenges' He Inherited." *USA Today*. October 13, 2012. https://www.usatoday.com/story/theoval/2012/10/13/obama-ad-morgan-freeman-politics-election-2012-mitt-romney/1631365/.
Jackson, Rosemary. *Fantasy: The Literature of Subversion*. London: Methuen, 1981.
Jamieson, Kathleen Hall. *Dirty Politics: Deception, Distraction, and Democracy*. New York: Oxford University Press, 1992.
Jamieson, Kathleen Hall. *Packaging the Presidency: A History and Criticism of Presidential Campaign Advertising*. New York: Oxford University Press, 1984.
Jancovich, Mark. "Gender, Sexuality, and the Horror Film." In *Horror, the Film Reader*, edited by Mark Jancovich, 57–59. London: Routledge, 2002.
Jancovich, Mark. "Horror in the 1940s." In *A Companion to the Horror Film*, edited by Harry M. Benshoff, 237–54. New York: Wiley Blackwell, 2014.
Jasinski, James. "A Constitutive Framework for Rhetorical Historiography: Toward an Understanding of the Discursive (Re)constitution of 'Constitution' in the Federalist Papers." In *Doing Rhetorical History: Concepts and Cases*, edited by Kathleen J. Turner, 72–92. Tuscaloosa: University of Alabama Press, 1998.
"Joe Biden." *Stuttering Foundation*. https://www.stutteringhelp.org/content/joe-biden.
Johnson, Jenell. *American Lobotomy: A Rhetorical History*. Ann Arbor: University of Michigan Press, 2015.
Jones, David R. "Why Bush Won." *CBS News*. November 3, 2004. https://www.cbsnews.com/news/why-bush-won-02-11-2004/.
Kendrick, James. "Slasher Films and Gore in the 1980s." In *A Companion to the Horror Film*, edited by Harry M. Benshoff, 310–28. New York: Wiley Blackwell, 2014.
Killough, Ashley. "The 'Daisy' Spot and Five Other Compelling Political Ads." *CNN*. September 7, 2014. https://www.cnn.com/2014/09/07/politics/political-ads/index.html.
King, Ernest W. and Franklin G. Mixon Jr. "Religiosity and the Political Economy of the Salem Witch Trials." *The Social Science Journal* 47, no. 3 (2010): 678–88.

Kracauer, Siegfried. *From Caligari to Hitler: A Psychological History of German Film*. Princeton, NJ: Princeton University Press, 2004.

Leonard, Ben. "Former Defense Secretary Miller Blames Trump's Speech for Jan. 6 Insurrection." *Politico*. March 11, 2021. https://www.politico.com/news/2021/03/11/chris-miller-trump-capitol-riot-475404.

Levina, Marina and Diem-My T. Bui. "Introduction: Toward a Comprehensive Monster Theory in the 21st Century." In *Monster Culture in the 21st Century: A Reader*, edited by Marina Levina and Diem-My T. Bui, 1–14. New York: Bloomsbury, 2013.

Levy, Michael. "United States Presidential Election of 2000." *Encyclopedia Britannica*. https://www.britannica.com/event/United-States-presidential-election-of-2000.

Lewis, Derek. "Voting Horrors: Youthful, Monstrous, and Worrying Agency in American Film." *The Popular Culture Studies Journal* 6, no. 2–3 (2018): 306–25.

Lewis, Sophie. "Joe Biden Breaks Obama's Record for Most Votes Ever Cast for a U.S. Presidential Candidate." *CBS News*. November 7, 2020. https://www.cbsnews.com/news/joe-biden-popular-vote-record-barack-obama-us-presidential-election-donald-trump/.

López, Ian Haney. *Dog Whistle Politics: How Coded Racial Appeals Have Reinvented Racism & Wrecked the Middle Class*. New York: Oxford University Press, 2014.

Mangan, Dan. "QAnon 'Shaman' Jacob Chansley Held Without Bail after Storming Senate during Capitol Riot by Trump Supporters." *CNBC*. January 15, 2021. https://www.cnbc.com/2021/01/15/trump-rioters-planned-to-kill-congress-members-fed-probe.html.

Matthews, Chris and Stephen Gandel. "Is the Economy Partying Like It's 1999?" *Fortune*. December 5, 2014. http://fortune.com/2014/12/05/us-economy-growth-1999-vs-2014/.

Maurantonio, Nicole. "'Reason to Hope?': The White Savior Myth and Progress in 'Post-Racial' America." *Journalism & Mass Communication Quarterly* 94, no. 4 (2017): 1130–45.

McCluskey, Megan. "Horror Films Have Always Tapped into Pop Culture's Most Urgent Fears. COVID-19 Will Be Their Next Inspiration." *Time*. October 7, 2020. https://time.com/5891305/horror-movies-coronavirus-history-genre/.

McCollum, Victoria. "Introduction." In *Make America Hate Again, Trump-Era Horror and the Politics of Fear*, edited by Victoria McCollum, 1–16. New York: Routledge, 2019.

McGee, Michael Calvin. "The 'Ideograph': A Link Between Rhetoric and Ideology." *Quarterly Journal of Speech* 66, no. 1 (1980): 1–16.

McIlwain, Charlton D. and Stephen M. Caliendo. "Mitt Romney's Racist Appeals: How Race Was Played in the 2012 Presidential Election." *American Behavioral Scientist* 58, no. 9 (2014): 1157–68.

McIlwain, Charlton D. and Stephen M. Caliendo. *Race Appeal: How Candidates Invoke Race in U.S. Political Campaigns*. Philadelphia, PA: Temple University Press, 2011.

Midsommar. DVD. Directed by Ari Aster. Lionsgate, 2019.

The Monolith Monsters. DVD. Directed by John Sherwood. Willette Acquisition Corp., 2015.

Montgomery, Fielding. "The Monstrous Election: Horror Framing in Televised Campaign Advertisements during the 2016 Presidential Election." *Rhetoric & Public Affairs* 22, no. 2 (2019): 281–321.

Montgomery, Fielding. "*Rogue One*: A U.S. Imperialism Story." *Journal of Popular Film and Television* 48, no. 1 (2020): 27–37.

Mueller, John and Mark Stewart. "Terrorism in the American Psyche: Why Fears of Attacks are So Overblown." *Foreign Affairs*. December 10, 2015. https://www.foreignaffairs.com/articles/united-states/2015-12-10/terrorism-american-psyche.

The Mummy. DVD. Directed by Karl Freund. Universal Studios Home Entertainment, 2016.

Museum of the Moving Image. *The Living Room Candidate: Presidential Campaign Commercials 1952–2020*. http://www.livingroomcandidate.org.

Mutz, Diana C. and Byron Reeves. "The New Videomalaise: Effects of Televised Incivility on Political Trust." *American Political Science Review* 99, no. 1 (2005): 1–15.

"National Exit Polls: How Different Groups Voted." *New York Times*. November 3, 2020. https://www.nytimes.com/interactive/2020/11/03/us/elections/exit-polls-president.html.

Naylor, Brian. "Read Trump's Jan. 6 Speech, A Key Part of Impeachment Trial." *NPR*. February 10, 2021. https://www.npr.org/2021/02/10/966396848/read-trumps-jan-6-speech-a-key-part-of-impeachment-trial.

Nelson, John S. and G. R. Boynton. *Video Rhetorics: Televised Advertising in American Politics*. Urbana: University of Illinois Press, 1997.

A Nightmare on Elm Street. Blu-ray. Directed by Wes Craven. New Line Home Video, 2010.

Night of the Living Dead. DVD. Directed by George A. Romero. Film Detective, 2018.

Nussbaum, Martha C. *The Monarchy of Fear: A Philosopher Looks at Our Political Crisis*. New York: Simon & Schuster, 2018.

Olson, Joshua and Muhammad Rashid. "Modern Drone Warfare: An Ethical Analysis," *2013 ASEE Southeast Section Conference*, 2013, http://se.asee.org/proceedings/ASEE2013/Papers2013/157.PDF.

Outbreak. DVD. Directed by Duncan Henderson. Warner Home Video, 2010.

Parry-Giles, Shawn J. and Trevor Parry-Giles. "Collective Memory, Political Nostalgia, and the Rhetorical Presidency: Bill Clinton's Commemoration of the March on Washington, August 28, 1998." *Quarterly Journal of Speech* 86, no. 4 (2000): 417–37.

Petley, Julian. "Horror and the Censors." In *A Companion to the Horror Film*, edited by Harry M. Benshoff, 130–47. New York: Wiley Blackwell, 2014.

Pementel, Michael. "Representations of Mental Health in Horror: From Establishing Stigmas to Tearing Them Down." *Bloody Disgusting*. August 2, 2018. https://bl

oody-disgusting.com/editorials/3513603/representations-mental-health-horror-establishing-stigmas-tearing/.
Pew Research Center. "4. Top Voting Issues in 2016 Election." July 7, 2016. http://www.people-press.org/2016/07/07/4-top-voting-issues-in-2016-election/.
Pew Research Center. "IV. What the Voters Want." July 13, 2000. http://www.people-press.org/2000/07/13/iv-what-the-voters-want/.
Pew Research Center. "Race Tightens Again, Kerry's Image Improves." October 20, 2004. https://www.people-press.org/2004/10/20/race-tightens-again-kerrys-image-improves/.
Pew Research Center. "Section 2: Issues of the 2012 Campaign," April 17, 2012. https://www.people-press.org/2012/04/17/section-2-issues-of-the-2012-campaign/.
Pew Research Center. "Section 3: Issues and the 2008 Election." August 21, 2008. http://www.people-press.org/2008/08/21/section-3-issues-and-the-2008-election/.
Phillips, Kendall. "Foreword." In *Make America Hate Again, Trump-Era Horror and the Politics of Fear*, edited by Victoria McCollum, ix–x. New York: Routledge, 2019.
Phillips, Kendall R. *A Place of Darkness: The Rhetoric of Horror in Early American Cinema*. Austin: University of Texas Press, 2018.
Phillips, Kendall R. *Projected Fears: Horror Films and American Culture*. Westport, CT: Praeger, 2005.
Picart, Caroline Joan (Kay) S. and David A. Frank. *Frames of Evil: The Holocaust as Horror in American Film*. Carbondale: Southern Illinois University Press, 2006.
Poltergeist. DVD. Directed by Tobe Hooper. Warner Home Video, 2010.
Pomper, Gerald M. "The 2000 Presidential Election: Why Gore Lost." *Political Science Quarterly* 116, no. 2 (2001): 201–23.
Poseidon. DVD. Directed by Wolfgang Peterson. Warner Home Video, 2010.
Prysby, Charles and Carmine Scavo. "Campaign Themes, Strategies, and Developments." In *American Political Science Association, and Inter-university Consortium for Political and Social Research. SETUPS: Voting Behavior: The 2008 Election*. Ann Arbor, MI: Inter-university Consortium for Political and Social Research, 2009.
Punter, David. *The Literature of Terror: A History of Gothic Fictions from 1765 to the Present Day*. London: Longman, 1980.
Punter, David and Glennis Byron. *The Gothic*. Malden, MA: Blackwell, 2004.
The Purge. DVD. Directed by James DeMonaco Universal Studios, 2013.
Putnam, Robert D. *Bowling Alone: The Collapse and Revival of American Community*. New York: Simon & Schuster, 2000.
Rebecca. DVD. Directed by Alfred Hitchcock. Criterion, 2017.
[Rec]. Blu-ray. Directed by Jaume Balagueró. Shout Factory, 2018.
Regan, Michael D. "What Does Voter Turnout Tell Us about the 2016 Election?" *PBS*. November 20, 2016. https://www.pbs.org/newshour/politics/voter-turnout-2016-elections.
Richardson, Glenn W., Jr. *Pulp Politics: How Political Advertising Tells the Stories of American Politics*. Lanham, MD: Rowman & Littlefield, 2008.
Richardson, Glenn W., Jr. "Pulp Politics: Popular Culture and Political Advertising." *Rhetoric & Public Affairs* 3, no. 4 (2000): 603–26.

The Ring. DVD. Directed by Gore Verbinski. Paramount Pictures, 2012.

Ringu. Blu-ray. Directed by Hideo Nakata. Arrow Video, 2019.

Roberts-Miller, Patricia. *Demagoguery and Democracy.* New York: The Experiment, 2017.

Rodriguez, Sabrina. "How Miami Cubans Disrupted Biden's Path to a Florida Win." *Politico.* November 4, 2020. https://www.politico.com/news/2020/11/04/biden-miami-cubans-election-2020-433999.

Rosenstone, Steven J. and John Mark Hansen. *Mobilization, Participation, and Democracy in America.* New York: Pearson, 2003.

Rutenberg, Jim, Jo Becker, Eric Lipton, Maggie Haberman, Jonathan Martin, Matthew Rosenberg, and Michael S. Schmidt. "77 Days: Trump's Campaign to Subvert the Election." *New York Times.* February 12, 2021. https://www.nytimes.com/2021/01/31/us/trump-election-lie.html.

Saad, Lydia. "Trump and Clinton Finish with Historically Poor Images." *Gallup.* November 8, 2016. http://news.gallup.com/poll/197231/trump-clinton-finish-historically-poor-images.aspx.

Saw. DVD. Directed by James Wan. Lionsgate, 2014.

Savage, Charlie. "Incitement to Riot? What Trump Told Supporters Before Mob Stormed Capitol." *New York Times.* January 12, 2021. https://www.nytimes.com/2021/01/10/us/trump-speech-riot.html.

Scream. Blu-ray. Directed by Wes Craven. Miramax, 2020.

Shaun of the Dead. DVD. Directed by Edgar Wright. Universal Home Video, 2007.

Sheckels, Theodore F. "Narrative Coherence and Antecedent Ethos in the Rhetoric of Attack Advertising: A Case Study of the Glendening vs. Sauerbrey Campaign." *Rhetoric & Public Affairs* 5, no. 3 (2002): 459–81.

The Silence of the Lambs. Blu-ray. Directed by Jonathan Demme. MGM, 2009.

The Sixth Sense. DVD. Directed by M. Night Shyamalan. Disney, 2000.

Skocpol, Theda and Morris P. Fiorina. *Civic Engagement in American Democracy.* Washington, DC: Brookings Institution, 1999.

Smuts, Aaron. "Cognitive and Philosophical Approaches to Horror." In *A Companion to the Horror Film*, edited by Harry M. Benshoff, 3–20. New York: Wiley Blackwell, 2014.

Sobchack, Vivian. "American Science Fiction Film: An Overview." In *A Companion to Science Fiction*, edited by David Seed, 261–74. Malden, MA: Blackwell Publishing, 2005.

Stuckey, Mary E. *Political Rhetoric.* London: Routledge, 2017.

Sutton, Matthew Avery. "The Capitol Riot Revealed the Darkest Nightmares of White Evangelical America." *New Republic.* January 14, 2021. https://newrepublic.com/article/160922/capitol-riot-revealed-darkest-nightmares-white-evangelical-america.

Swanson, Alexander. "Audience Reaction Movie Trailers and the Paranormal Activity Franchise." *Transformative Works and Cultures* 18 (2015).

Tarantula. DVD. Directed by Jack Arnold. Universal Studios Home Entertainment, 2013.

Tavernise, Sabrina and Matthew Rosenberg. "These Are the Rioters Who Stormed the Nation's Capitol." *New York Times.* January 7, 2021. https://www.nytimes.com/2021/01/07/us/names-of-rioters-capitol.html.

The Texas Chainsaw Massacre. DVD. Directed by Tobe Hooper. Dark Sky, 2014.
Them! DVD. Directed by Gordon Douglas. Warner Brothers Pictures, 2020.
Titanic. DVD. Directed by James Cameron. Paramount Home Video, 2012.
United States of America v. Jessica Marie Watkins, Donovan Ray Crowl, Thomas Edward Caldwell. Case: 1:21-mj-00119—Amended Criminal Complaint—District Court. United States District Court for the District of Columbia, 2021.
United States of America v. Joshua Matthew Black. Case 2:21-mj-00010—Memorandum in Support of Pretrial Detention—District Court. United States District Court for the Northern District of Alabama, 2021.
Us. Blu-ray. Directed by Jordan Peele. Universal Studios, 2019.
The Vatican Tapes. DVD. Directed by Mark Neveldine. Lionsgate Home Entertainment, 2015.
Wallace, Gregory. "Voter Turnout at 20-year Low in 2016." *CNN*. November 30, 2016. https://www.cnn.com/2016/11/11/politics/popular-vote-turnout-2016/index.html.
Walpole, Horace. *The Castle of Otranto*. Edinburgh: James Ballantyne & Co., 1811.
War of the Worlds. DVD. Directed by Byron Haskin. Paramount Pictures, 1999.
War of the Worlds. DVD. Directed by Steven Spielberg. Paramount Home Entertainment, 2005.
West, James. "Get Out (of the White House): The Trump Administration and YouTube Horror Parody as Social Commentary." In *Make America Hate Again, Trump-Era Horror and the Politics of Fear*, edited by Victoria McCollum, 152–63. New York: Routledge, 2019.
"What is Noir?" *Film Noir Foundation*. http://www.filmnoirfoundation.org/filmnoir.html.
Whissel, Kristen. "Tales of Upward Mobility: The New Verticality and Digital Special Effects." *Film Quarterly* 59, no. 4 (2006): 23–34.
White Zombie. DVD. Directed by Victor Halperin. Music Video Dist., 2014.
Williams, Debbie Jay and Kalyn L. Prince. *The Monstrous Discourse in the Donald Trump Campaign: Implications for National Discourse*. Lanham, MD: Lexington Books, 2018.
Wilson, Scott and Philip Rucker. "The Strategy that Paved a Winning Path." *Washington Post*. November 7, 2012. https://www.washingtonpost.com/politics/decision2012/the-strategy-that-paved-a-winning-path/2012/11/07/0a1201c8-2769-11e2-b2a0-ae18d6159439_story.html?noredirect=on&utm_term=.d45faa08d05a.
Witte, Kim. "Putting the Fear Back into Fear Appeals: The Extended Parallel Process Model." *Communication Monographs* 59, no. 4 (1992): 329–49.
The Wolf Man. DVD. Directed by George Waggner. Universal Pictures Home Entertainment, 2016.
Wood, Robin. "An Introduction to the American Horror Film." In *The American Nightmare*, edited by Robin Wood and Richard Lippe, 7–33. Toronto: Festival of Festivals Publications, 1979.
Worland, Rick. "The Gothic Revival (1957–1974)." In *A Companion to the Horror Film*, edited by Harry M. Benshoff, 273–91. New York: Wiley Blackwell, 2014.
Wynn, L.L. "Shape Shifting Lizard People, Israelite Slaves, and Other Theories of Pyramid Building." *Journal of Social Archaeology* 8, no. 2 (2008): 272–95.

Index

abortion, 104
accomplishments, 26, 27, 107–8; economic, 16; past, 4, 35, 187
accountability, 28
"Accountability" (Gore advertisement), 27–28
action, mob, 116, 136
actors, Black, 76
advertisements: personal testimony, 83, 119, 124–25, 128; spot, 9. *See also* attack advertisements; *specific advertisements*
advertising, campaign, 1; archive of, 15, 23n128; coherence of, 10–11, 86; consistency in, 86; negative, 9; prior research on, 9–12; spending, 116–17. *See also* attack advertisements; positive campaign advertising
airdates, campaign advertisement: Biden, *146*; Bush, *26*, *48*; Clinton, H., *116*; Gore, *26*; Kerry, *48*; McCain, *72*; Obama, *72*, *94*; Romney, *94*; Trump, D., *116*, *146*
Akron, Ohio, 171
"Always" (Obama advertisement), 104–5
"America First! #MAGA" (Trump, D., advertisement), 153, 154
Americans, Black, 125, 167–70

American Southwest, 6
analysis, 17, 98, 109, 124, 135–36, 159, 191; of *Cat People*, 128; consistency of, 110n21, 112n60; of genres, 11–12; modes of, 14
anxiety, 6, 173; mass, 192; music inducing, 158; about young voters, 39, 78
appeals: of efficacy, 133–35, 168, 170, 171; fear, 64, 65, 136–37, 187; racial, 169, 190–91; racist, 155
aptitude, mental, 146, 147, 156
archive, of campaign advertising, 15, 23n128
arguments, 9, 15, 31, 56, 105, 131; dual narrative, 78; as insidious, 76; moral, 60; tropes and, 195, 196; visual, 128, 148, 154, 165–66, 172–73
artifacts, visual, 12
attack advertisements: of Bush campaign, 40–41, 62; of Clinton, H., campaign, 118, 136; of Kerry campaign, 55; of Trump, D., campaign, 132, 150–52
audience reaction marketing, 103
authority, 3–4
Axelrod, David, 96

"Backbone" (Biden advertisement), 174

Baier, Bret, 157
Bain Capital, 100
banality, 40–41
"Barbershop" (Clinton, H., advertisement), 124–25
"Bean Counter" (Gore advertisement), 27, 30
Benshoff, Harry M., 3
"Better America" (Biden advertisement), 167–69
Biden, Joe, 17, 145, 190–91, 196, 199; campaign advertisement airdates, *146*; classic horror framing of, 164, 166–69, 172–73, 174; conflicted horror framing of, 162–66; efficacy appeals of, 169–71; on pandemic, 164–66; positive campaign advertising of, 164, 174–75
"Biden Lied" (Trump, D., advertisement), 156–57
Big Bird, 101
"Big Bird" (Obama advertisement), 100–101
The Birds (1963), 131
Black actors, 76
Black Americans, 125, 167–68
Black communities, 162
Black Lives Matter, 145, 154, 155, 158, 168, 169
blackness, in horror, 76
Bloodsworth-Lugo, Mary K., 192
body horror, 8, 32, 149–50
bomb, 121
boxes, 96–97
boycotts, 171
Boynton, G. R., 11, 194
bracketing: spatial, 53–55, 131; temporal, 13, 53–54, 85, 126, 135, 168–69
Bram Stoker's Dracula (1992), 123
broadcast speeches, 9
"Broken" (McCain advertisement), 73–74
brutality, police, 145, 163, 168

Bush, George W., 15–16, 25–26, 47, 80, 187–88; attack advertisements of, 40–41, 62; campaign advertisement airdates, *26*, *48*; classic horror framing of, 37–39, 57–61, 64; conflicted horror framing of, 40–41, 61–64; monstrosities of, 37–39; positive campaign advertising of, 34–36, 41, 63; as Texas hero, 35–36
Butler, Ivan, 128

The Cabinet of Dr. Caligari (1920), 3–4, 38, 73, 117, 121, 151
Calafell, Bernadette Marie, 148, 169
Caliendo, Stephen M., 95
cameos, 155
campaign advertising. *See* advertising, campaign
campaign workers, 108
"Cancer" (Romney advertisement), 96
candidates, election, 23n128. *See also specific candidates*
Capitol riots, 187, 196–97
"Captain Kahn" (Clinton, H., advertisement), 119
"Carefully" (Trump, D., advertisement), 161–62
The Castle of Otranto, 38, 45n88, 121, 139n64
Castro, Fidel, 160
Cat People (1942), 5, 6, 128
"Celeb" (McCain advertisement), 76–77
celebrity, 76, 77, 81, 87, 107, 108
censorship, 123–24
centrist science fiction, 6, 170
certification, of election results, 196, 197
"Challenges" (Obama advertisement), 105–6
changes, fear of, 59
"Changing World" (Bush advertisement), 58–59
Chansley, Jacob, 197
"The Cheaters" (Obama advertisement), 102

children, 81–82
China, 84, 96–97, 102
"Choice" (Trump, D., advertisement), 128–30
Cisnero, J. David, 127
Civil Rights Movement, 168
civil unrest, 155
classic horror framing, 26, 188–90, 193, 195; of Biden campaign, 165–69, 172–74; of Bush campaign, 37–39, 57–61, 64; of Clinton, H., campaign, 120–23, 135; of Gore campaign, 28–34; of Kerry campaign, 52–56, 64–65; of McCain campaign, 72–76, 86; of Obama campaign, 83–87, 100–101; of Romney campaign, 93–98, 108–9; of Trump, D., campaign, 126–33, 135, 136, 149–50, 154–56, 158–61, 176
clichés, 98–99
Clinton, Bill, 25, 39, 95, 98, 105, 106
Clinton, Hilary, 17, 71, 115, 189–90; attack advertisements of, 118, 136; campaign advertisement airdates, *116*; classic horror framing of, 120–23, 135; conflicted horror framing of, 117–20, 135, 136; mixed horror framing of, 123–24; positive campaign advertising attempted by, 124–26
close-ups, 159
coherence, in campaign advertising, 10–11, 86
Coleman, Robin R. Means, 76
collective memory, 153
color, women of, 148, 190
comedy, 14, 63–64, 100–101, 107, 167–68
communities, Black, 162
companies, insurance, 27
"Compare (R)" (McCain advertisement), 79
conflicted horror framing, 13–14, 17, 26, 188, 189, 193–94; of Biden campaign, 163–66; of Bush campaign, 40–41, 61–64; of Clinton, H., campaign, 117–20, 136; of Gore campaign, 33–34; of McCain campaign, 76–80, 86; of Obama campaign, 80–83, 87, 101–4, 108, 109; of Romney campaign, 98; of Trump, D., campaign, 152–53, 157, 176
consistency, 81; of analysis, 110n21, 112n60; in campaign advertising, 86; in efficacy appeals, 126; inconsistency, 95; narrative, 133, 136
conspiracy theories, 196
constitutive forces, 195–99
construction workers, 162
Cooper, Anderson, 104
corruption, 33, 73, 81, 122, 129, 130
"Country I Believe In" (Obama advertisement), 84
"Country I Love" (Obama advertisement), 80
coup, 196, 197
COVID-19, 17, 145, 161–62, 164–67, 176
credibility, 29
crime, safety and, 145, 146
crises: financial, 16, 71, 82, 83, 107, 188; framing of, 169–71; multiple, 1–2, 190
"Crisis" (McCain advertisement), 74
"Crossroads" (Biden advertisement), 163–64
culture, popular, 2–3
The Curse of Frankenstein (1957), 123
Cutter, Stephanie, 96

"Daisy" (Clinton, H., advertisement), 122–23, 189
"Dangerous" (McCain advertisement), 78
"Dangerous World" (Bush advertisement), 37
Dante, Alighieri, 166
debates, 54–55

decay, 9, 84, 102, 129–30, 199
decline, economic, 33
decrepitness, 147–48, 190
"Defining Moment" (Obama advertisement), 84–85
dehumanization, 14, 15, 96, 193; of immigrants, 148; tactics, 59
demagoguery, 192, 193, 195, 197, 198
Demo, Anne, 127–28
democracy, 58
depictions, of voters, 132
"Deplorables" (Trump, D., advertisement), 132
"Determination" (Obama advertisement), 106
dictators, 160
Dirty Politics (Jamieson), 10
disaster films, 79
discrepancies, funding, 94
disfigurements, 118
distortion, 117–19, 129, 130, 149
"Dome" (McCain advertisement), 74–75
domestic safety, 54
"Donald Trump Failed to Protect Us From COVID-19" (Biden advertisement), 165–66
"Donald Trump's Argument for America" (Trump, D., advertisement), 129–31, 133
"Don't Let Them Ruin America" (Trump, D., advertisement), 155–56
doom, 199
"Down" (Gore advertisement), 31–32
Dracula (1931), 3, 4, 53, 97, *131*
Dr. Caligari (fictional character), 3–4
dual narrative arguments, 78
Ducklo, TJ, 156–57

economic accomplishments, 16
economic decline, 33, 129–32
economics, trickle-down, 31
economy, as voting issue, 48, 56, 57, 71, 93, 115, 145

education, 77–78; accountability in, 28; Obama campaign on, 81–82; recession, 37, 39
"Education" (McCain advertisement), 77–78
"Education Recession" (Bush advertisement), 39
Edwards, John, 51
efficacy, 10–11, 16, 71, 85, 107, 190; Biden campaign appealing to, 169–71; consistency in, 126; Trump, D., campaign appealing to, 133–35
Egyptian mythology, 133
election, presidential, 1; 2000, 15–16, 25, 26, 187–88; 2004, 15, 47, 188; 2008, 16, 71, 87, 109, 188; 2012, 17, 93, 94, 189; 2016, 17, 115, 189–90; 2020, 17, 93, 145, 176–77, 190–91; candidates, 23n128; certification of, 196, 197. *See also specific topics*
elements, of visual rhetoric, 12
elevated horror, 8
email scandal, 133
"Embrace" (Obama advertisement), 80–81
energy, 4, 71
engagement, political, 194–95
enthymeme, 154, 163, 175
environment, 28
the establishment, 130, 132–33, 136
evangelicalism, 198
Evil Dead II (1987), 63
exit polls, 65, 145, 177n1
The Exorcist (1973), 30, *31*, 33, 73, 78, 124, 150
experts, 166
explicitness, 124
Expressionism, German, 3, 5, 7, 38, 73, 121, 129
extremism, 7

factory, 101–2
factory workers, 103, 131

"Failing American Workers" (Romney advertisement), 96–97
"Failing America's Families" (Romney advertisement), 97
Fauci, Anthony, 161
fear, 1, 120–21, 163; appeals, 64, 65, 136–37, 187; of changes, 59; exponential growth of, 42; rationality of, 10
Feldman, Lauren, 177, 194
feminist horror, 8
Ferrell, Will, 107
film noir, 5–6
films: disaster, 79; film noir, 5–6; slasher, 7, 86; zombie horror, 164–65
filter, red, 59
financial crises, 16, 71, 82, 83, 107, 188
"Firms" (Obama advertisement), 100
"First Choice" (Bush advertisement), 59–60
Floyd, George, 145
foolishness, 116–18, 120
forces, constitutive, 195–99
foreignness, 53, 160
foreign policy, 104
foreign trade, 131
"47 Percent" (Obama advertisement), 102–3
"47 Years of Failure" (Trump, D., advertisement), 147–48
found footage genre, 8
Frank, David A., 13–14, 53, 131, 168
Frankenstein (1931), 3, *5*, 102, 122, 128
Frankenstein (Shelley), 3
"Freedom" (McCain advertisement), 75–76
Freeman, Morgan, 105
"Fundamentals" (Obama advertisement), 82
funding: discrepancy, 94; military, 61; police, 149
future policies, of Gore, 26–27

gas tax, 62
gendered horror framing, 152–54
genre, 14; analysis of, 11–12; critical conception of, 13; defining, 12–13. *See also* horror genre
German Expressionism, 3, 5, 7, 38, 73, 121, 129
Get Out (2017), 173, *174*
"Give Me a Break" (Romney advertisement), 98
global interconnectedness, 6
global pandemic. *See* pandemic, global
global warming, 28
"Go from There" (Biden advertisement), 175
Goodyear, 171
Gore, Al, 15–16, 25, 187–88; campaign advertisement airdates, *26*; classic horror framing of, 28–34; conflicted horror framing of, 33–34; future policies of, 26–27; monstrosities of, 28–33; positive campaign advertising, 27–28, 34, 41
gothic horror, 7, 38, 45n88
gothic manors/castles, 4, 139n64
graphicness, 7
Gronbeck, Bruce E., 124
groups, minority, 125
growth, of fear, 42
The Grudge (2004), 53, *53*
guilt, 153

Halloween (1978), 85–86
Hammer Films, 7
Hantke, Steffen, 13–14, 118
Harris, Kamala, 150–51, 155, 159, 162, 169–70, 190
Hart, P. Sol, 177, 194
health, mental, 151, 152
healthcare, 169
healthcare workers, 163, 164, 166, 169, 190
Health Maintenance Organizations (HMOs), 27, 30
"Heart" (Kerry advertisement), 49
Hell, 155, 165
henchman, 82, 83

"Heroes" (Kerry advertisement), 51–52
heroism, 35–36, 51, 52, 191
"He's Got It Right" (Obama advertisement), 106–7
"He's Lost, He's Desperate" (Kerry advertisement), 54–56
history: of horror genre, 2–8; images of, 170
Hitchcock, Alfred, 131
HMOs. *See* Health Maintenance Organizations
Hollywood, 2–3
"Honor" (Obama advertisement), 82
hope, 85
"Hopeful" (Bush advertisement), 35–36
"horrality," 7
horror framing, 12–14; arguments on, 15; as demonic, 192–93; gendered, 152–54; implications of, 2, 191–95; as insidious, 193–94; invasiveness of, 193; justified, 18, 198, 199; mixed, 123–24, 147–49, 153–54, 158; nihilism of, 194–95; normativity of, 191–92; omnipresence of, 42, 191; polarizations of, 176, 192; subtle, 150. *See also* classic horror framing; conflicted horror framing
horror genre, 1, 18n10; blackness in, 76; disaster, 79; elevated, 8; feminist, 8; film noir hybridized with, 6; found footage, 8; gothic, 7; history of, 2–8; J-horror, 8; as mirror, 199; racial, 8; science fiction hybridized with, 6; slasher, 7, 86; slump in, 8–9; Third Golden Age of Horror in, 192–93; zombie, 164–65. *See also specific topics*
"How to Build Back Better" (Biden advertisement), 170–71
Hughey, Matthew W., 162
Humphrey, Daniel, 124
hypnosis, 95–96, 109
hysteria, 1

"Ian" (Gore advertisement), 30–31
illegal immigration, 127, 129, 158
illness, mental, 4
images, historical, 170
immigrants, 134; dehumanization of, 148; as monstrosities, 127–29
immigration, illegal, 127, 129, 158
implications, of horror framing, 2, 191–95
inconsistency, 95
Independence Day (1996), 74–75
inequality, racial, 145, 146
Inferno (Dante), 166
influences, 1, 148
innovation, technological, 57
insurance companies, 27
interconnectedness, global, 6
invasion, 6, 150
Invasion of the Body Snatchers (1956), 150
Iraq war, 48–52
irrationality, 10
"It Is What It Is" (Biden advertisement), 164–66

Jackson, Samuel L., 172–74
Jamieson, Kathleen Hall, 9–10, 86, 119, 136
Jancovich, Mark, 6, 19n40, 119
Jasinski, James, 195–96
J-horror, 8
"The Joe Biden They Are Hiding From You" (Trump, D., advertisement), 158–59
Johnson, Lyndon B, 191
justice, mob, 76, 129, 131–32
justified horror framing, 187, 198, 199
"Just One" (Clinton, H., advertisement), 121
"Juvenile" (Kerry advertisement), 54

"Kamala Harris: Vice President Announcement" (Biden advertisement), 169–70

Kendrick, James, 7
Kennedy, John F., 170
Kerry, John, 16, 47, 176, 188; attack advertisements of, 55; campaign advertisement airdates, *48*; classic horror framing of, 52–56, 64–65; positive campaign advertising of, 49–52, 56; restrained approach, 48–56; self-praise, 49–50
King, Martin Luther, Jr., 172
Krauthammer, Charles, 120

landslide, 87, 109
Latinx voters, 160, 167–68
"Laura" (Trump, D., advertisement), 128
Lehman Brothers, 82, 83
Lewis, Derek, 78
Lewton, Val, 4–5, 128
The Living Room Candidate (Museum of the Moving Image), 15, 23n128, 110n10
lobbyists, 81
López, Ian Haney, 154
"Low Opinion" (Clinton, H., advertisement), 118
Lugo-Lugo, Carmen R., 192
Luiz, Monique Corzilius, 122

"Make Life Better" (Biden advertisement), 175
Malone, Christine, 30, 31
Malone, Ian, 30
"Mandatory" (Obama advertisement), 103
manors/castles, gothic, 4, 139n64
marketing, audience reaction, 103
masks, 154, 161–62
mass anxiety, 192
"Matters" (Gore advertisement), 28
maverick, McCain as, 72–74, 81
McCain, John, 16, 59–60, 71, 188; campaign advertisement airdates, *72*; classic horror framing of, 72–76, 86; conflicted horror framing of, 76–80, 86; as maverick, 72–74, 81; monstrosities of, 75; self-praise, 74

McCarthyism, 160
McCollum, Victoria, 193
McConnell, Mitch, 173
McIlwain, Charlton D., 95, 169
mediation, visual, 159–60
medicine, socialized, 150
"Meet Phony Kamala Harris!" (Trump, D., advertisement), 150–51
memory, 123, 153
mental aptitude, 146, 147, 156
mental health, 151, 152
mental illness, 4
mentors, 84
Middle East, 72–73, 99
Midsommar (2019), 8, *8*
military, 37, 61, 118, 152
miners, 103
minority groups, 125
mirror, horror genre as, 199
"Mirrors" (Clinton, H., advertisement), 118–19
misogyny, 119
missiles, 37
mixed horror framing: of Clinton, H. campaign, 123–24; of Trump, D. campaign, 147–49, 153, 158
mob action, 116, 136
mob justice, 76, 129, 131–32
"The Moment" (Romney advertisement), 98–99, 108, 109
monstrosities, 2–3; of Bush campaign, 37–39; corruption as, 73; of Gore campaign, 28–33; immigrants as, 127–29; in McCain campaign, 75; suggestion of, 5, 6; temporal bracketing of, 13
moral arguments, 60
moral values, 56
"Morph" (Gore advertisement), 32
"Motherhood" (Trump, D., advertisement), 134
"Movement" (Trump, D., advertisement), 133–34
"Muchas Gracias" (Bush advertisement), 36

The Mummy (1932), 133
Museum of the Moving Image, 15
music, anxiety inducing, 158
Mutz, Diana C., 159
mystery, 6, 19n40
mythology, Egyptian, 133

narcissism, 193
narratives: of Bush, 34–41; consistency in, 133, 136; dual narrative arguments, 78; white savior, 162
"Need Education" (Obama advertisement), 83
negative campaign advertising, 9
negativity, 15
Nelson, John S., 11, 194
Night of the Living Dead (1968), 76, *77*
nihilism: of horror framing, 194–95; political, 177
9/11 attacks, 57, 192
"1969" (Gore advertisement), 28–29
"No Maverick" (Obama advertisement), 81
normativity, of horror framing, 191–92
nostalgia, 107, 170, 171
nuclear terror, 72–73
nuclear weapons, 120, 121
Nussbaum, Martha C., 177, 195

Obama, Barack, 16–17, 71, 93, 165, 173, 188–89; campaign advertisement airdates, *72*, *94*; classic horror framing of, 83–87, 100–101; conflicted horror framing of, 80–83, 87, 101–4, 108, 109; on education, 81–82; otherization of, 95–96; positive campaign advertising of, 104–8
"Obligation" (Kerry advertisement), 55
Ocasio-Cortez, Alexandria, 148, 149, 151, 153, 176, 190, 197
Ohio, 32, 171
Omar, Ilhan, 148, 149, 151, 153, 176, 190, 197

omnipresence, of horror framing, 42, 191
"The One" (McCain advertisement), 77
optimism, 50, 58, 63
"Optimists" (Kerry advertisement), 50
"Original Mavericks" (McCain advertisement), 74
otherness, 1, 6, 13, 73, 95–96, 192

Palin, Sarah, 74, 81
pandemic, global, 1, 2, 17, 145, 147, 160–61; Biden on, 165–66; Black Americans and, 168
Parry-Giles, Shawn J., 153, 170
Parry-Giles, Trevor, 153, 170
partisanship, 195
past: accomplishments, 4, 35, 187; actions, 30
patriotism, 52, 98–99
"Peace Little Girl (Daisy)" (advertisement), 122, *122*
Pelosi, Nancy, 153, 197
Pementel, Michael, 151
"Pero Ya No" (Biden advertisement), 167
"Personal" (Biden advertisement), 178n5
personal testimony advertisements, 83, 119, 124–25, 128
persuasion, 13, 22n115, 135
"Pessimism" (Bush advertisement), 63
Petley, Julian, 123
Pew Research Center, 25, 71, 115
Phillips, Kendall R., 38, 53, 133, 192–93
Picart, Caroline Joan S., 13–14, 53, 131, 168
polarizations, of horror framing, 176, 192
police, 127, 150, 167, 169, 170; brutality, 145, 163, 168; reform, 149; riot, 29, 149
"Policy" (Obama advertisement), 103–4
political engagement, 194–95

political nihilism, 177
"Political Payoffs and Middle Class Layoffs" (Romney advertisement), 95–96
polls, 25, 65, 100, 115, 145, 177n1, 192
Poltergeist (1982), 150
popular culture, 2–3
positive campaign advertising, 25, 187–89, 191; of Biden campaign, 163–64, 174–75; of Bush campaign, 34–36, 41, 63; Clinton, H., campaign attempting, 124–26; of Gore campaign, 27–28, 34, 41; of Kerry campaign, 49–52, 56; of Obama campaign, 104–8; of Romney campaign, 98–99; of Trump, D. campaign, 134, 135, 153–54, 160–63
possession, 32, 39, 78, 97, 123–24, 150
power, visualizing, 165
"Predators" (Trump, D., advertisement), 132
prescriptions, 37, 38
presidential elections. *See* election, presidential
priorities, 36
"Priorities" (Bush advertisement), 36
"Priority MD RNC" (Bush advertisement), 38–39
"Progresista" (Trump, D., advertisement), 159–60, 178n5
promises, 35
prosperity, 26
protagonists, 73, 80, 84, 105
protests, 145, 155, 197
Prysby, Charles, 72, 80, 85
Puerto Rico, 167, 168
The Purge (2013), 149

QAnon, 198
"Question" (Gore advertisement), 33–34

racial appeals, 169, 190–91
racial horror, 8
racial inequality, 145, 146
racism, 80, 86, 95–96, 155–56, 159, 194

racist appeals, 155
Radical Left, 17, 148–51, 153, 162
radical science fiction, 6–7
Rankin, Tony, 162
Rassman, Jim, 52, 53
"Rassman" (Kerry advertisement), 52–54
rationality, of fear, 10
reaction, audience, 103
Reagan, Ronald, 60–61, 126, 191
"The Real Biden Plan" (Trump, D., advertisement), 157–58
"Really MD" (Bush advertisement), 40
"Rearview Mirror" (Obama advertisement), 85–86
recession, education, 37, 39
"Record Smashing" (Trump, D., advertisement), 160–61
recounts, vote, 42
red filter, 59
Reeves, Byron, 159
reform, police, 149
research, on campaign advertisements, 9–12
"Respected" (Clinton, H., advertisement), 119
rhetoric, visual, 12–14
Richardson, Glenn W., Jr., 11, 29, 35, 52, 188, 198
riot police, 29, 149
"Risk" (Kerry advertisement), 50
Roberts-Miller, Patricia, 192
Roe v. Wade, 104
"Role Models" (Clinton, H., advertisement), 123–24
Romney, Mitt, 17, 110n10, 189; campaign advertisement airdates, 94; classic horror framing of, 93–98, 108–9; conflicted horror framing of, 98; positive campaign advertising of, 98–99
Roosevelt, Franklin D., 170
Ryan, Paul, 99

"Sacred" (Biden advertisement), 171–72

"Sacrifice" (Clinton, H., advertisement), 118
"Safer, Stronger" (Bush advertisement), 57
safety, 152; crime and, 145, 146; domestic, 54
"Same Old" (Biden advertisement), 172–73
Sanders, Bernie, 132, 148–51, 158, 160
sarcasm, 77
satire, 101
savior, 75, 162–63
scandals, 25, 133
Scavo, Carmine, 72, 80, 85
science, 162, 170
science fiction: centrist, 6, 171; radical, 6–7
scientists, 167, 170
Scranton, Pennsylvania, 174
"Second Chance" (Trump, D., advertisement), 162
"Seen" (Obama advertisement), 104
self-praise, 29, 34–35, 116; Harris, 169; Kerry, 49–50; McCain, 74; of past actions, 30
setting, victimization and, 4
sexual energy, 4
sexual violence, 119
shadows, 74–75
Sheckels, Theodore F., 9
Shelley, Mary, 3
singing, 95, 100
Siren, 95, 100
The Sixth Sense (1999), 106
slasher films, 7, 86
socialized medicine, 150
Social Security, 25, 29, 34, 36, 83, 172
soldiers, 61, 62
"Something" (Obama advertisement), 85
Southwest, American, 6
Spanish, 36, 160, 167
spatial bracketing, 53–55, 131
"Special" (McCain advertisement), 75

speeches, broadcast, 9
spending, campaign advertising, 116–17
"Spending Spree" (Obama advertisement), 83–84
spheres, merging of, 41
spot advertisements, 9
steel, 101–2
"Storm" (McCain advertisement), 79
"Strength" (Kerry advertisement), 50–51
strife, 145, 147
Stuckey, Mary E., 12
subtle horror framing, 150
"Successful Leader" (Bush advertisement), 35
suggestion, of monstrosity, 5, 6
super PAC, 110n10
supplies, 58
suppression, voter, 172–73
"Sweat Equity" (McCain advertisement), 78–79
synecdoche, 130

tactics, dehumanization, 59
"Takeover" (Trump, D., advertisement), 149–50
Tarantula (1955), 118
taxes, 149, 158; cuts to, 31, 36; gas, 62
technological innovation, 57
teleprompter, 157
"Teleprompter Joe" (Trump, D., advertisement), 156–57
temporal bracketing, 13, 53–54, 85, 126, 135, 168–69
terror, 37–38, 51; nuclear, 72–73; triumph over, 58
terrorism, 47, 50, 56, 57, 59–60, 115
testimony, personal, 83
Texas, 32, 35–36
The Texas Chainsaw Massacre (1974), 33
Texas hero, Bush as, 35–36
Texas workers, 32
Them! (1954), 121

Third Golden Age of Horror, 192–93
"This Is a Clear Choice" (Obama advertisement), 105
"This Year" (Obama advertisement), 84, 188
"Three Minutes" (Kerry advertisement), 51
"Tomorrow" (Clinton, H., advertisement), 125–26
trade, foreign, 131
trickle-down economics, 31
"Troops" (Bush advertisement), 61
tropes: arguments and, 195, 196; body horror, 32; disaster film, 79; mental health as, 151; use of, 188
Trump, Donald, 17, 115, 145, 189–90, 196–98; attack advertisements of, 132, 150–52; campaign advertisement airdates, *116*; classic horror framing of, 126–33, 135, 136, 149–50, 155–56, 158–61, 176; conflicted horror framing of, 151–52, 157–58, 176; on economic decline, 129–32; efficacy appeals of, 133–35; on immigrants, 127–29; mixed horror framing of, 147–49, 153, 158; positive campaign advertising of, 134, 135, 154, 161–63; subtle horror framing of, 151
Trump, Ivanka, 134
"Trump's Boycott—Goodyear OH" (Biden advertisement), 171–72
"Truth :60" (Biden advertisement), 166–67
turmoil, 29
turnout, voter, 177
"27 Million Strong" (Clinton, H., advertisement), 125
"$2.2 Trillion" (Bush advertisement), 40–41
"Two Americas: Economy" (Trump, D., advertisement), 129–30
"Two Americas: Immigration" (Trump, D., advertisement), 127

2000 election, 15–16, 25, 26, 187–88
2004 election, 15, 47, 188
2008 election, 16, 71, 87, 109, 188
2012 election, 17, 93, 94, 189
"2013" (McCain advertisement), 72–73
2016 election, 17, 115, 189–90
2020 election, 17, 93, 145, 176–77, 190–91

"Understands" (Obama advertisement), 101–2
unemployment, 33, 130
"Unfit (D)" (Clinton, H., advertisement), 120–21
"Unfit (R)" (Trump, D., advertisement), 132–33, 189–90
"United" (Trump, D., advertisement), 134
unity, 175
Universal Studios, 3
unrest, civil, 155

valor, 51
values, moral, 56
vampire, 97, 130
verticality, 165
victimization, 120; setting and, 4; of women, 118, 119
"Victory" (Bush advertisement), 58
Video Rhetorics (Nelson and Boynton), 11
Vietnam War, 49, 51–54
villains, 6–7, 30, 40, 55, 102, 127
violence, sexual, 119
visual arguments, 128, 148, 154, 166, 173
visual artifacts, 12
visual mediation, 159–60
visual rhetoric, 12–14
voodoo, 76–77
voters, 10; Black American, 167–68; depictions of, 132; economy as issue for, 48, 56, 57, 71, 93, 115, 145; Latinx, 159, 167; suppression of, 172–73; turnout of, 177; young, 39, 78

votes, 42, 61, 109

"Wacky" (Bush advertisement), *62*, 61–63
Wall Street, 73, 74, 101, 174
Walpole, Horace, 38, 45n88, 121, 139n64
war: Iraq, 48–52; War on Terror, 15, 47, 57–60, 176
warmongering, 126
War of the Worlds (1953), 121
War on Terror, 15, 47, 57–60, 176
"Watch: Past vs Present" (Trump, D., advertisement), 151–52
weakness, 60
wealth, spread of, 79
weapons, nuclear, 120, 121
"Weapons (Florida)" (Bush advertisement), 57–58
"We Are America" (Clinton, H., advertisement), 119–20
West, James, 163
Weyrich, Paul, 172
"Whatever It Takes" (Bush advertisement), 60
"What Kind" (Obama advertisement), 81–82
"What We're Fighting For" (Obama advertisement), 107–8
Whissel, Kristen, 165

white savior narratives, 162–63
White Zombie (1932), 76–77
"Who We Are" (Clinton, H., advertisement), 117–18
Wilkerson, Laura, 128
"Will Ferrell Will Do Anything To Get You To Vote" (Obama advertisement), 107
"Windsurfing" (Bush advertisement), 63–64
Witte, Kim, 10, 128, 136
The Wolf Man (1941), 4, 5, 61, 84
wolves, 60
"Wolves" (Bush advertisement), 60–61
women: of color, 148, 190; victimization of, 118, 119
"Word" (Gore advertisement), 33
workers, 33, 105, 130, 160–61, 171; campaign, 108; construction, 162; factory, 103, 131; healthcare, 163, 164, 166, 169, 190; Texas, 32; young, 34

xenophobia, 4
Xi Jinping, 147, 154

young voters, 39, 78
young workers, 34

zombie horror films, 164–65

About the Author

Fielding Montgomery is a PhD student in the Department of Communication at the University of Maryland, College Park. He earned his Master of Arts in communication, as well as his Bachelor of Arts, from Baylor University. Fielding's research interests include presidential rhetoric, campaigning, disinformation, and popular culture. He is especially interested in research that examines where those topics intersect. He has published on these and other topics in *Rhetoric & Public Affairs*, the *Journal of Popular Film and Television*, and *International Political Science Review*.

www.ingramcontent.com/pod-product-compliance
Lightning Source LLC
Chambersburg PA
CBHW061711300426
44115CB00014B/2650